CAR WARS

CAR WARS

Fifty Years of Greed, Treachery, and Skulduggery in the Global Marketplace

JONATHAN MANTLE

Arcade Publishing • New York

FIRST U.S. EDITION

Library of Congress Cataloging-in-Publication Data

Mantle, Jonathan.
Car wars : fifty years of greed, treachery, and skulduggery in the global marketplace / [by Jonathan Mantle]. — 1st U.S. ed.
p.   cm.
Includes bibliographical references and index.
ISBN 1-55970-333-4
1. Automobile industry and trade — History.   2. International business enterprises — History.   3. Competition, International — History.   I. Title.
HD9710.A2M35   1996
338.4'7629222 — dc20   95-53184

Published in the United States by Arcade Publishing, Inc., New York

Distributed by Little, Brown and Company

10 9 8 7 6 5 4 3 2 1

BP

PRINTED IN THE UNITED STATES OF AMERICA

To Bill Nicholson
Fellow traveler on the roads

Contents

Acknowledgments   xi

Prologue   xiii

PART 1: *The Struggle Begins with Peace*

1. Hitler: The Dictator in the Driver's Seat   3
2. Japan: Samurai into Sedans   21
3. Agnelli, FIAT, and the *Cinquecento*   28
4. Les Chemins de la Liberté et les Deux Chevaux   33
5. A Very British People's Car   36

PART 2: *America and the Rise of Europe*

6. An American in Europe   43
7. *Il Boom:* Italy and Agnelli on the *Autostrada*   48
8. De Gaulle and "The Goddess"   54
9. Mercedes-Benz and the Economic Miracle   57
10. BMW and the Pride of Bavaria   60
11. Dr. Porsche and Other People's Cars   64

PART 3: *America, Europe, and the Rise of Japan*

12. The Men in Motown   75
13. Auto da Fé: Snapshots from the Suicide of the British Auto Industry   81

14. The Last of the Line Leaves Wolfsburg 90

15. Collision: The Autocrat and the Commissars 95

16. The Coming of Age of the Samurai Sedan 102

PART 4: *The Battle for World Domination*

17. Brand Loyalty and the Bedouin: Mercedes-Benz and General Motors in the Middle East 109

18. Marx, Mao, and Motoring: Internal Combustion at Renault and Peugeot-Citroën 116

19. Toyota, Mazda, Datsun, and the Drive Upmarket 123

20. Inside Castle Volvo: PG, ET, and the Company That Outgrew a Country 127

21. Radial Chic: The Coming of Age of Four-Wheel Drive 132

22. "How Much of Your Garden Are You Going to Give to the Japanese?" Roger Smith and the New Ghost Towns of the Midwest 136

23. Fallen by the Roadside: Trabant and Zil in a Disintegrating Europe 143

PART 5: *The End of History and the Beginning of the Global Market*

24. Contenders: Malaysia and South Korea 151

25. "This Is an Economic Pearl Harbor": General Motors and the Downsizing of Detroit 156

26. Supermodels and "Superlopez": The Catwalk and the Covert Car Wars 162

27. How the Rise of Japan and the Fall of the Wall Brought the Germans to South Carolina 172

28. Send for "Motorhead": The Empire Strikes Back 181

29. Capitalist Roads: The Wild East and the
    New Frontiers   187

30. Lawless Roads: The Illegal Traffic in Western
    Cars to Eastern Europe and the Far East   202

    Epilogue: The People's Car — Yesterday,
    Today, and Forever   213

    Appendix 1. A Selective A–Z of the World's
    Car Companies   223

    Appendix 2. A Selective A–Z of Overseas
    Operations and Automobile Alliances   225

    Notes   227

    Select Bibliography   235

    Index   239

Acknowledgments

Car Wars has been made possible with the help of many people in many countries. The author wishes to thank the following individuals and institutions in particular for their assistance in his researches for this book.

William Armstrong, Keith Arundale, BMW AG, Mark Berry, Tim Bishop, Carole Blake, Jo Burge, Ricardo Cerdan, Rupert Christiansen, Alan Crowther, FCO, Detective Kieron Freeburn and the Metropolitan Police Stolen Car Investigation Wing, Julian Friedmann, Jonathan Glancey, Haymarket Publishing, John Henry, Ivan Hirst, Beatrice Howald, Rainer Hupe, Hyundai, Terry Kirby, Hans-Georg and Christa Lehmann, Robin Lough, Alice Louis, MC Micro Compact Car AG, Teresa Ma, Douglas Brian Martin, David Martyn, Jim Mather and the Royal Hong Kong Police Anti-Smuggling Task Force, Mercedes-Benz AG, Phil Milner-Barry, Alex Nicoll, Jenny Osorio, Carol Page, Charles Pearce, Roland Philips, Richard Preston, Jonathan Prichard, Gareth Renowden, John Robins, Royal Institute of International Affairs, SMH Société Suisse de Microélectronique et de l'Horlogerie SA, Catharine Sanders, Edda Tasiemka, Tony Timbs, Lady Turnbull, Volkswagen, Charles Ware, Bill West.

Prologue

IN THE TWO THOUSAND YEARS since the death of Jesus Christ, there have been only two main forms of personal transport: the horse and the automobile. The automobile has existed for only the last one hundred years, and in that short time, unlike the horse, it has transformed the lives of peoples, countries, and continents.

This is the story of individuals and nations in the second half of this century through the rise of the worldwide automobile manufacturers. It is the story of a struggle that began with the end of one war and developed into the economic and political equivalent of another — for just as there has never been an invention as revolutionary as the automobile, there has never been an industry like the automobile industry.

The automakers are the largest manufacturing industry in the world, employing 4 million people and investing hundreds of billions of dollars in America, Europe, and Japan. One hundred years ago, there were six experimental cars in France and Germany. Today, jammed bumper to bumper on a six-lane highway, the earth's 350 million cars would stretch for 200,000 miles, eight times around the world and two thirds of the way to the moon.

Against this potentially cataclysmic environmental scenario, with its contribution to the greenhouse effect, must be set the indispensability of the automobile and the internal combustion engine. In 1928, Bruce Barton — author, salesman, and early industrial guru — spelled out to the oilmen of America the significance of the automobile:

> Stand for an hour beside one of your filling stations. Talk to the people who come in to buy gas. Discover for yourself what magic a dollar's worth of gasoline a week has worked in their lives.
>
> My friends, it is the juice of the fountain of eternal youth that you

are selling. It is health. It is comfort. It is success. And you have sold merely a bad smelling liquid at so many cents per gallon . . . You must put yourself in the place of the men and women in whose lives your gasoline has worked miracles.

The miracle was that of freedom and mobility. For the first time in their lives, people could go where they wanted. The automobile transformed the daily life of America, and the demand it created for freedom and mobility transformed the American car manufacturers. General Motors and Ford became synonymous with the American dream; with the rise of the multinational corporation; with the power of the individual executive and the family dynasty; and with American supremacy in the postwar world.

But it only began in America. After the end of the Second World War, that freedom was brought to millions in Europe and the rest of the world. Today, parked down any street in any developed or developing country on the planet, is a map of the world in the form of automobiles. The miracle Barton was preaching has transcended national and international barriers to become the barometer of individual prosperity and of the wealth of nations.

In the 1960s, the automobile manufacturers fueled and drove the economic miracles of postwar Europe. In the 1970s, the flaws in those industries and the first of the great oil shocks took America and Europe by surprise and enabled the beginning of the rise to power of Japan. In the 1980s, America and Europe were joined by Japan as world powers and the battle was on for world domination.

In the 1990s, the car companies have grown to such supranational status that the traditional stuff of history — migration of labor, of national and international frontiers — no longer applies to them. The automakers have created the first truly global marketplace in the history of the world.

In the last years of this century, the remaining space in this marketplace is being filled by the Far East and China. The struggle that began with the end of one war has developed into another. A new kind of war, with its own origins and momentum and combatants and alliances, has begun.

The automobile is as integral to war as to peace, and to poverty as to prosperity. It is the vehicle of progress and its nemesis. It is a proposition of this book that whenever that balance between necessity and excess begins to teeter toward the latter, it begins to right itself, and the automobile reverts toward its utilitarian origins as "the people's car."

This book is a political biography of the automobile, and an automotive history of the world in the second half of the twentieth century. It establishes the automobile as the vehicle of modern history. To do so, it travels from Berlin in 1945 to Shanghai and Los Angeles in the 1990s and traces the people and the political and technological developments behind this story. It charts the victories and defeats in what has become a global contest for a prize of unprecedented proportions.

It reveals the role of industrial espionage in the competition between rival manufacturers on both a national and an international scale. It explores the political and economic forces at work in the world's first global marketplace, and the quest of the individual for that miracle of freedom and mobility, for which as yet no better answer is to be found.

1

The Struggle Begins
with Peace

1

Hitler

The Dictator in the Driver's Seat

MUSSOLINI, STALIN, PÉTAIN, and Mao Tse-tung have not gone down in motoring history. Alone among twentieth-century tyrants, totalitarians, anti-democrats, and dictators, this distinction rests with Adolf Hitler. Although he never learned to drive, his legacy to a shattered world was a car. They called the company that would make it Volkswagenwerk: "The People's Car Company."

The *New York Times* reported in 1936 that Hitler was believed "to reel off a higher annual motor mileage than any other ruler or head of State." In 1933 he opened the annual Berlin Motor Show, and did so every year thereafter until 1939. Each year he made a new grandiose statement about the car industry.

At the opening of the 1935 show, he declared that Messrs. Daimler and Benz were "among the great pioneers of humanity in the sphere of transport." His remark stemmed not least from the fact that the company gave the dictator a substantial discount on its most powerful model.

But the next year he admired the powerful new BMW 326. He

announced that Germany had "effectively solved the problem of producing synthetic gasoline."

Hitler was overambitious in this, as in so many other respects, but he had launched a campaign to build a network of autobahns and limited-access highways across the country. These, as he declared, would mark "a turning point in the history of German automobile traffic."

Hitler's most ambitious project was already under way. By 1934, more than one in five Americans owned their own cars. But in Germany the figure was barely one in fifty, and half of all road transport was still horse-driven. In the same year, Hitler had commissioned Dr. Ferdinand Porsche and others to design a people's car. It was to cost under one thousand reichsmarks (the equivalent of $140 at the time), and have an air-cooled engine and a top speed of sixty miles per hour. The low-revving, high-geared engine was specifically designed for the great autobahns that Hitler and his chief architect, Albert Speer, envisaged would stretch from Berlin to Moscow with gas stations every thirty miles.

Hitler himself admitted, "All strategic roads were built by tyrants — for the Romans, the Prussians, or the French. They go straight across country. All the other roads wind like processions and waste everybody's time."

According to Porsche, Hitler said the car should "look like a beetle."

A Town Called Strength Through Joy: Germany, 1938

By 1935, testing of a prototype car was taking place. The original suggestion was that Volkswagenwerk should be built near Nuremberg, so that customers could collect their cars after attending Nazi Party rallies. This suggestion had proved impractical. It was decided instead to build a gigantic factory and town on Lüneberg Heath.

The plant was modeled on the great Ford factory at Rouge River, Detroit, in the United States. Henry Ford had revolutionized automobile production in the early years of the twentieth century, putting America on wheels and changing the social and economic structure of America and the world. Hitler much admired *Der Fordismus* and pronounced this to be the German way. As we shall see, the mutual admiration between Hitler and Ford took on terrifying forms about which the American company remains silent alongside its paeans to its all-American heritage.

The German plant was financed with funds confiscated from trade unions, and built by Italian construction workers on loan from Mussolini. In 1938, at a huge rally hung with Nazi banners, Hitler laid the cornerstone: "It is for the broad masses that this car has been built," he declared. "Its purpose is to answer their transportation needs, and it is intended to give them joy." Hitler added that the car was to be known as *"der KdF (Kraft-durch-Freude)-Wagen"* — short for "the Strength-Through-Joy Car." The name dismayed Hitler's marketing men.

The *KdF-Wagen* was displayed for the first time at the Berlin Motor Show in 1939. Work on *KdF-Stadt*, or Strength-Through-Joy Town, went slowly, and marketing became increasingly important in order to maintain public interest. A novel savings scheme was developed that typified the threatening atmosphere of the times. Prospective *KdF* drivers could reserve a Strength-Through-Joy Car by paying five reichsmarks a week to the German Labor Front. Once they had paid 990 marks, they could take delivery of their car.

The fact that it was as yet unbuilt, in a factory that was as yet unfinished, was no concern of the ordinary citizens of the Third Reich. This was to be the new Europe's Model T. In another nod to Henry Ford, they could have any color they liked, as long as it was gray-blue.

Full payment would take four years, although extra payments could be made to procure earlier delivery. A single missed payment, however, would result in the cancellation of the entire agreement. Children could save five reichsmarks a month. The company was still compensating some of them thirty years later.

By 1939, 336,668 subscribers had paid 110 million reichsmarks into a Berlin bank account.

At the Berlin Motor Show in the same year, Hitler was approached by a Dutchman named Ben Pon. Pon secured the official distributorship for the Strength-Through-Joy Car in the Netherlands. The Dutchman returned home pleased with the deal, and awaited the next move.

It did not come quite as he expected. On August 28, 1939, the Netherlands were forced to mobilize their armed forces. On

September 1, Germany invaded Poland, and by May 10, 1940, German troops were on Dutch soil.

The Dutch royal family fled to London. Less than two weeks later, Rotterdam was captured and the Netherlands surrendered to the victorious forces of the man Ben Pon had met at the Berlin Motor Show.

By the outbreak of the Second World War, KdF-Stadt had produced very few of the *KdF-Wagen*. The management, Dr. Porsche and his son Ferry, preserved their positions by putting the plant into wartime production.

KdF-Stadt produced the *Kubelwagen*, or "bucket car," a German version of the cross-country Jeep. It went into mass production after the invasion of the Soviet Union and found particular favor with Rommel's forces in Africa. The *Kubelwagen* could not, however, cross water; this obstacle was surmounted by the *Schwimmwagen*, which was built of welded steel with rubber seals in crucial places. The wheels remained turning in the water, but propulsion was provided by a rear-mounted propeller.

The few *KdF-Wagen* produced were not delivered to subscribers, but supplied as staff cars to Nazi Party officials. As fuel became scarce, many were converted to run on coal, coke, bottled gas, anthracite, and even peat.

As the war dragged on, KdF-Stadt depended increasingly on slave labor from concentration camps and Russian prisoners of war. The plant became one of the dark engine rooms of the Reich. To the west, it dispatched the fuselage and wings of the V-1 flying bomb. To the east, it dispatched sheet-metal army stoves to the Russian front.

The VW had mutated, like Doctor Frankenstein's creation, into the V-1. One of them, fittingly, played its part in the last days of the dictator who, less than seven years earlier, had launched the little car that had turned into a flying bomb.

Hitler's Last Ride

The heroic quest had turned into a nightmare. This was the final, inevitable travesty of the Hitlerian ideal that had begun only six years earlier. Warsaw had fallen to the Red Army; Roosevelt, Stalin, and Churchill had met at Yalta to divide the world without Hitler. Dresden had been destroyed in an Allied firestorm, and Cologne had fallen to the Allies.

When, in the spring of 1945, Hitler made a last, desperate visit to rally his troops on the Eastern Front, the war was already lost. His chauffeur, Erich Kempka, drove him east from Berlin in a modified version of the *KdF-wagen*. The Type 87 *Kommandeurwagen* was a four-wheel-drive vehicle fitted with a roller at the front to clear large obstacles out of the way. There was no questioning the engineering principles behind the vehicle, but the logistical obstacles loomed larger in its path.

This was the end of the strategic road built by the tyrant, the great autobahn that Hitler had envisaged would one day run all the way from Berlin to Moscow.

Six weeks after his return from the Eastern Front, Hitler and Eva Braun committed suicide in their bunker in Berlin. In a fitting end, their bodies were doused with gasoline, also provided by the chauffeur, and ignited.

Although his last journey was in a *KdF-Wagen*, Hitler had preferred to tour his territories in his 7.7-liter supercharged Mercedes-Benz. His favorite architect, Albert Speer, preferred the faster, lighter BMW. The difference between Mercedes-Benz and BMW was as great as that between Hitler and Speer; and this difference would outlive the Führer, Speer, and the Thousand Year Reich.

BMW — *Bayerische Motoren Werke*, Bavarian Motor Works — had been founded shortly before the First World War by Franz-Josef Popp. The company sported a circular blue and white badge symbolizing an aircraft propeller against the blue and white of the Bavarian flag, also the colors of the cloud and sky.

BMW built airplane engines. One of these quickly established its reputation in high-altitude combat: "Its only flaw," said Lieutenant Ernst Udet of the Richthofen Fighter Squadron, who scored thirty victories, "was that it arrived too late."

After the First World War, BMW was prohibited from manufacturing airplane engines, and turned to motorcycles. A British-made Douglas was acquired and stripped down in order to see how it worked. The company later returned to airplane engines as well. In the late 1920s it made its first venture into car manufacture. Unlike the Japanese, who would obtain a British Austin Seven, strip it down, and use it as a model for their own car, BMW had built the Austin Seven under license as the "Dixi."

Germany's resurgence in the 1930s put BMW back on the map. The BMWs were the fastest production cars in the world. BMW motorcycles triumphed on the racetrack at home and abroad.

The Second World War saw BMW concentrating again on airplane engines. The other area of expertise was V-2 rocket development — another innovation that came too late.

But the founders and principal patrons of BMW were no Nazis. "At times, you've got to make a pact with the devil, for aviation's sake, provided he doesn't have you for dinner," wrote Lieutenant Udet of the pressure placed on him by Goering, after the Luftwaffe failed to dominate the skies. In December 1941, Udet shot himself.

BMW management was engulfed in the evil momentum of the Reich. The plant at Allach in Bavaria used slave labor from Dachau and other concentration camps. Inmates suffered unspeakable barbarities and found the plant no refuge from the Nazi extermination policy of *Nacht und Nebel* . . . night and fog.

By 1945, BMW was high on the invading Allies' war crimes list. The plants in the west, like Allach, were stripped of their machinery and put to work making pots and pans and bicycles.

The BMW plant at Eisenach, which had spent the war producing cars and motorcycles, was also in the path of the liberating forces. But instead of being destroyed, it was to be preserved for a different fate: night and fog were to be replaced by the red star.

Eisenach, Germany, April 1945

Albert Siedler saw the first tank and breathed a sigh of relief that the tank was American. He was chief engineer for BMW at Eisenach, and the German military had ordered him to blow up anything that was still standing before surrendering the plant to the enemy. The fact that the Americans were here meant he could ignore his orders without fear of being put up against the nearest wall.

Eisenach, the old town under Wartburg Castle, was already largely destroyed by bombs. The plant too was a place of smashed windows, ruined boiler houses, derelict repair shops, and broken-down walls.

Siedler and the small group of colleagues put down their white flag. The Sherman rolled to halt at the factory gate. An officer clambered out of the tank, which was from the Sixth American Armored Division. A GI in a Jeep took Siedler back to what remained of his home. Siedler told his wife the joyful news.

By the same afternoon he was back at the plant, under instructions to start work. The printing shop could produce leaflets to broadcast the town commandant's appeals for help from the local population. Enough men were alive to form a skeleton workforce. Enough vehicles existed to form a small vehicle pool.

Siedler did not mind what form this work took. This was the first time in six years that he could work without fear.

By June 1945, the interest of the Americans in Eisenach was waning. Siedler took this as a sign that things were getting back to normal. In fact, this was because they had gathered sufficient information about BMW's role in the German rocket program at its other plants, information that would play a crucial role in the American space program.

The Americans left Thuringia and Saxony at the end of June.

Siedler was asked if he would prefer to go back to BMW headquarters in Munich. He thought about this, and decided he would. He filled a van with the family possessions and prepared to take to the road.

But early on the morning of July 1, an American GI roared up to his office on a BMW motorcycle. The GI wanted to know if he could still have the cylinder heads he needed. Siedler wondered what he meant by "still" — but did not give it a second thought. He nodded to the GI. "Come on," he said.

"Nix come on." The GI shook his head. He pointed to the warehouse. The Russians were there, he said.

The Russians? Siedler rushed to the shed where he had parked the van, ready for his departure.

The door to the shed was open. Siedler looked in. The van was gone.

"Poshol!" a voice behind him called. "Come on! You boss here?" the voice demanded.

Siedler closed and bolted the door, although there was nothing left to guard inside.

He turned around. "Yes," he said slowly, "me boss here."

The GI on the motorcycle had disappeared. In his place stood a Russian soldier with a Kalashnikov.

The chief engineer's chances of working in an environment free of fear had disappeared. The Russian major who approached him and politely asked him to repair his captured BMW 321 did not have to resort to social niceties. The Russians were there to stay.

Siedler protested only once, and realized that the alternative to cooperation was the Russian equivalent of night and fog. It was a short, but fatal, step from being a hostage valued for his expertise to being a "capitalist lackey" and a "saboteur."

Over the next few days, he saw the expressions of terror on the faces of those who were summoned to the Russian Commandant's building at Eisenach. Most of them never returned. One day, he, too, was summoned. He said good-bye to his wife.

The Russians locked him in a cellar without heat or light or food. They kept him there for some time. Then they unlocked the door and dragged him out.

"Can you make motorcycles?" they asked.

"With pleasure," Siedler replied weakly.

"We need two hundred a month."

"How? With what?"

"You don't want to do it?"

Siedler knew the penalty for the wrong answer. "Of course I do," he said.

Siedler told the Russians what they wanted to know. BMW had hidden spare parts and tools in a potash mine near what was now the border of the Russian and Allied zones. The Russians took him there under heavy escort. He clambered down into the bowels of the earth, marked what he needed, and the Russians took it back to Eisenach. The rest of the contents of the mine were dispatched by rail to Russia. En route, the rail wagons were looted, and the contents never reached their destination.

Siedler and his wife lived on millet gruel and cabbage. He worked day and night. He made motorcycles. He made cars. Huge wooden boxes were made from timber cut in the nearby Thuringian Forest, in which the cars were crated up and sent to Russia. A Russian state-owned company, Avtovelo, took over Eisenach. Unknown to Siedler and his employees, the Russian company marketed the cars as if they were still Bavarian-made BMWs. They sold them for hard currency, through dealers in France, Switzerland, West Germany, and other parts of free Europe.

Siedler was often summoned to interrogations by his superiors. Sometimes the interrogations went on for days without food or sleep. Sometimes they took place in Soviet-held East Berlin, in a building guarded by machine guns. Siedler never knew where or when the next interrogation would be, or if he would emerge alive. Siedler and his wife survived in this way for four and a half years.

The border between the Russian and Allied zones was heavily fortified and patrolled by tracker dogs and guards instructed to fire on sight. Many had died crossing or helping others to do so. The Siedlers would never reveal the place where they eventually crossed, or the names of those who risked their lives to enable them to do so. In the spring of 1950 they arrived in a free, resurrected Germany with only two small suitcases and the clothes they stood up in.

Sometimes Albert Siedler wondered what had happened to that GI on the motorcycle, four and a half years earlier, after he rode away.

A Town Called Strength Through Joy: Germany, 1945

By 1945, KdF-Stadt had become a place of phantoms in the mists of Lüneburg Heath. One hundred fifty miles north of Eisenach, and only a few miles to the west of the advancing Red Army, the plant had escaped serious damage until the last months of the war, when Allied bombers had taken revenge for the destruction wrought on British cities by the V-1. Two thirds of the plant had been destroyed. The body plant was a heap of twisted metal.

Roof girders, *Kubelwagen* and *Schwimmwagen* — and the odd *KdF-Wagen* — had melted in the heat. The slave laborers, concentration camp inmates, and Russian prisoners of war had gone, but the fact of their presence here would not so easily go away.

Helmut Amtenbrink was not a slave laborer, or a concentration camp inmate, or a prisoner of war. He had been a member of the Hitler Youth. Amtenbrink had been a courier for the Luftwaffe when he was ordered by a retreating Nazi Party official to stay and fight a rearguard action against the Allies. Amtenbrink declined the invitation. He threw away the hated swastika armband and surrendered to British troops near his hometown of Soltau.

Soltau was sixty-five miles from KdF-Stadt. It was one of several dispersal sites to which Volkswagenwerk had sent parts and equipment during the bombing raids. Shortly after the town surrendered, Amtenbrink managed to get a job cleaning up the mess.

On his first day at work, his supervisor told him to go home — what was left of it — and fetch his swimming trunks. "Swimming trunks?" said Amtenbrink.

The supervisor said there was a pond that needed clearing. Amtenbrink did as he was told: like Siedler at Eisenach, he knew that, for the first time in five years, he would not face death if he refused.

The pond had been used to pump water for firefighting and was flecked with oil. Amtenbrink emerged, oily but triumphant, clutching bits of differential and gear assemblies.

After a few months at Soltau, however, the novelty had begun to wear off. He went back to school. The teachers were at pains to distance themselves from the Nazi period. By then, the pond was empty.

Amtenbrink had decided his future lay with Volkswagenwerk, seventy-five miles away. With some friends, he set out on foot. At night they slept in barns. Many of the rail bridges had been blown up, either by the retreating Wehrmacht or the advancing Allies. After two days, they arrived at KdF-Stadt.

In the summer of 1945, Helmut Amtenbrink was sixteen years old.

KdF-Stadt was high on the list of plants to be dismantled. Its machinery was scheduled to go as war reparations to the Allies. The Soviets too were hungry for reparations in any shape or form. The Americans saw no place for the plant under the Morgenthau Plan, which aimed to punish Germany by restricting its industry and reconstructing it as a predominantly agricultural country.

The management and staff of the plant consisted of Nazi sympathizers, displaced persons, and demoralized engineers. Conditions were primitive, and people fended for themselves as best they could.

Helmut Amtenbrink and his fellow apprentice mechanics lived in freezing wooden huts. They were always hungry. They wore U.S. Army boots and dark green British Army trousers. They stole potatoes from the surrounding fields.

The new geography of Germany also militated against the plant's recovery. Ten miles to the east was the end of the British zone and the beginning of the Soviet zone. Henry Ford, who had announced at the outbreak of the war that "we do not regard ourselves as a national company, but solely as a multinational organization," took one look at KdF-Stadt on the map and declared, "What we're being offered here isn't worth a damn." To Ford, automobile production was out of the question in a place so close to the Reds.

While the occupying forces wondered what to do, the plant and town were given a change of name. Strength-Through-Joy Town became Wolfsburg, after Count von Schulenburg of Wolfsburg, on whose estate the factory had been built.

Wolfsburg was under the control of the military government of the Allied zone. A British detachment of Royal Electrical and Mechanical Engineers was posted to the plant to set up a repair base for captured enemy vehicles.

As far as the Americans were concerned, the plant was destined for the dustbin of history. But the British, though they were the weaker partner in the occupying Allied forces, disagreed with the Morgenthau Plan. They saw the idea of reconstructing Germany as an agricultural economy as precisely the kind of punishment that had created the climate of bitterness that gave rise to the Nazis. They regarded the rebuilding of German industry as essential to creating a bulwark against Soviet Communism in postwar Europe.

They also needed cars.

In the summer of 1945, a young British officer arrived at Wolfsburg from Belgium, where he had been running a tank depot. He had been seconded to Wolfsburg by the military government of the Allied zone.

He was a grammar-school boy from the north of England who believed in fair play, enjoyed driving "rather grand" automobiles, and spoke schoolboy German. Regarded by his British superiors as possessing a remarkable, if suspect, talent for persuading foreigners of different nationalities to work together, he had a mission that was almost certainly doomed to failure. His name was Major Ivan Hirst.

One of the first things Major Ivan Hirst did when he arrived at Wolfsburg was to weed out the Nazi Party members still present in the management of Volkswagenwerk. Major Hirst knew about the Nazi concentration camps and the use of slave labor at KdF-Stadt. He regarded the Wolfsburg Nazis as fortunate, insofar as their fates, whatever they might be, would never equal that of the victims of *Nacht und Nebel.*

Hirst's mission was to get a vehicle — any vehicle — into production. Communicating in his schoolboy German, he sifted through the wreckage of the shattered plant. He and his colleagues, Colonel Charles Radclyffe, Alastair McInnes, and Major Michael McEvoy, unearthed the *Kubelwagen.* They unearthed the *Schwimm-wagen.*

Some of these British officers, and their deceased friends and comrades-in-arms, had greatly admired the performance of the sturdy, air-cooled *Kubelwagen* in the brilliant campaign waged by Rommel and his Afrika Korps in the North African desert. The German campaign had not foundered through lack of military skill or hardware, but through lack of gasoline. The Americans had even issued a manual — *The German Jeep* — with instructions on how, once they had captured one, Allied troops should drive and maintain it.

Major Hirst and his colleagues found something else in the wreckage: the bomb-damaged remains of a car — although it looked more like a beetle. It so happened that some of the other officers had seen and admired this vehicle at the 1938 Berlin Motor Show.

They repaired it, painted it dark green, and sent it for inspection to Army Headquarters of the Military Government of the Allied Zone.

The Americans still wanted Wolfsburg dismantled as part of war reparations. So did the Russians. Henry Ford himself had dismissed the plant as too close to the new Communist peril. So had the French, who had instead imported Dr. Porsche to France. The Australians had tried and failed to buy the plant and ship it, lock, stock, and barrel, to Australia.

Major Hirst, his colleagues, and their ragged German management and workforce were visited by Lord Rootes, the British motor magnate. "This vehicle," Lord Rootes told Major Hirst, "is quite unattractive to the average buyer. It is too ugly and too noisy. If you think you're going to build cars in this place, young man, you're a bloody fool."

Shortly afterwards, a message from the military government of the Allied Zone came back to Major Hirst at Wolfsburg. They wanted twenty thousand cars as soon as possible. The clients advanced 20 million marks in working capital.

Lord Rootes's remarks had stung Major Hirst. The American comptrollers, the British military authorities, and the German management had reckoned without the competitiveness inherent in the English class system. Major Hirst sought out raw materials and organized components and spares. He had German prisoners of war transferred to the production line. By the end of 1945, in spite of appalling conditions and setbacks, they had managed to make fifty-eight cars. They called the car the Volkswagen Type One; it was known simply as the Volkswagen.

The vehicle they had found in the wreckage was the vehicle through which Hirst still hoped to fulfill his mission. But the future remained uncertain.

In 1946 the plant again came under threat. Under the reparations orders and the Morgenthau Plan, no repairs could be made to the plant. At the same time, in a sort of catch-22, it was announced that the plant would be dismantled if production was not increased to one thousand cars a month.

Major Hirst began to despair. Perhaps Henry Ford, the Russians, the French, the Australians, and Lord Rootes were right after all. Perhaps it was impossible that the best light transport for the military government of the Allied Zone of a shattered Germany was the ugly, noisy inspiration of the deceased dictator of the Third Reich.

But Major Hirst had two aces in the hole: Richard Berryman, the British Royal Air Force officer who had worked for General Motors, and Ben Pon, the Dutchman who had met Adolf Hitler at the Berlin Motor Show.

Berryman had experience in mass production. He persuaded the workforce at Wolfsburg that it was in their interests to increase production. Somehow he obtained more food and blankets; when they slept more soundly in their huts, and meat was added to their lunchtime soup, the workforce responded. They managed to increase production to 1,003 cars a month, just four above the fateful minimum.

Hirst, Berryman, and their colleagues employed every trick in the book to circumvent the obstacles that continually appeared in their path. Supplies and parts were often obtained in return for the promise of a car. When the source of carburetors dried up, they made their own housings with components made by a local camera manufacturer.

Their spirits were raised by the return of the Dutchman, Ben Pon. Pon signed a contract enabling Volkswagenwerk to release five cars for him to ship to Holland. This small transaction, conducted between two aliens on disputed soil, marked the rebirth of Germany as an exporting nation.

Pon imported the cars to Holland in 1947. In the same year, Hirst interviewed a German for a managerial position at Wolfsburg. His name was Heinrich Nordhoff. Later he would become known as "King" Nordhoff. Hirst would describe Nordhoff as "a cat who liked to walk alone. I don't think he ever had a really close friend. He was a solitary soul."

Nordhoff had worked with the General Motors subsidiary Opel, but was barred from returning to the parent company by the American authorities because of his wartime role in producing trucks for the Wehrmacht. Nordhoff was scornful of the Volkswagen. "It has more faults than a dog has fleas," he said, and added that the few prewar cars that had been made were "custom-built at a cost per unit similar to that of a Rolls-Royce."

In the bitter winter of 1947, the ice froze on the inside of the huts. But as winter gave way to spring, Morgenthau gave way to Marshall. The Marshall Plan changed the Allied scheme for postwar Germany from a punitive agricultural economy to a reinvigorated industrial bulwark against Communism in Western Europe. The occupying forces transferred control of Wolfsburg to the federal government in Bonn, who in turn passed it on to the province of Lower Saxony.

The reform of the German currency, when the reichsmark was replaced by the deutsche mark at the astonishing rate of fifteen to one, unleashed the long-suppressed buying power of the German people. Wolfsburg was flooded with orders for cars.

Major Hirst handed over Volkswagenwerk to Nordhoff, who became its *Generaldirektor.* Nordhoff reinforced the morale of the workforce with hard work, art exhibitions, and music. Herbert von Karajan came to conduct in a former works kitchen, and complimented him on the excellent acoustics. The Volkswagen was at last on the autobahn.

Major Hirst had changed the course of history.

He changed the course of history and went home to England, a tired, bankrupt country where the *Volkswagen*, unlike history, was in short supply.

A British Army officer and his colleagues had realized the vision of Hitler. They had finished what Dr. Porsche had begun. But had Dr. Porsche really invented the *Volkswagen* in the first place?

Koprivnice, Czechoslovakia, 1946

Dr. Porsche was not the only person to work on the *Volkswagen* in the years leading up to World War II. So did Franz-Josef Popp, of BMW, and Hans Ledwinka, among others.

Popp and BMW soon pulled away from the *Volkswagen* project, and Dr. Porsche took the central role in its development.

Hans Ledwinka became technical chief of a company that was, and is, one of the oldest surviving automakers in the world: Tatra of Czechoslovakia. Ledwinka, it turned out, was an innovative genius, whose designs dominated the prewar history of the company.

Chief among his creations were the big, powerful, air-cooled, streamlined, rear-engined V-8 Tatra sedans. In 1933, Hitler himself had done all his election campaigning for the chancellorship in an elegant Tatra T11, covering thousands of miles across Germany without a hitch. As the new Reich Chancellor, he was an ardent admirer.

At Berlin Motor Shows, Hitler always went straight from the Daimler-Benz and BMW stands, which he applauded so publicly, to the Tatra stand. There he would respectfully greet Ledwinka and grill him on every detail of his latest creations.

Hitler declared that any new German *Volkswagen* should be worthy of the strong, air-cooled Tatra: *"Das ist der Wagen für meine Straßen!"* ("This is the car for my roads!") he would declare to all who cared to listen, including Dr. Porsche.

Dr. Porsche, although perceived as an Austrian citizen and therefore acceptable, was in reality of Czech Bohemian extraction, a fact about which he preferred to keep quiet as relations deteriorated between the Czechoslovak Republic and Germany. Ironically, although Ledwinka was really of Austrian birth, he was perceived as a Czech because he was based in Moravia. This led to his being seen as a political embarrassment to the new Reichsführer by the Nazi Party, who prevented Hitler from being seen in public with him at subsequent Berlin Motor Shows.

Hitler's ambitions, as he would shortly demonstrate, transcended mere national frontiers. Not to be outdone by his Party *Gauleiter*, the Reichsführer invited Hans Ledwinka and his son Erich to his private apartments, where they talked late into the night about the Volkswagen.

Ledwinka gave Hitler a detailed drawing. It was based on a small, air-cooled, rear-engined car, the prototype of which he had designed and built some years earlier. It was called the V570.

Hitler lost no time passing this drawing to Dr. Porsche.

After the Munich Agreement of 1938, the Czech city of Koprivnica, where the Tatra plant was located, fell just inside the boundaries of the Sudetenland. Tatra, its factory, its prototypes, designs, and working cars all became part of the Third Reich.

Tatra was ordered to stop production of everything but spare parts by Hermann Goering, and its patents were confiscated. Ledwinka always believed this resulted from lobbying by BMW and Daimler-Benz, German car companies fearful of his success in Germany.

After the outbreak of World War II, Tatra was put back into production of military cars and trucks. The astonishing V-8 Tatra T87s exacted a fearsome toll on German Army officer joyriders. So many were killed in these powerful cars that the German high command stopped production.

Ledwinka's reputation as a designer and engineer had already impressed the Führer himself. Now, in the latter days of the war, the

Germans ordered him to convert the plant at Koprivnica to munitions manufacture. Like many others in his position, he had little choice.

At the end of the Second World War, Ledwinka was arrested and imprisoned by the Czech puppet administration, on the orders of the Russians, for alleged collaboration with the Nazis. He was acquitted twice, but in spite of widespread local testimony to his innocence, he was eventually sentenced to six years' imprisonment on the charge of arms manufacture and supplying trucks to the German army.

Many Tatra employees had already fled Russian-occupied Czechoslovakia for Germany, where dozens swiftly found employment in what had been KdF-Stadt, at Wolfsburg on Lüneburg Heath. The Americans, too, had retreated behind the new frontier of a divided Europe.

Dr. Porsche had traveled to France, been arrested and briefly imprisoned, and would return to West Germany by 1947. In East Germany, the Red Army dug in to stay. Hundreds of miles to the east, Ledwinka, Tatra, and Koprivnica, with their designs, cars, and prototypes, disappeared behind the Iron Curtain.

Vienna, Austria, 1948

American efforts to smuggle German rocket scientists out from behind the Iron Curtain continued long after they had gleaned everything they wanted from BMW and abandoned the likes of Albert Siedler to his fate at Eisenach. Their junior partners in this clandestine trade were the British, and the battleground of this secret war was the divided city of Vienna.

The agreement between the Allies and the Russians meant that the Allies could drive to and from Vienna and West Germany. Intelligence officers and their agents secured a fleet of closed moving vans and loaded them with Tatra T87s painted in Russian colors.

Once in Vienna, the agents would unload a car in a darkened side street and drive it through the Russian checkpoint to a prearranged rendezvous. There they would pick up a fleeing scientist, drive back through the Russian checkpoints, and load the Tatra back inside its moving van. Then they would drive the lorry, the car, and the scientist back to West Germany for debriefing and a new life in the West.

British Intelligence had eleven Tatras at the height of this novel removal operation, which would remain officially secret nearly fifty years later. By that time, in a very different war zone, Tatra would have featured again in the secret history of the Cold War.

2

Japan

Samurai into Sedans

BY THE 1990s it would be said in some quarters that within a few years Japan would be capable of making all the world's cars.

Insofar as this prognosis inspired every reaction except indifference, Japan was already the world's dominant automobile manufacturer. Not only was Japan the most successful exporter of automobiles on earth; the automobile had made it one of the earth's most powerful nations.

Yet in 1945, Japan, like Germany, was a shattered nation, whose punishment for attempting to emulate the imperialist style of the West had been military defeat and the nuclear bombing of Hiroshima and Nagasaki.

America nursed bitter memories of the humiliation of Pearl Harbor and outrage at Japanese atrocities toward prisoners and civilians in the Pacific. It harbored plans for a peace so punitive that the Morgenthau Plan for Germany looked mild by comparison. In 1944, a Gallup poll in the United States revealed that 13 percent of the American public favored exterminating all Japanese. In 1945, Senator Lister Hill of Alabama urged the Allies to "gut the heart of

Japan with fire." Shortly after the surrender, the racist demagogue senator from Mississippi, Theodore Bilbo, wrote to General Douglas MacArthur urging the sterilization of all Japanese.

Elliott Roosevelt, the son of the president, told former vice-president and current secretary of commerce Henry A. Wallace that the United States should "keep on bombing until we have destroyed about half the Japanese population."

Even President Roosevelt, the great libertarian, showed interest in a scheme to crossbreed the Japanese with docile Pacific island-ers. This, Roosevelt told Smithsonian anthropologist Ales Hrdlička, might eradicate the "primitive" brains and "barbarism" of the enemy. President Truman, Roosevelt's successor, had no hesitation in de-scribing the Japanese as "vicious and cruel savages" who deserved nuclear extermination at Hiroshima and Nagasaki.

Those sentiments would endure in the United States well into the 1950s. In the parts of Asia that had endured the nightmare of Japanese occupation, they would last far longer. Yet the bombing, forcible crossbreeding, and sterilization of Japan prescribed by many Americans never took place either in literal or metaphorical form.

How did the Japanese rebuild themselves and their companies after such a shattering defeat? Was wartime defeat the key to their seemingly remorseless postwar rise and victory? Or were they some-how destined by time and temperament to succeed?

Tokyo, Japan, 1945

From their headquarters inside the Dai Ichi Insurance Building, one of the few left standing in downtown Tokyo, the Allied Supreme Commander in Japan, General Douglas MacArthur, and his staff set about implementing the American plan for postwar Japan.

By August 1945, 2 million Japanese had died as a result of the war. One quarter of that number were civilians. Americans arriving in Japan found themselves in an eerie, desolate land. Japanese gov-ernment officials and their corporate allies had looted the stockpiles of supplies built up during the war. Forty percent of Japanese cities were destroyed, and even the harvests failed.

The American plan was punitive but ultimately idealistic, in that it aimed to destroy what remained of Japanese military power and create a liberal, demilitarized Japan in which the influence of the long-established *zaibatsu* ("money cliques") such as Kawasaki, Sumitomo, Mitsui, and Mitsubishi would be ended. Instead of these giant industrial monopolies linked by webs of family relationships and nepotism, and characterized by cartels, fixed prices, and anti-competitive hidden agendas, there would be an egalitarian economy in which citizens enjoyed greater opportunities for advancement and participation in the means of production.

This was President Roosevelt's New Deal for Nippon. Yet less than two years later the plan had perished along with the president. As the Cold War intensified in Europe, Roosevelt had given way to Truman, and Morgenthau had given way to Marshall. In Germany, the plan for a return to a prewar agricultural economy had been cast aside in favor of a political and economic reconstruction program of unprecedented proportions.

In Japan, the representatives of the *zaibatsu* who had retained power during and after the war skillfully exploited the differences within Washington and between Truman and MacArthur over the Cold War, and encouraged the new American notion of Japan as a bulwark against Soviet and Chinese Communist expansion in Asia.

By 1948 the voices of concern were heard in Washington over the rising costs of the American occupation, compared with the long-term benefits of a reconstructed, highly centralized regional power. The early idealism of Roosevelt was discarded in favor of a pragmatic alliance between America and the conservative forces within Japan.

In 1949 the Americans even collaborated with the conservative Yoshida government to purge from Japanese industry "leftist" workers whose position would have been upheld only three years earlier as living proof of the need for reforms. The result was a postwar Japan that bore, as many American commentators later observed ruefully, an uncanny resemblance to the Japan that had existed before the war.

The Japanese had founded their automobile industry with the help of a crude but effective piece of industrial espionage. In 1930, Nissan, then known as Datsun, obtained a British Austin Seven, stripped it down, and used it as a model for the company's first car. Sir Herbert

Austin, the head of the British company, was so outraged when he heard about it that he had a Datsun shipped to England to see if the Japanese could be sued for patent infringement. This proved to be impossible.

American companies had dominated the Japanese market until 1936, when they were squeezed by restrictions. In 1939 the Japanese military government expelled them from the market altogether.

After the war, Japan, as an occupied country, was cut off from its traditional markets and suppliers and was dependent on American aid. Between 1946 and 1953, the country exported just twenty-two cars. By the same token, imports of American cars were minimal. American auto companies returned to mainland Japan, but because of the protectionist policies of the *zaibatsu*, they did not return to their prewar dominance. Instead, within a very few years they were squeezed out again by the Japanese government and by tariffs and bans on foreign investment.

Elsewhere the American automobile reigned supreme, thanks to the cheapness of oil and gasoline. America was the most powerful nation on earth. At home, Americans lived the American Dream. Abroad, they were the agents of the new Pax Americana. But the division of Europe, the Cold War in Europe and Asia, and the rise of the Soviet Union and China led to American involvement in countries far afield.

First and foremost among these countries was Korea, where America would soon be in dire need of a great many cars and trucks on very short notice. One of the great ironies of modern history is that the rebirth and rise to power of postwar Japan did not begin in Tokyo or Hiroshima, but in Washington, D.C., and Detroit, Michigan.

Detroit, Michigan, 1950

The Toyota Motor Sales Company was a part of the Mitsui *zaibatsu*. Toyota was a Nagoya-based company that had started life in the nineteenth century as a loom manufacturer with the help of technology from Oldham, in Britain. In the twentieth century, Toyota made cars and trucks.

In 1950 the company was almost broke. One plant switched production to flour and bread to feed its workers. Others made pots and pans. The CEO, Shotaro Kamiya, made the long journey to the United States in the hope of striking a deal with the great Ford Motor Company.

Kamiya was desperate. Toyota was selling fewer than three hundred trucks a month, and it had stopped making cars altogether. If he failed to line up a deal with Ford, Toyota would fail. But Ford was not interested. The Defense Department, too, opposed this kind of deal on the grounds that it would distract from domestic American production.

To Kamiya, the journey home to Japan was even longer. By the time he arrived home, however, the Korean War had broken out. Japan's proximity to Korea made it an ally of America in the war against Communist China. Kamiya was greeted with an order from the Pentagon for 1,500 trucks a month.

The war dividend had saved Toyota and many other Japanese companies.

The profits from the Pentagon's truck purchases enabled Kamiya and Eiji Toyoda, a descendant of Toyota's founder, to contemplate a return to making cars.

Toyoda traveled to America, to Ford's Rouge River plant in Detroit, the home of the Model T and the Model A, and the heartland of the American automobile industry. He stayed in Detroit for three months and absorbed many things. When he arrived back in Japan he had made up his mind. He had seen the most modern, most efficient, most successful car manufacturing plant in the world, but he had not seen what he believed should be the Japanese way.

Der Fordismus treated people like subhumans, or *Untermenschen,* which was what had inspired Hitler to re-create Rouge River at KdF-Stadt on Lüneburg Heath. Ford laid workers off at short notice and subordinated them to an inflexible production line designed for a broad mass market. Toyoda could not do this with his Japanese workers. His Japanese workers were newly aware of their rights — ironically, because Japan's American occupiers had laid down more liberal labor laws.

Then there was the question of mass production of identical items. If Toyota was to make cars again, it would have to cater first to the small and fragmented Japanese domestic market. The company could not afford to keep in stock the huge quantities of parts Toyoda saw stored at Rouge River. This new adaptability would also involve inventing new ways of changing at short notice the machinery on the production line.

The dies on the presses at Rouge River were not designed to be changed, except with considerable difficulty, while the labor force was laid off or sat around with nothing to do. Mistakes were mass-produced and only discovered months later. This, too, was not the Japanese way.

Eiji Toyoda and his chief production engineer, Taiichi Ohno, set to work addressing these problems. They obtained some second-hand American presses and modified them. They told their workers to turn out the parts for each stage of the manufacturing process "just in time" for when they were needed.

They encouraged their workers to form self-sufficient teams and to be their own supervisors, technicians, quality controllers, and cleaners. If they saw a car going down the line with a part missing or defectively installed, they were empowered to stop the line by pulling a cord so that the fault could be corrected.

At first the result was chaos. The line kept stopping whenever somebody thought they spotted a defect or ran out of parts, and pulled the cord. But soon the line began to run more smoothly, and with miraculous results. Not only did the individual workers begin to experience greater self-respect, but they functioned as a self-sufficient team on and off the production line.

The teams took pride in their work, and it showed in the lower cost and higher quality of the cars that came off the production line. Soon other Japanese automakers, such as Datsun, were following Toyota's example. They called it the Toyota Production System. Many years later, Westerners christened it "lean production."

By this time, many Westerners made the pilgrimage to Nagoya, but few Japanese made the pilgrimage to Detroit in return.

In 1958 the Korean War had been over for five years. One million Chinese, 600,000 Koreans, and 54,246 Americans had died. The border between North and South Korea remained where it had been, on the Thirty-eighth Parallel. The only tangible political consequence was America's decision to go to the support of France in fighting Communism in Vietnam.

The cost of the Korean War in financial terms had been colossal. Although it was little publicized at the time, the U.S. Special Procurements program pumped $3.5 billion into Japan. With other U.S. funds, Japan received as much as the Marshall Plan had invested in West Germany.

By 1958, Japan was producing 200,000 cars a year. In the same year it began exporting cars to the United States — although Datsun and Toyota each sold fewer than one hundred cars a year in that market.

Toyota was not the only Japanese car company jump-started by the foreign policy of the United States of America. But Toyota was the first, and it would become the biggest. To Kamiya, who had made the long and initially dispiriting journey to Detroit, the tragedy of Korea was "Toyota's salvation," although he added that he felt a sense of guilt that he "was rejoicing over another country's war."

Twenty-five years later, Japanese journalists would write how "even today Japanese businessmen shudder at the thought of what would have happened if there had been no war in Korea." The governor of the Bank of Japan would go so far as to describe the Special Procurements program as "divine aid."

The children of the American taxpayers who had unwittingly paid for the Special Procurements program, however, would reap the bitter harvest their parents had sown. In the unemployment lines and ghost towns that spread across Middle America, they would rue the day America ever helped Toyota, Nissan, Honda, and Mitsubishi discover the Japanese way.

3

Agnelli, FIAT, and the *Cinquecento*

I TALY, IN THE IMMEDIATE POSTWAR YEARS, seemed the least likely candidate for an economic miracle. The people were impoverished, the country was fragmented, the king was in exile, and the government was demoralized. Hopes for the future were torn between American aid and the Mafia. Yet out of this Mediterranean melting pot came a national success story based on one of the most resilient economies of all time.

The key players were a handful of extraordinary individuals. They included the late dictator, *Il Duce* Benito Mussolini, and the top managers at FIAT: the late tycoon Giovanni Agnelli; the designer, Dante Giacosa; the vice president, *Il Professore* Vittorio Valletta; and the playboy-turned-heir-apparent, Gianni *L'Avvocato* Agnelli.

The key to the story lay in the prewar years. The Agnelli family and FIAT — *Fabbrica Italiana Automobili Torino* — had dominated the Italian automobile industry since the early part of the century. They had formed profitable alliances with overseas powers such as Russia. They had built most of the Italian army's First World War trucks, and during the Second World War they had furnished Mussolini's military with its requirements. Although *Il Duce* personally preferred the elegant, powerful machines designed by Vincenzo Lancia — one of which he had built especially to impress

Hitler during the latter's visit to Rome to sign the "Pact of Steel" in 1938 — he rewarded FIAT with tariff protection and freedom from strikes.

In 1939, young Gianni Agnelli was sent on an automobile tour of the United States. "We always wanted to know," he recalled, "what was going on in Detroit."

Appropriately for a man whose empire would transcend frontiers and ideologies, Agnelli saw the Second World War from both sides. First, he served as a tank officer on the Russian front. After Italy withdrew from the war, he served as an officer in an Italian outfit that fought alongside the Fifth Army of General Mark Clark.

His vice president, Dr. Vittorio Valletta, had a wartime role that was even more prophetic of FIAT's postwar balancing act. In April 1944, three months after the Allies landed at Anzio, he undertook a hazardous journey across the Alps to reveal to the American intelligence chief Allen Dulles that the geographical position of Italy and its cheap labor force made it an "interesting opportunity" to the United States.

Shortly afterwards, FIAT began sending copies of the German production requests to the Allies, and negotiated with the Allies what levels would be acceptable. At the same time, Dr. Valletta was careful not to antagonize the Germans, and made no effort to protect anti-Fascist workers in his factories.

In June 1944, as the Allies entered Rome, the retreating Germans stepped up their reprisals against FIAT workers in the north who were active in the resistance. FIAT truck plants were flattened from the air by Allied air raids. By the spring of 1945, the car and truck plants of Turin had become a stronghold of the Italian national insurrection.

In April 1945, *Il Duce* was captured by partisans while trying to escape disguised as a German soldier in a motorized column on the *autostrada*. Mussolini and his mistress, Clara Petacci, were shot and their bodies suspended upside-down from lampposts in the Piazza Loreto in Milan.

In the same month, Italian anti-Fascist partisans went to Dr. Valletta's villa to arrest him as a wartime collaborator. When they arrived, they found a British officer already there, with a safe-conduct pass issued on Valletta's behalf.

∾

At the end of the war, Gianni Agnelli's grandfather and father were dead, and Agnelli junior was too occupied with the life of a playboy to take much interest in the family business. This period at FIAT was known as the Regency. The key figures were *Il Professore* Valletta and the designer Dante Giacosa.

Their diminutive prewar 500-cc Topolino had been designed and built at Lingotto, a Futurist-style factory with a racetrack on the roof. *Il Topolino* had cost between four and five months' earnings for the average worker. The automobile in question was nicknamed "Little Mouse," after the Italian name for Disney's Mickey Mouse. It brought mobility within reach of the Italian people.

The origins of the Italian people's car lay in a series of classic Italian contradictions. Valletta, a diminutive, autocratic former mathematics professor who had been one of Mussolini's closest associates, needed all the protection the Allies could afford him in the climate of suspicion of immediate postwar Italy. As late as 1948, *Il Professore* would be taken hostage by FIAT workers in sympathy with striking miners during a bloody battle with police in Turin.

Giacosa, the brilliant engineer from a poor background, knew what the people wanted. He despised the gas-guzzling monsters dreamed up in Detroit. The postwar success of FIAT was rooted in Giacosa's egalitarian vision of the automobile as a safe and economical means of transport for the average Italian family, combined with Valletta's adroitness in switching from arms manufacture back to automobiles.

It still took several years — and a playboy's car accident — for the combined forces of Valletta, Giacosa, and Agnelli to produce the definitive Italian people's car. "Have a fling for a few years," Agnelli's grandfather had told him. "Get it out of your system."

His grandson took him at his word. By 1952, Gianni Agnelli was one of the premier playboys of the western world. He commuted between palazzo, casino, and ski slope, by fast car, helicopter, and power boat. At 5:00 A.M. one day in 1952, he was on his way from a party in Cannes to Monte Carlo. His car skidded at high speed and crashed into a meat truck. The result was a permanent limp and a change of attitude.

Within a year, Agnelli had married a Neapolitan princess, settled in Turin, and gone to work in the family company. The playboy had become *L'Avvocato*, the dedicated businessman and dealmaker.

In 1957 the FIAT triumvirate unveiled the *Nuova Cinquecento*. The tiny but perfectly formed two-cylinder, air-cooled, rear-engined, four-seat *Cinquecento* was Giacosa's masterpiece. Yet it had taken him only ten months to design. Hypnotized by the motor scooter created by the helicopter designer D'Ascanio, he was convinced that what Italians wanted was a four-wheeled Vespa scooter. This, in the form of the *Cinquecento*, was what they got.

At home in Italy, *Il Professore* Valletta remained the dominant figure in FIAT's Regency. Abroad, he continued to show his mastery of the political tightrope.

In 1954, the American ambassador to Italy, Clare Boothe Luce, had a meeting with Dr. Valletta in Rome. The ambassador was unhappy that "in spite of the great sacrifices made by the U.S.A. (to the tune of more than one billion dollars), Communism in Italy instead of declining seemed to be making continuous progress." She said many members of the U.S. Congress were alarmed by this fact.

Dr. Valletta reassured the ambassador, and wrote to American diplomats. He told them of FIAT's efforts to introduce each year into the factories three hundred new workers who had been "well trained in the company's professional schools" and who the company hoped would be the foremen of the future.

"Turbulent elements," continued Dr. Valletta, had been sacked, and troublemakers against whom no exact charges could be made to stick were confined to the notorious spare parts section of the plant.

By 1962, Dr. Valletta was all too aware of the wind of change blowing through Italy in the form of center-left Christian Democracy. In the same year, he went to visit President Kennedy.

Kennedy was as perplexed as Clare Boothe Luce had been eight years earlier. He wanted to know which horse America should back in Italy. Dr. Valletta told him to support the Socialists financially — and added that he should do so through the Christian Democrats, so that they in turn could use the money "as a lever to extract the cooperation of the Socialist party."

By this time FIAT was synonymous with Italy's postwar economic miracle, but few Italians had heard of Giacosa. The launch of the *Cinquecento* made him a national hero. Three and a half million of the cars were made between 1957 and 1975. Like the Volkswagen, it is one of the very few cars to have transcended its origins and become synonymous with a landscape, a people, and a way of life.

Dante Giacosa retired as chief engineer and designer in 1970. At the end of his career, he wrote, "The automobile has become a mobile living-space . . . The car designer is now comparable to an architect."

If anybody could have made such a claim for himself, it was Giacosa. But he was too modest. Besides, he was too busy. Until his death in 1996 at the age of ninety-one, he lived and worked as a consultant for FIAT in Turin.

4

Les Chemins de la Liberté et les Deux Chevaux

WHEN THE GERMANS MARCHED INTO PARIS in 1940, Pierre Boulanger knew exactly what to do.

Boulanger was chief engineer and designer to André Citroën, France's premier private automobile manufacturer. For several years he and his team had been working on the prototypes of a revolutionary new car that would bring motoring within reach of the average French family. Since the average French family was agricultural and rural, there were certain criteria to be met.

Boulanger's brief to his team had been simple. The car had to be able to carry four peasants, a hundred pounds of potatoes, and a basket of eggs across a plowed field, without breaking the eggs. The top speed should be only thirty-four miles per hour — any faster than that would be dangerous.

A tall man, Boulanger also stipulated that the car had to have a roofline high enough for a man wearing a hat.

Citroën's new car was unveiled at the 1948 Paris Motor Show. They called it the Deux Chevaux (2CV) — literally, "two horses" — because of André Lefevbre's two-horsepower 375-cc engine. The billowing, swooping bodywork was sculpted by the Italian Flaminio Bertoni. The aerodynamics and construction were borrowed from aircraft design; Boulanger had been a much-decorated First World War fighter pilot.

André Citroën called it "the ugly duckling." Boulanger said it looked like "an umbrella on wheels." The Parisian press were even less kind: "Where," they asked, "is the can opener?"

The car they were describing did indeed look like nothing else ever seen. The driver peered through the night with the help of a single bug-eyed headlight. The engine was started by pulling on a rope. Later models added a second light and an electric starter. The roof could be peeled back like a sardine can. There were no outside door handles, and the internal ones frequently broke off. Many people got in and out through the roof.

Boulanger would not allow shock absorbers because, he said, they were an expensive luxury (his design team added them in secret). The seats were slung from the roof like hammocks, and there was a single hand-operated windshield wiper. Later, more sophisticated models ran the wiper from the speedometer. The faster you drove, the faster it wiped. When you stopped at traffic lights, the wiper stopped too.

Yet the reception by the public of these cars was remarkable. The engine had the fewest moving parts of any automobile power unit, used very little fuel, and, the manufacturer stressed, it could be run at full power all day without blowing up. (The inference was that Frenchmen always drove that way.) Those who managed to buy the early 2CVs were indeed fortunate because they had to satisfy Citroën that they were a country doctor, a farmer, or a vet. An inspector would call on would-be purchasers to check.

The 2CV was manufactured a mile from the Eiffel Tower at Levallois, formerly a Victorian bicycle factory. During the 1950s, the engine grew first to 425 cc and then to 602 cc. The windows also grew marginally bigger, and more instruments were added. A twin-engined, four-wheel-drive version was developed for the Sahara, and a plastic-bodied, open-topped version for the beach.

In the Atacama Desert of Chile, a 2CV driver lost all his crankcase oil and filled the crankcase with bananas. He drove safely to the first garage he saw — 185 miles away.

In the Himalayan state of Sikkim, the monarchy adopted the

2CV as its royal car. In Chad, 2CVs had their bodywork replaced with wicker to improve air cooling. In Holland, a farmer in North Brabant used his 2CV to pull his plow. In Andorra, a "stretch" 2CV was used as a hearse.

In France, the 2CV was used in a novel way by the Provençal forest fire department: The front halves of two 2CVs were joined back to back; faced with an advancing fire on a narrow trail, with no room to turn around, the driver simply switched off the forward-pointing engine, moved to the rearward-pointing half of the car, with its seat, engine, windshield, and steering wheel, and drove away.

The *Deuche*, short for *Deux Chevaux*, as it became known, was hailed as "the minimum French car." No other car powered by the internal combustion engine would enjoy such favor from the green movement for its low energy cost and relative generosity to the ozone layer.

Meanwhile, what of that fateful day in 1940 when the Germans marched into Paris? Boulanger had sent the designs into safekeeping and ordered the 250 prototypes of the new car destroyed. A single vehicle was crated up in parts and stashed in a Parisian sewer. After the war, no one could remember where it was. It was eventually discovered in 1970. When reassembled, it ran on the first attempt to start it.

5

A Very British People's Car

THE SUEZ CRISIS OF 1956 led to gasoline rationing in Europe for the first time since World War II. In Britain there was a sudden vogue for German "bubble cars" manufactured by Messerschmitt and Heinkel — names that had bombed and strafed British cities only a decade and a half earlier.

Sir Leonard Lord was head of the British Motor Corporation. Lord decided that a British small car was needed, one that would match the Germans for fuel economy, but would also accommodate the family and their luggage. This was to be the first of the small-car wars, and the last to be won by a totally British car.

The car in question would not only see off the German bubble cars, but also make the Volkswagen look pedestrian. It would set off a host of counteroffensives by competitors such as Renault, FIAT, Citroën, and, above all, Ford of Britain. It was also the last car to be effectively designed by one man — and that man was Alec Issigonis.

He was an exile and an emigré, and his imagination likewise knew no frontiers. He was born in 1906 in Smyrna, now Izmir, in Western Turkey. His early life is obscure. By 1933 he was a British citizen, and a draftsman for Rootes Motors. By 1936 he was Morris Motors' suspension engineer. Shortly afterwards, he became Morris's chief engineer.

Issigonis had already become a legend at BMC as the father of the Morris Minor, a quintessentially British motor car shaped like a teapot without a handle or spout. Although BMC would end up selling over a million Minors, the car would remain a benevolent cult object that never possessed the universal appeal of the Volkswagen or the unquenchable *brio* of the *Cinquecento*. The Morris Minor suited archbishops of Canterbury and retired prime ministers, like Clement Attlee. A new car was needed, and Lord Issigonis was given a free hand to design it.

The new project was commissioned in March 1957. The German threat was perceived to be sufficient to increase the normally modest level of secrecy around it. They called it ADO 15.

Two and a half years later, it was ready. This was about half the usual time it took to create a new car. It recalled Giacosa's inspired burst of creativity that, in the same year that Issigonis began work, had produced the *Nuova Cinquecento*.

Issigonis took Lord for a drive in the car. Lord's reaction was immediate. "We'll make it," he said.

The novelty of the car lay in its having so much space within such a small body. It was only ten feet long, and yet four adults could sit inside. There was even a trunk. Issigonis had mounted the engine sideways, so that it took up less room (a trick first used in 1911, in a long-forgotten British car called the FD). The gearbox of the ADO 15 fitted underneath, and there was no transmission tunnel; the car had front-wheel drive.

There were other unusual features. The wheels were only ten inches in diameter, and the suspension was "independent." The doors were equipped with bins for carrying odd bits and pieces. The side windows slid open, instead of winding down, a design, the ad-men would later explain, that would keep the breeze from spoiling a woman's hairdo.

Between 1950 and 1959 the number of cars on British roads had risen from 2.5 million to 9 million. One third of these were driven by women. The journalism of the time reflected the preoccupation with balancing freedom and femininity:

> What every woman wants is a car with gently circulating fresh air, which does not make a complete bird's nest of her hair-do . . .

The main virtue of owning a car is that it gets you from A to B
immaculately. A virtue which is lost if you have to stop on the way and
struggle with a wheel in your pencil-slim skirt and white gloves . . .

The new BMC "baby," as the press called it, was launched in
August 1959. It cost less than eight hundred dollars. Although BMC
was an amalgamation of Austin and Morris, the two companies
retained separate dealerships. The car was marketed under two
badges — Austin and Morris — and the vehicles were identical except for the radiator grille.

One was called the Austin Seven, after the popular if primitive
little car of the 1920s, plagiarized by Datsun and paraphrased by
BMW as the "Dixi." The other was named after the Minor, which was
still in production. "Minor" meant small, so an extra word was
needed to emphasize the fact that the new car was even smaller;
hence it became the Morris Mini-Minor.

This was the machine that Lord and Issigonis hoped would
repair the damage that Messerschmitt and Heinkel had done to
Britain. By 1962, both the Austin Seven and the Morris Mini-Minor
were popularly known as the Mini.

Before the Mini, cars were small, medium-sized, or large, and
their size was a direct measure of wealth and status. The German
bubble cars epitomized the lowest end of the scale, and were
doomed to remain there through lack of space and pace. The Mini
had plenty of both, and succeeded beyond all expectations in fulfill-
ing the intentions of Sir Leonard Lord to see off the descendants of
the Luftwaffe.

By the end of the 1960s, the Mini would be synonymous with the
changes and contradictions that overturned the conventions of half
a century and an entire country in a single decade. This "people's
car," which cost less than five hundred pounds, was bought not only
by people who could afford no more than this, but also by affluent
Londoners as a second car to overcome the problems of traffic and
parking. The Mini was the first truly classless British car, the second-
best-selling car in history after the Volkswagen, and the best-selling
British car of all time.

In the 1969 movie *The Italian Job*, Michael Caine and his fellow
British crooks stage a traffic jam in the heart of Turin. The aim is to
pull off a bullion robbery. The success of the enterprise and of the

film at the box office depended on a small, fast, and photogenic getaway car.

Turin was the home of FIAT. But although the Italian giant lent the producers the test track on the roof of its Lingotto factory for stunt sequences, there was never any chance of the drive-on scenes being stolen by the *Cinquecento*. To take on the Italians on their home territory and win — this was surely the Mini's finest hour.

In the 1990s, Minis and their drivers from all over the world would begin to converge on Turin for an annual rally and *Italian Job* rerun. Less plausible, but true and far more criminal to many than the activities of the fictitious characters in the movie, was the fact that Michael Caine and his fellow actors would make more profits in a single day's acting than their world-beating getaway car would make in the thirty-five years of its unbroken real-life production.

2

America and the Rise of Europe

6

An American in Europe

B<small>Y THE</small> 1960s, the people's car was a worldwide reality. The race was on to penetrate the richer levels of the American and European markets. This was the limit of the known mass-market automobile world.

The big manufacturers — Ford, Volkswagen, FIAT, Citroën, and General Motors — and luxury car makers such as Mercedes-Benz, BMW, and Porsche — had invested billions of dollars in developing designs that their domestic markets alone could not sustain. The battle for the new domestic and export markets had begun, and it was not merely based on engineering excellence, but also on marketing and design.

The 1960s were a period of unparalleled affluence in America and Europe. The automobile was unique in that it both fueled and drove that boom and was the boom's most conspicuous and significant product. To the American and European automakers there seemed no limit to how far they would go.

The success of the cheap, economical, and well-made "people's cars" from Germany, Italy, France, and Britain in the late 1950s and early 1960s did not escape the attention of the industrial giant that had developed the world's first mass-market automobile. Ford of

Dearborn, Michigan, had never lived down the success of the Model T "Tin Lizzie," and had never quite recovered from it. People from all over the world still made the pilgrimage to Rouge River in the footsteps of Agnelli and Toyoda. But Ford had no plans to become an automobile museum.

Ford was second in size only to General Motors, and similar in culture and outlook. Like General Motors, Ford had had substantial operations in Nazi Germany that remained in production throughout the Second World War.

Adolf Hitler and Henry Ford went back a long way. Hitler kept a life-size portrait of Ford in his Munich Nazi Party Headquarters and offered to bring his storm troopers to America to support Ford's presidential ambitions in the 1920s. Ford mass-produced not only cars, but anti-Jewish hate literature, which he distributed through his newspaper *The Dearborn Independent* and through Ford dealerships across America. The most vicious example of this was "The International Jew," much of which Ford himself had cribbed from the notorious turn-of-the-century forgery "The Protocols of the Elders of Zion," concocted by the Russian Czarist secret police. Hitler, who, as we have seen, did not hesitate to appropriate an idea when he saw it, in turn cribbed much of the rhetoric and "theory" of anti-Semitism advanced in Ford's book and incorporated it in his own *Mein Kampf.*

In 1939, Henry Ford sent Hitler a check for fifty thousand dollars on the dictator's fiftieth birthday. Hitler was already a millionaire from the royalties of *Mein Kampf.* This was a message of congratulations from Ford to Hitler for putting Germany back on its feet.

Henry Ford's comment at the beginning of World War II might just as well have been made by Hitler: "We do not regard ourselves as a national company, but solely as a multinational organization."

In 1940, Ford met Sosthene Behn, the founder of ITT, and Gerhardt Westrick, a prominent Nazi lawyer, in New York. Westrick had been authorized by German foreign secretary Joachim von Ribbentrop to ask Ford and Behn to do everything they could to persuade Britain to surrender. Ford and Behn attempted to explore this possibility in communications with Prime Minister Winston Churchill.

Throughout the Second World War, Ford subsidiaries, with subsidiaries of General Motors, made 90 percent of the half-track troop transports and 70 percent of the trucks for Hitler's Wehrmacht. The British Secret Intelligence Service regarded these vehicles as "the backbone of the German Army's transport system."

At the end of the war, Ford declared Volkswagenwerk at Wolfsburg to be too close to the new frontier with the Reds. But Ford was keen to extract compensation for the damage done to its own plants inside the Third Reich.

In 1967, Ford would receive $1 million, in the form of tax exemption on profits, for the damage done to its military truck lines in Cologne. Today, thirty years later, the Ford Motor Company is reviving the sanitized, homespun image of Henry Ford as the American icon in its television advertising. The Ford whom Hitler called "my inspiration" has been airbrushed out of the official history, in a manner worthy of the Russian Communist propaganda machine that Ford himself would have been the first to condemn.

In the 1950s and early 1960s, apart from General Motors, the Ford Motor Company was still bigger than nearly all the European car manufacturers put together. In the 1960s, under the driving force of the brilliant salesman Lee Iacocca, the Ford Falcon and the legendary Ford Mustang brought the perfect car to young aspirational America and brought to the men in Michigan who had put the world on wheels with the "Tin Lizzie" and created *der Fordismus* the glamour associated with the high-performance sports car.

In Europe, Ford was the most successful foreign automobile manufacturer. The interprovincial rivalry between its bridgeheads in Britain and Germany was so intense that they maintained separate dealer networks. But the Europeans were getting a jump on the Americans with their new, affordable utility cars. There was no telling the limit of this market. There were signs that the Europeans were developing sexier and sportier variations on the Americans' themes.

The BMC Minis, in particular, were grabbing greater and greater shares of the European market. The Minis had been developed by John Cooper into the most glamorous and popular Monte Carlo rally winners for decades. Even the little FIATs were being transformed by Abarth into road racers. At Ford headquarters in Dearborn, the feeling was that something had to be done about their European market.

Ford of Britain was nervous. The investment in a new model was colossal, and would commit the resources of the company for years to come. If the investment went wrong, there would be no way to abandon the project fast enough and start again. Only when Ford of Britain heard from Dearborn and other sources that Ford of Germany was also contemplating a new model did the British suddenly become fired up. The two companies may have been part of the same American multinational corporation, but the rivalry remained, and it was still only fifteen years since the end of World War II.

Ford of Britain wanted to break into the market with a car that would not follow where the others had gone. The car had to be faster and lighter than the others, and also bigger and sportier, with the hint that there was even more to come. The engineers and the stylists set to work, in conditions that were, by today's standards, positively indiscreet.

The car, code-named Archbishop, was developed by Ford's product planning staff under Terence Beckett. John Barber, who would go on to head the British Leyland Motor Corporation, estimated the cost of every component in every potential competitor's cars so that the new car could be designed and built more competitively. The chief product analyst on the new car was an ambitious young Scot named Alex Trotman.

The engine and the strong, light body were developed in line with the existing European market, and with an eye to the growth of the high-speed highway, *autoroute*, *autobahn*, and *autostrada*. It was in Italy that Ford of Britain finally found the idea for marketing the new car that would be linked to the brave new Europe. Ford of Britain chose the name of a small town in the Dolomites — Cortina.

The Cortina was an immediate success at the 1962 London Motor Show. The first American-developed popular car to dominate the European markets since before the Second World War, it was Ford of Britain's best-selling car for over a decade.

The Cortina did everything that the German, French, Italian, and British "people's cars" did, but on a more sophisticated scale. It became an established rally car and road racer. As a vehicle big enough for courting couples, it also made a substantial contribution to the British baby boom.

Thirty years later, Terence Beckett had been knighted, John

Barber would be apportioning blame for the collective suicide of British Leyland Motor Corporation, and Alex Trotman would be chairman and CEO of the Ford Motor Company.

The Cortina's descendants would still be selling heavily on the strength of the name. Like the half-tracks and trucks of Hitler's Wehrmacht, and many of the sentiments of *Mein Kampf*, the most profitable British car ever would, in reality, be American.

7

Il Boom

Italy and Agnelli on the *Autostrada*

FORD'S CHOICE OF A SMALL TOWN IN ITALY for the name of its new car in Europe was a compliment. Under the triumvirate of Valletta, Agnelli, and Giacosa, FIAT had become the automobile manufacturer more closely associated with the rise of a nation than any other car company in the world.

By the 1960s, FIAT was a car kingdom, and industrial Italy was FIAT by any other name. They had done this by satisfying the desire for greater freedom of the ordinary person with the automobile. The *Nuova Cinquecento* and nine other models in twenty body styles had meant that, by 1963, one in seventeen Italians owned a car, compared with one in ninety a dozen years earlier. Not only that, but 63 percent of them owned a FIAT. There were 350,000 serious accidents in the same year, in which nine thousand people were killed — a fatality rate five times that of the United States.

FIAT was turning out nearly a million cars a year by 1963, just ten thousand fewer than Chrysler in America. This made FIAT number five among the world's automobile manufacturers, and the tenth biggest corporation in Europe. Within Italy itself, FIAT was not only a state within a state, but was inextricably intertwined with Italian political and economic life. FIAT's 130,000 employees enjoyed the best wages and benefits in Italy, including private health care and summer camps for the children.

FIAT controlled the Turin-based newspaper *La Stampa*, one of the most influential in Italy. The company was paternalistic yet progressive, altruistic yet all-powerful; and most employees seemed to like it that way. They called what was happening in Italy *Il Boom — Il Miracolo*.

But in Turin, *Il Professore* Valletta was worried about foreign competition. "When you eat at someone else's table," he growled, "you should be very careful to take only your own portion."

Dr. Valletta was eighty-one years old and still putting in an eleven-hour workday. He liked to see what was going on for himself. On an inspection of the company's summer camp for children on the Tyrrhenian Sea, he had personally tested all the taps and lavatories. *Il Professore* had emerged from the building soaked from head to foot.

Dr. Valletta was worried. The new Common Market meant that Italians were buying more and more foreign cars: "We have no objection to a certain amount of foreign competition," said Dr. Valletta, "but foreign car sales in Italy are at the 26 percent level . . . they are only 10 percent in the rest of Europe and only 4 percent in the United States."

The man who had advised Mussolini, survived the attentions of anti-Fascist partisans, rebuilt FIAT's bombed factories, reassured American ambassadors, and guided President Kennedy was as spry and straight-backed as ever, but there were others who said he was out of touch. Gianni Agnelli, *L'Avvocato*, was diplomatically soothing about Italians who succumbed to the foreign competition. "It's like a married man who commits an act of unfaithfulness and returns to his wife," said the world-renowned playboy. "After fifty years of being married to FIAT, Italy can be forgiven one infidelity."

Agnelli was playing down the question of who would succeed Dr. Valletta as chairman and managing director. Valletta was grooming his longtime assistant Gaudenzio Bono. Agnelli did not publicly disagree. "I haven't the slightest idea how to build a car," he said. "FIAT is a machine which needs a chief who is an expert in all phases of its operations, as is Bono."

But in 1966, when *Il Professore* retired, the playboy pounced. "I decided that I was the best person," Agnelli said, "and I took over."

Under Agnelli's chairmanship, FIAT and Italy consolidated their relationship at home and abroad. It took the fast lane to the international markets of the *autostrada*. No other car company, before or since, presented such a dazzling contrast, in terms of size, sophistication, and continuity, to the relatively small, undeveloped, and unstable country of its birth.

In the same year, 1966, Agnelli made his most spectacular deal yet.

Moscow, 1966

FIAT's presence in prerevolutionary Moscow was a dim memory, but it had not altogether lapsed with the Bolshevik revolution and the coming to power of Lenin and Stalin. Agnelli had at least fought on the side of the Allies in the latter years of World War II. Germany, not Italy, was the battleground of the Cold War, and Soviet-Italian relations were cordial, if frequently confused, throughout the 1950s. The Russians knew it was not enough merely to make fake BMWs at places like Eisenach.

In the early 1960s, Premier Nikita Khrushchev had visited FIAT's plants in Turin. As a farmer's son, he had shown great interest in FIAT's tractors. Khrushchev had not entirely disapproved of the automobile, but, like Dr. Valletta, he was shocked by the wastefulness of American automobiles. As president of the Soviet Union, he feared the capacity of the automobile to unleash the individualism pent up in the Soviet peoples; he wanted it restricted to approved collective use in giant car pools.

Khrushchev's successor, President Kosygin, was more attuned to the automobile as a vehicle for change. A change was certainly needed. In spite of its vast population of over 200 million people, the Soviet Union still classified the automobile industry as a subsidiary of the machine-making industry. Buses and trucks dominated automobile production; car production was limited to 200,000 a year: 2 percent of that of Western Europe.

The first postwar Soviet car was the *Pobieda*. By the 1960s it was manufactured and sold in Poland as the *Warszawa*. Few Poles could afford even this, and many opted for the two-cylinder, two-cycle *Syrena*, the tiny, rear-engined *Mikrus* sedan, or the even tinier *Smyk* two-seater. In the Soviet Union, another tiny, rear-engined car, the *Zaporogiets*, carried four people and a gas-burning heater against the subarctic winters.

Soviet auto plants in Moscow and Gorky produced the small, obsolete *Moskvich* sedan and the larger, equally obsolete and sinister *Zim*, the preferred means of transport of the KGB. In spite of the vaunted phenomenon of the Soviet people, there was no Soviet people's car.

In 1966, Kosygin's Minister for Cars, Tarasov, also visited Turin. Unlike Khrushchev, Tarasov was not a farmer's son, and he showed more interest in cars than in tractors — particularly the middle-sized FIAT 124.

Three months later, *Il Professore* Valletta went to Moscow to complete the deal. The Italian government granted the Soviet Union export credits worth $450 million to enable FIAT to build a plant capable of manufacturing 600,000 cars a year — more than half of FIAT's total output and three times the total current Russian production — on the River Volga. The car would be a modified version of the FIAT 124. Work would begin straightaway.

Kuybyshev, Soviet Union, 1966

Six hundred miles southeast of Moscow, on the left bank of the River Volga and bounded by the Zhiguli Mountains, on the main road to the Urals, Siberia, and Soviet Central Asia, was the port town of Kuybyshev. The town and its surrounding *oblast*, or independent administrative region, was a place of forested plains and humid uplands; of dry steppes rich in black soil and mineral resources; of wheat, beet, barley, and pigs. It was a major industrial center, dominated by its hydroelectric power plant.

Until 1935, Kuybyshev was known as Samara. It was renamed in that year after Valerian Vladimirovich Kuybyshev, a prominent Bolshevik and organizer of the armed revolt in Samara during the revolution. Kuybyshev had been a Politburo member and supporter of Stalin in the latter's struggle with Trotsky — for which his reward was death under "mysterious circumstances" in 1935.

Kuybyshev and its eponymous *oblast* was a place of long, cold winters and short, hot summers. The actual site of the planned plant and complex was Stavropol, two hours from Kuybyshev, on the Volga. It was here, in the early months of the winter of 1966, that work began on a massive construction project encompassing a plant capable of manufacturing more than half a million cars a year, and a high-rise complex capable of housing 100,000 workers and their families.

This was the result of the unprecedented coalition between the Mediterranean capitalists and the Communist commissars. In keeping with the name of the mountains that overlooked this remote, windswept spot, it was announced that the new car, in reality the modified FIAT 124, would be named the *Zhiguli*. In overseas markets, it would be better known as the Lada.

Other Western automobile manufacturers had been approached by the Russians before they decided on FIAT. They claimed that the deal was no more than a barter arrangement between governments. But the fact was that no other Western automaker had had such a long association with Russia as FIAT, and no other car company chairman wielded such personal charisma and political influence as Agnelli.

FIAT, the lifelong enemy of the Italian Communist trade unions, was an ally of Moscow. "It is hard," said one Roman economist, "for Italian Communists to complain about Agnelli. After all, if FIAT is good for Russia, why shouldn't it be good for Italy?"

The Italian Communists feared an attempt by FIAT to circumvent the trade unions at home, and export its own cars from a cheaper labor market back to Italy. They complained, all the same. So did the anti-Communist Italian prime minister, when the Russians, in honor of the recently deceased Italian Communist leader, Palmiro Togliatti, insisted on calling the new car plant "Togliattigrad."

Il Boom — Il Miracolo — L'Avvocato. By 1969, Agnelli was *numero uno* at FIAT, and FIAT was number one in Italy. Every Friday, 4 million Italians crammed baggage and *bambini* into their cars and set off on the *stradas* and *autostradas* for *Il Weekend*.

There were 54 million people in Italy, and 8 million cars, and most of those cars were made by FIAT. FIAT was a city-state with

157,000 people at work in twenty-two plants around smog-covered Turin. FIAT outproduced Volkswagen and ranked as the biggest automobile manufacturer outside the United States. Even in Germany, one car in thirteen was a FIAT.

The Agnelli family's holding company, IFI (*Instituto Finanzario Industriale*), controlled FIAT and much of Italian industry and the stock market. "Agnelli," wrote the British journalist Anthony Sampson in *The New Europeans*, "has a mythology not unlike President Kennedy's. Clearly his presence fills some kind of psychological gap."

In 1969, Italy's twenty-sixth government since 1945 was forced to step down. There was a one-day general strike, followed by similar strikes in more than twenty cities. In the *autunno caldo* — "hot autumn" — of that year, the giant FIAT Mirafiori plant in Turin became the headquarters for an alliance of militant students and young workers from the south of Italy coordinating strikes for better conditions. A demonstration several thousand strong assembled at the gates of Mirafiori and set out with a slogan that sent a shiver down the spines of the businessmen of Turin: *"Che cosa vogliamo? Tutto!"* ("What do we want? Everything!")

Many Italians, especially in the south, still lived in appalling poverty. In Rome, judges and lawyers staged an angry demonstration outside the Palace of Justice to protest the archaic penal codes — they included imprisonment for adulterous women, but not for men — and an overloaded court system.

Yet, like the Italians on the *autostrada*, Agnelli always wanted to go faster. He negotiated the complex merger of FIAT and Citroën with his friends, the Michelin family, and effectively took control of a combine with sales of $3 billion and production of 2 million cars a year.

Agnelli still drove his $500,000 Ferrari at speeds of up to 180 miles per hour, his lame leg propped on the dashboard.

He feared the failure of the rest of Italy to keep up. "The trouble is," he said, "that we have to compete with Detroit, but the government in Rome doesn't have to compete with Washington."

In the 1970s his worst fears — for FIAT and Italy — would come dangerously true.

8

De Gaulle and "The Goddess"

AFTER THAT DAY AT PETIT-CLAMART in August 1962, for President
de Gaulle the "Goddess" could do no wrong.

General Salan, the figurehead of the French settlers in Algiers,
had been arrested. De Gaulle himself would shortly win a referen-
dum for the direct election of the president. To the anti-Gaulleist
OAS (Organisation Armée Secrète), this only made him more of an
enemy.

The OAS hitmen waiting on the road between the Elysée Palace
and Orly Airport riddled the president's car with 140 bullets and
killed two of his motorcycle bodyguards. One shot passed within an
inch of the president's head. In a remarkable feat of driving, de
Gaulle's chauffeur kept the car under control with four punctured
tires and the president, Madame de Gaulle, and his chauffeur survived.

They called it the DS 19 — *La Déesse*. Seven years earlier it had
caused a sensation at the 1955 Paris Motor Show. Within forty-five
minutes of its unveiling, Citroën had 750 firm orders, which grew to
twelve thousand by the end of the day. There was almost nothing
that was not new about this car, and what was not new was still
better engineered than the competition.

The DS 19 was the first production car with such an elegant and advanced aerodynamic shape and so much technical innovation. All the major systems — gearshift, clutch, steering, and brakes — were power-assisted. The Déesse had a new suspension system that automatically adjusted the height of the car. It had a powerful 1.9-liter engine and a one-spoke steering wheel designed to increase safety. It had fenders that could be released by turning a single nut. It was the antithesis of Citroën's equally revolutionary "ugly duckling," the 2CV.

Citroën made one and a half million of these cars in the next twenty years. A sixteen-year-old trainee mechanic working in a Citroën garage could scarcely contain himself: "When the first DS came in, it was just an utter amazement. It was so wonderful to look at and so far advanced in its engineering that it made other cars of the time look completely dull."

Over the following decade, the automotive press was equally lost for words: "Unique in style . . . The years-ahead car . . . The car of the future . . . The most advanced car of its time . . . A car that made history . . . Still waiting for the others to catch up after nine years . . ."

The 1966 movie *Un Homme et une femme* by Claude Lelouch, starring Anouk Aimée and featuring a haunting soundtrack by Francis Lai, unleashed the world's repressed Francophilia. The movie made fashionable all things French in America and elsewhere. One of its tracks was entitled "A 200 à l'heure" ("Two hundred kilometers an hour").

The avant-garde filmmaker Jean-Luc Godard struck back in the celluloid car wars with *Weekend,* a chronicle of unrelenting carnage set on the *autoroutes* and *routes nationales* and aimed squarely at the embodiment of capitalist evil in the form of the French automobile.

But despite all the commotion, outside France the quintessentially French "Goddess" would remain a car for the connoisseur. Inside France it was the unchallenged vehicle of choice for the wealthy and the privileged.

This included President de Gaulle.

In 1962 his life had been saved by the Goddess and his chauffeur. In 1969 de Gaulle was informed that the Michelin family, who owned Citroën, was contemplating selling the company to FIAT and the Italian tycoon Agnelli. De Gaulle, who had some years earlier dismissed the visiting Japanese prime minister Ikeda as a "little transistor salesman," reacted to the suggestion that Citroën was in danger of slipping into foreign hands with characteristic bluntness. There would be no outright sale of France's premier private car manufacturer to the Italians.

While Agnelli was telling his friends that "the merger is complete," the French government limited FIAT to a 15-percent stake. As far as President de Gaulle was concerned, he had saved the day for *La belle France*, as the "Goddess" had done for him. In the end, Agnelli and FIAT would win effective control of Citroën through a complex holding company arrangement.

The French distrust of Italy lingered. In the Fred Zinneman movie about the attempt to assassinate de Gaulle, *The Day of the Jackal*, the OAS contract killer symbolically crossed the border into France from Italy in an Italian Alfa Romeo — a company controlled by FIAT.

The real President de Gaulle, meanwhile, was taking no chances. He had his later "Goddesses" bulletproofed and mineproofed, just in case.

9

Mercedes-Benz and the Economic Miracle

THEY NAMED WHAT HAPPENED IN GERMANY in the 1950s and 1960s the *Wirtschaftswunder*; the "economic miracle." They named the car that was to become an emblem of that miracle after the eleven-year-old daughter of the Austrian consul-general in Nice, Emil Jellinek.

In 1900, Jellinek ordered a car from Gottfried Daimler's motor company. The consul-general wanted a car that was fast and low to the ground. It had to be named Mercedes, after his daughter. Daimler obliged, and the car was so successful that all Daimler cars subsequently bore the Mercedes name.

Gottfried Daimler and Karl Benz never met, although they lived only sixty miles apart in Stuttgart and Mannheim. In 1926, when the real-life Mercedes was thirty-seven years old, the Daimler and Benz companies merged to form Daimler-Benz AG. The Mercedes became the Mercedes-Benz.

Hitler had admired the powerful sports cars made by BMW and secretly coveted the Tatra; he had commissioned the *KdF-Wagen*; he had made the last car journey of his life in one. But the automobile manufacturer whom he had declared to be "among the great pioneers of humanity" was Daimler-Benz. The car in which he had generally toured his territories in happier times was the super-charged 7.7-liter, 230-horsepower Mercedes-Benz.

Daimler-Benz, the parent company, enthusiastically returned the Führer's compliment. The company gave the dictator a discount on his favorite car. It combined with the General Motors subsidiary Opel to build Blitz trucks for the Wehrmacht. It supplied the engine for the Messerschmitt ME-109 fighter. It built tanks, ships' engines, torpedo heads, and components for Hitler's ultimate secret weapon, the V-2. It was preeminent among the dark engine rooms and work-shops of the Thousand Year Reich.

The Reich was equally indispensable to the life and economy of the company. Daimler-Benz management opposed the republican government of Weimar, welcomed Hitler, applauded his destruction of the multiparty state, and encouraged German rearmament. On festive occasions, the company's insignia was displayed alongside the swastika.

The three-pointed star framed by a circle symbolized the su-premacy of Daimler-Benz engines on land and sea and in the air. If the Russians had not redrawn the postwar map of Europe and triggered the Cold War, and if the Western Allies had implemented the Morgenthau Plan to return Germany to a prewar agricultural economy, the biggest casualty of peace would have been Daimler-Benz, the Führer's favorite automaker.

After the Second World War and the coming of the Cold War, Daimler-Benz was a prime beneficiary of the Marshall Plan. With the reconstruction of industrial Germany, Mercedes-Benz soon resumed its dominant place on the autobahns.

The Mercedes-Benz range featured uniformity of engineering excellence from the bottom to the top. The same rounded finish and effortless power characterized the middle-range sedans and the high-end sports cars.

At the summit was the Mercedes-Benz 600, the fantastic new peak of automotive luxury. The 600 had hydraulically operated doors that closed at the touch of a fingertip, a rear lounge with two rows of hydraulically adjustable facing seats and a 6.3-liter engine. Had things turned out differently, this surely was the car that would have conveyed the aging Führer and Frau Hitler along the autobahn from Berlin to Moscow.

However, unlike BMW in Germany and FIAT in Italy, the origin of its name was the nearest Mercedes-Benz came to a personality. The Mercedes-Benz plant and management and staff at Stuttgart, like the car, were the ultimate machine. One in ten employees was concerned with quality control. If a single scratch or chip in its finish was discovered, the entire vehicle was resprayed.

Mercedes-Benz was the first choice of the postwar German *nouveaux riches*. Ninety-five out of every hundred buyers subsequently reordered a Mercedes-Benz. One man picked up his new model from the plant at Stuttgart and drove it sixty miles up the autobahn to Karlsruhe before he realized he had left his wife behind.

The highest mileage ever recorded by a car by the 1980s has been put at 1,184,880. The car was a Mercedes-Benz. In the developing countries of Africa, the name *Wabenzi* would be given to the new power elite, after the first status item they tended to purchase. Across the wild new automobile frontiers of the 1990s, the Mercedes-Benz would be the most smuggled car in the world.

Yet few in earlier times bought it for its looks. Many could not have done so, because they ordered "blind" years in advance. Such was the popularity of Mercedes-Benz that new models sold out months before they appeared on the market.

Occasionally a fin would appear on a new model, a Teutonic concession to the latest American gas-guzzler from Detroit. But it took Mercedes-Benz five years to design a new car and another six years to put it into production. The car was designed and produced to last at least fifteen years. The last things that concerned the men in Stuttgart were fins and fashion.

Mercedes-Benz was the epitome of German engineering excellence at a time when Germany was driving Europe's postwar industrial recovery. Money was no object for the company and the customer. As long as the Berlin Wall remained up, the Western investment remained in, and the Russians and East Germans remained out, Mercedes-Benz — and Germany — could do no wrong.

The *Wirtschaftswunder* and Mercedes-Benz were synonymous to the point where they were inseparable, unthinkable without each other. If Mercedes-Benz ever experienced difficulties, there could be only one explanation — Germany must be in trouble.

10

BMW and the Pride of Bavaria

By 1960, when the rest of Germany had been swept up in the economic miracle, BMW could regard it as a miracle that the company still existed at all. The main BMW plant at Eisenach had fallen into the hands of the Russians, who kidnapped BMW staff members like Albert Siedler and many others and forced them to work for Avtovelo, making bogus BMWs behind the Iron Curtain. The Red Army had also taken over and stripped what remained of the BMW plant at Spandau in East Berlin. The Allach plant near Munich was intact, but part of the plant at nearby Milbertshofen had been destroyed by Allied air raids. The rest of it had been saved from total destruction at the hands of the Allies and of vengeful former slave laborers from Dachau concentration camp by its wartime director, Kurt Donath.

BMW designs had not only been plundered by the Russians, but also by the Allies. In 1949 the British Bristol 400 road racer, also made by an aircraft company, was successful in the Italian *Mille Miglia*, raising British spirits with the help of a stolen BMW design.

BMW had just barely survived the immediate postwar years in West Germany. Without the equivalent of Volkswagenwerk's Major Hirst, the company made bicycles, saucepans, and agricultural equipment from aluminum parts salvaged from its airplane engine lines. It repaired U.S. Army trucks. Like its employees, the company lived from day to day.

Ultimately, the replacement of the Morgenthau Plan by the Marshall Plan saved BMW as it saved Volkswagenwerk and Daimler-Benz. The plants in West Germany slowly crept back into motorcycle production. But the 1950s had not been kind to the pride of Bavaria.

In 1952, BMW in West Germany produced its first car since before the Second World War. The 501 competed with and failed in terms of performance, price, and engineering excellence to match the middle-range sedans made by Mercedes-Benz. The 502 was a still more dismal failure. In the years that followed, BMW management made every mistake in the book. They launched expensive new luxury models with temperamental high-performance engines in a country that had not yet recovered its prewar confidence. They suffered huge losses, panicked, and attempted to escape down-market by making "bubble cars" under license for an Italian company, Isetta.

These cars had some success in postimperial Britain, where there was no Marshall Plan and the Suez Crisis brought on the first of many oil shocks. But Germany in the late 1950s was enjoying the fruits of the *Wirtschaftswunder*. The country that had been in ruins only ten years earlier was no longer poor enough for the BMW Isetta Motor-Coupé, known colloquially, but never popularly, as "the egg."

BMW tried and failed to launch the 507 sports car to compete with the Corvettes and Thunderbirds in America, and fell into crisis. The lack of income meant a lack of investment in the new models that were the only way ahead. Concerned that BMW could never make it on its own, Deutsche Bank and others kept the company alive just in order to find a buyer. By 1959 they believed they had found one. Daimler-Benz in Stuttgart needed more capacity for components manufacture. The sale was expected to be a formality at the shareholders' meeting in Munich in December 1959.

Rescue was unexpectedly at hand.

Herbert Quandt was a major shareholder. Quandt was a member of a great German industrial dynasty whose companies produced the Varta battery. He was almost blind but loved cars. He would run his hands over them for a feel of their design.

Quandt convinced Kurt Golda, the chairman of the BMW works

council, that the company could prosper with Quandt's money and the right management. He also convinced the Bavarian Finance Ministry. The small shareholders listened and threw out the Daimler-Benz proposal. They placed their fate in the hands of Quandt and Golda.

The faith of the small shareholders in Quandt and Golda was rewarded in the departure of the old management and the arrival of a new car. The BMW 1500 sedan not only restored the fortunes of the company, but was hailed as a landmark in automobile design at the 1961 Frankfurt Motor Show.

In fact, the BMW 1500, along with new cars from NSU and Panhard, based its "new" body design on an American car, the Chevrolet Corvair, which debuted in 1959. While the Corvair emulated the Volkswagen (and Porsche) in having a rear-mounted, air-cooled engine, the body of the car was pure, clean, simple, and inexpensive to manufacture — and to copy.

Wilhelm Hofmeister, the designer, had also rediscovered and updated all the qualities of BMW before the Second World War. Hofmeister's consultant, Giovanni Michelotti, went on to help style the British Triumph Herald and Spitfire. The new BMW had aircraft-type instrumentation, elegant aerodynamic style, and a sense of security at high speeds. It also frightened Mercedes-Benz and placed BMW back in the fast lane.

Quandt, Hofmeister, and the marketing man "Niche Paul" Hahnemann identified and exploited the markets for sexy and up-market cars to be driven by the children of the *Wirtschaftswunder.* These were the newly affluent young, for whom Mercedes-Benz was synonymous with stuffiness, while BMW was synonymous with a glamorous prewar racing heritage and high-altitude dogfights.

In the 1960s, BMW went from success to success. In 1970 Quandt picked a forty-one-year-old from inside the company to become managing director. Eberhard von Kuenheim soon edged out Paul Hahnemann. BMW built towering new headquarters in the shape of four engine cylinders in Munich. The drive in search of the international customer had begun.

Herbert Quandt died in 1982. Eberhard von Kuenheim gave the memorial address, an eloquent refutation of many of the myths that have grown up concerning the industrial giants of postwar Germany:

He was no dictator, ordering his subordinates to make reports. He was no prince holding court, nor a man tempted to create a sphere of influence for despotism in which only his will counted. There was nothing of that.

He was much more a man who did not want to be judged solely on the successes of a product, nor only on the figures from profit-and-loss accounts and from balance sheets, but on the consequences which his decisions had on human beings.

These were the consumers, the customers, just as much as those directly answerable to him, including those dependent on him and working under him. They transformed his investments directed at the business world into market results.

Quandt had had a vision of the automobile industry as straight as an autobahn. The success of BMW was achieved through the rediscovery of a style and performance directly descended from the company's style and performance in war.

Other German manufacturers would find their wartime heritage a less marketable and more problematic commodity.

11

Dr. Porsche and Other People's Cars

By 1963, more Volkswagens were sold in the United States than in Germany. The same year, the Porsche 911 was introduced into the American market and immediately took its place as the standard against which all performance cars would be judged for years to come. Together, the Volkswagen and the Porsche would help to realize Hitler's Autopian vision of the great autobahn that would run from Berlin to Moscow — but on the West Coast of the United States and the freeways of L.A. Both cars were inextricably linked to the checkered history of the man Hitler had commissioned to fulfill his dream, Dr. Ferdinand Porsche.

Between 1923 and 1929, Dr. Porsche had been technical director and a board member of the Führer's favorite car company, Daimler-Benz. He had been a member of both the Nazi Party and the SS. Under his supervision, KdF-Stadt had employed slave labor during the war to make military vehicles, aircraft parts, and rockets for the Third Reich. A company archivist at Wolfsburg, Klaus-Jorg Siegfried, later unearthed and published evidence to this effect.

Toward the end of the war, Porsche and his son-in-law Anton Piech, who had overseen KDF-Stadt from 1940 on, were commissioned by France's Vichy government to create a French *Volkswagen* or people's car. Then the Vichy government fell, and the new government arrested Porsche and Piech in connection with their wartime attempts to take over Peugeot, several of whose managers had died in concentration camps.

Hans Ledwinka, the head of Tatra, who had worked on the Volkswagen before the war, had been falsely imprisoned by the Russians. Was *Herr Doktor Ingenieur Porsche*, by contrast, a Nazi collaborator who got away scot-free?

"I don't think so," said Professor Hans Mommsen, Professor of Modern European History at the Ruhr University in Bochum, Germany. In 1988, fifty years after Hitler laid the foundation stone at KdF-Stadt, Professor Mommsen organized a symposium titled *Wolfsburg Under the Swastika*. "He was not the type to be a Nazi. He was anyway a different generation from most Nazi fanatics, and was already in his sixties when the war broke out. Porsche," Mommsen went on, "was a cunning Austrian who used the opportunity provided by the Nazis to achieve what he wanted: to build civilian cars."

At a second symposium in 1990, Mommsen suggested that Dr. Porsche had tried to improve the lot of forced laborers at KdF-Stadt during the Second World War. Mommsen referred to wartime KdF-Stadt as a "multicultural" society and described as "illegal" Dr. Porsche's detention by the French government after the war.

Mommsen's last remarks, and the fact that Volkswagenwerk had commissioned him to answer these and other awkward questions about Volkswagenwerk, caused outrage. Mommsen and his team were accused of betraying their academic credentials for thirty pieces of silver — or, in this case, 3 million deutsche marks.

In Wolfsburg, Mommsen's remarks provoked journalists and foreign workers to call for the removal of Dr. Porsche's name from streets and institutions dedicated to his memory.

In Paris, Mommsen's remarks provoked Professor Joseph Rovan, professor emeritus of German History at the Sorbonne, to write to *Die Zeit*. Rovan was a former prisoner at Dachau.

That a "respected" historian could describe the emaciated, starving, demoralized mass of foreign workers, Soviet POWs, and concentration camp inmates as a "multicultural society" and still defend his insensitive blunder despite the indignation which his use of the words provoked, is further proof of the inability of the historian to grasp what happened.

In London, they provoked Dr. Michael Burleigh, lecturer in International History at the London School of Economics, to write critically of Mommsen in the influential magazine *History Today*.

In Bochum, Professor Mommsen wrote to *History Today* criticizing Dr. Burleigh's criticisms.

In London, Dr. Burleigh wrote to *History Today* criticizing Professor Mommsen's criticisms of him and holding his ground.

And in Wolfsburg, one of Dr. Porsche's grandsons, Ferdinand Piech, succeeded Carl Hahn as head of Volkswagenwerk.

So what was the truth about Dr. Porsche?

In 1978, Dr. Porsche's son Ferry had described how his father had made a number of Austrian factory visits with Hitler's chief architect and armaments minister, Albert Speer. On one such occasion they had driven near a concentration camp near Linz, where prisoners were working in a quarry.

Speer had remarked, "If you don't follow us, Herr Professor, there is still room for you here . . ."

The probable truth, if such a phrase can be used, is that Porsche was an amoral technocrat, a phrase used to describe him at the 1990 symposium by two board members of Volkswagenwerk. Porsche was a man whose amorality and technological ambitions were precisely suited to the ambitions of Hitler and Speer. He was the chosen *Reichskonstrukteur*.

In 1947, Porsche and Piech had been released by the French and returned to Germany. They had launched the *KdF-Wagen* at KdF-Stadt, but had no inkling of the miracles wrought at Wolfsburg by the foreigners working together under Major Hirst. Once across the German border, the two men were astonished to see that six out of every ten cars they saw on the autobahn were Volkswagens.

The *Volkswagen*, indelibly associated with Dr. Porsche, had become the West German people's car. The *Wirtschaftswunder* wrought by Major Hirst at Wolfsburg and taken forward by Heinrich Nordhoff had put Volkswagenwerk on the international map. By 1950 there was a waiting list for the car. There was also a shortage of U.S. dollars, the only currency that would enable investment to be made in greater production. U.S. dollars could only be gained from American exports. Volkswagenwerk had not broken into this market, and there seemed little chance of its doing so.

Ben Pon had survived the invasion of Holland that had followed his close encounter with Hitler at the 1939 Berlin Motor Show. Pon had taken one of the cars to the United States in 1949. The lack of interest was such that Pon had had to sell the car as a curiosity to pay for his return ticket.

By 1953, a handful of Volkswagens were being sold through Max Hoffman, a specialist in imported cars in New York City.

Max Edwin Hoffman was known to his friends throughout the automobile world as "Maxie" or "the baron of Park Avenue." He loved the high life of Manhattan, and liked to do business at the Waldorf Astoria. "He is the Duveen [the famous art dealer] of the automobile business," said an associate, "a great entrepreneur. He has tremendous vision, loves cars, and he's a fantastic salesman."

Hoffman was not the salesman to sell the people's car in the American mass market. Only when Nordhoff sent a hundred Volkswagenwerk personnel to America to form a proper export department did sales slowly began to rise. But the breakthrough came in 1959, when Nordhoff appointed a new head of Volkswagenwerk operations in America. His name was Carl Hahn.

Carl Hahn's decision to advertise the Volkswagen led to one of the most successful advertising campaigns ever mounted in America. Doyle Dane Bernbach, Inc. (DDB), devised a campaign that presented the American people with the pioneering "honest" style of advertising, in contrast to the grandiose automobile advertising of the time.

DDB sold the Volkswagen on its virtues of quality and dependability. It poked fun at the pomposities and pretensions of car ownership in post-Eisenhower America. By implication, it presented the Volkswagen as a classless alternative to the superficial glamour and built-in obsolescence of the American car. By 1960, the five-hundred-thousandth Volkswagen had arrived in the United States. By 1963, the Beetle had captured the collective imagination of the state of California:

> Say, isn't that your old Aunt Nabby who just passed you in the outer
> lane of the Berdoo at eighty? There she is, six months in Southern

California, and already she's got the glued-up ash-blond hair, the wrap-around shades, the tight pants, and . . . a chrome yellow Volkswagen with reversed wheels and a voom-voom exhaust . . .

But the Beetle was not the only creation of Ferdinand Porsche to take America by storm.

Gmund, Austria, 1930

The first postwar Porsche plant was at Gmund, in Lower Austria, in a disused sawmill. Here, Porsche set about making the sports car he had been planning since the 1930s. Many of the early mechanical features, including engine blocks, transmissions, headlights, and suspension, came straight from the Volkswagen. Other parts had to be smuggled from Switzerland in order to circumvent the import restrictions imposed by the Allies.

The first chassis for what became the Porsche 356 ran in 1948. Only when Porsche's son, Ferdinand "Ferry" Porsche, was satisfied with its handling on the mountain roads did he build a body for it. At one stage it collapsed and had to be repaired with scrap iron borrowed from a road repair worker.

The Porsche 356 originally had a mid-mounted engine. This was changed to a problematic rear-mounted engine (in the style of the Volkswagen and the Tatra) for production, due to excessive noise from the air-cooled engine. This tended to make the rear end swing away around corners, unlike the people's car, which had one of the lowest crash rates in the history of automobiles. The downside of the Porsche was that, in the wrong hands, it was an unguided missile just like the Tatra.

The Porsche 356 was launched in 1950. By 1951, five hundred had been sold, although the car cost as much as a Cadillac. Thirty-two went to America. By 1955, Porsche had sold five thousand cars, over one third of these in the United States. The company built a new and bigger plant at Zuffenhausen. The sales figure had doubled by the following year. This was a measure of the growing froth on the economic miracle and the growing appetite on the other side of the Atlantic for high-priced, high-performance German cars.

Part of the Porsche appeal was the danger factor. In 1955, the death of the American movie heartthrob James Dean at the wheel of his Porsche 550 Spyder, after a head-on collision with a pickup truck, sealed the Porsche and the star into legend. In fact, Dean was not at fault in the accident and probably would have died regardless of what sports car he was driving. The Porsche 550 Spyder was an aluminum-bodied, mid-engined sports car, tuned more for the race-track than the street, and had none of the traditional Porsche handling flaws. Dean was also well within the speed limit at the time.

By 1963, the Porsche 356 was being phased out and replaced by the 911. Designed by Dr. Porsche's grandson, Fernando Alexander "Butzi" Porsche, the 911 was an updated version of the 356. The 911 retained the driving characteristics that had given rise to the car's formidable reputation. The American market stipulated that the trunk — which was, of course, under the hood — had to be big enough for a set of golf clubs, but the car had other modifications as well, including a cast-iron weight, described as a "bumper reinforcement," which was placed behind the front bumper to correct the car's rearward bias. The assumption grew that the Porsche was a car that the driver expected to have to work to drive. The use of the Porsche by many Grand Prix drivers as their private cars reinforced this image as crudely and as effectively as the iron bar.

Porsche's success as a high-performance sports-car designer in America and Germany put clear tarmac between him and his Nazi past. In the 1950s and 1960s, this past was unlikely to hurt his reputation in Germany, which had done its utmost to obliterate images of the Nazi period in the rearview mirror, and accelerated forward at high speed under the Marshall Plan.

Like Professor Mommsen, the Germans could always point to the accepted wisdom that Dr. Porsche was an Austrian. In the unlikely event that Porsche drivers were embarrassed, they were more likely to be so by the possibility that he had designed the Volkswagen than that he was a war criminal.

On the east side of a divided Germany, however, behind the Iron Curtain, it was a different story.

Koprivnica, Czechoslovakia, 1951

Dr. Porsche and his eponymous, powerful, rear-engined sports cars were flourishing. But what had happened to Hans Ledwinka?

The former Republic of Czechoslovakia was under the Soviet yoke. Ledwinka was in jail, but allowed to finish his sentence working in the fields. Throughout his captivity he continued to work on car designs and protest his innocence of any collaboration with the Nazis.

The Czechoslovak Communist government released him in 1951, and asked him to go back and run Tatra at Koprivnica. Ledwinka refused, and left Czechoslovakia for Austria. He settled in Vienna, where his most remarkable creation, the powerful V-8 T87 sedan, had played its role in the secret war.

In 1954 he moved to Munich.

Tatra had been nationalized by the Soviets, and had gone back into production making trucks and high-powered sedans for the Czech, East German, and Soviet political and diplomatic *nomenklatura*. Unlike the cars made by Volkswagenwerk and Dr. Porsche, few of these trucks and cars appeared in the West. Tatra was forced to look eastward, a captive supplier to the apparently endless Soviet market.

In Munich, Ledwinka pursued his campaign for justice. The heirs of the Ringhoffer family, who had owned Tatra since 1923, had received a secret, large, out-of-court postwar settlement from Porsche and Volkswagen for patent infringements relating to the people's car. Ledwinka's testimony helped win this settlement, but he was by this time too poor to hire a lawyer to represent his personal interests. A friend learned of Ledwinka's predicament and offered the services of his own counsel. But it was too late.

Dr. Porsche and members of his family had contacted Ledwinka, according to Ledwinka's son Erich, in order to reassure themselves that the settlement with Ringhoffer-Tatra had silenced any further talk of Ledwinka's role in the creation of the people's car. Porsche and Volkswagenwerk remain intensely sensitive about the matter to this day.

Hans Ledwinka died in 1967, the forgotten man of automobiles. He had lost his fortune and several hundred patents. He was never rehabilitated by the Czech Communist government.

Tatra remained in production at Koprivnica. In the small museum there, the prototype also remained of the people's car Hans Ledwinka had designed years earlier, before the war. The events of the first years of peace had swallowed up Ledwinka and his car in the march of history.

Zwickau, East Germany, 1958

Before the Second World War, the Zwickau plant had made the exquisite Horch limousines and the majestic racing cars of Auto Union. After the Second World War, like BMW, one hundred miles to the west at Eisenach, and Tatra at Koprivnica, Zwickau was engulfed by the advancing Red Army and disappeared behind the Iron Curtain.

East Germany was crippled by war reparations to the Soviet Union, which refused to allow East Germany to produce four-cycle engines, and rationed fuel. In 1957, the year Giacosa in Turin produced the *Nuova Cinquecento* and Issigonis in Oxford began work on the Mini-Minor, a socialist collective at Sachsenring of Zwickau began to manufacture the Trabant. The name meant "Satellite." This was at the height of the Cold War and the age of the *Sputnik.*

The Trabant had a 594-cc, two-cycle engine and a body made of plastic, brown paper, and shredded cotton waste. It accelerated from zero to sixty kilometers per hour in thirty-two seconds. The engine burned a mixture of gasoline and oil, and gave off ten times the hydrocarbon level of other cars. It had no fuel gauge and no interior light.

The manufacturing process was equally disturbing. A dozen prewar presses, each weighing over two hundred tons, lined either side of the vast workshop. As each press stamped its steel sheet into the required shape, it sent a minor earthquake through the solid floor. Workers at Zwickau had to open the presses five times in each eight-minute cycle, releasing toxic fumes each time. Many Trabant workers became ill and died as a result.

In East Berlin, on Tucholsky Street, the car became synonymous with the drab consolations snatched by workers on their way home from work. The Trabant was ideally suited to curb-crawling, and the street where prostitutes met johns became known as "the Trabi beat."

This was the East German *Volkswagen* — the other German people's car. At one point, the waiting period for a Trabant was fourteen years. The waiting period for real freedom would be more than twice as long.

3

America, Europe, and the Rise of Japan

12

The Men in Motown

B Y THE BEGINNING OF THE 1970s, the automobile industries were beginning to display the strengths and weaknesses that would define their behavior in the global marketplace in the last decade of the twentieth century. The astonishing prosperity of America and the rise of Europe would be followed by crises in both these markets and pressure from the Japanese.

As this pressure grew, it exposed the flaws in both America and Europe, and revealed the colossal potential of Japan. In an industry in which success depended on short-term flexibility and long-term planning, the stakes were highest in Detroit, Michigan. "Motown" was the car capital of America, and its most important industrial center. The men in Motown most closely identified with the health and wealth of the nation were at General Motors, whose share price was one of the barometers of Wall Street, and which was the biggest and most powerful automobile manufacturer on earth.

GM had started life in 1908 as an amalgamation of several struggling car companies. Like many, its fortunes had been boosted by the 1914–18 war. The end of the war plunged the United States into recession. By 1920, GM was close to insolvency. The man who rescued GM, when it acquired his Hyatt Roller Bearing Company, was Alfred P. Sloan Jr.

Sloan was an austere man who neither smoked nor drank. He espoused extreme right-wing opinions, even by the standards of his day. Sloan disliked blacks, liberals, trade unions, and Jews. He hired a private police force recruited by the Detroit Mafia to break strikes and put down protests among his 700,000 employees. Such was the unifying effect of these actions on American workers that today it is possible to point to the automobile industry as the crucible of the American labor movement, the birthplace of the unions that became models for organized labor all over the world.

In 1938, Los Angeles was still a city of clean Pacific Ocean air. It had the largest electric rail system in the world. The "Big Red Cars" of Pacific Electric serviced the San Fernando Valley; more than one thousand trains left the downtown area each day. General Motors, joining with Standard Oil of California (Socal) and Firestone, the tire manufacturer, bought up the transit company and closed it down. Los Angeles grew around the roads and not the railroads. A few remnants of the transit system are still visible alongside the clogged freeways today.

General Motors did the same with other oil companies in other American cities, ensuring that the inhabitants would be dependent upon the automobile. The subjugation by General Motors of Pacific Electric was conclusive proof, if proof was still needed, of a powerful and discomfiting truth. In the twentieth century the automobile had asserted itself in the role of the one industry above all others. It was synonymous with the development of nations, analogous to, but far exceeding, the nineteenth-century role of the train.

At the outbreak of World War II, Sloan reassured his shareholders. "We are too big," he said, "to be inconvenienced by these pitiful international squabbles."

General Motors, like Ford, was not a national corporation; it was a multinational organization. Throughout the Second World War, GM and Ford in Detroit continued to benefit from their operations in Germany and Japan and other territories controlled by the Axis powers.

GM's Opel plant at Brandenburg in Nazi Germany built, with Daimler-Benz, the Blitz truck. The Blitz was the workhorse of the

Wehrmacht in their slaughter of American GIs in the Battle of the Bulge and the rearguard action on the road to Berlin. GM's Opel plants at Rüsselsheim manufactured 50 percent of the propulsion systems for the Junkers 88, the bomber used in the Luftwaffe's mass air raids on civilians.

In 1943, while GM's American subsidiaries were supplying the United States Air Force, its German subsidiaries were developing and manufacturing engines for the Messerschmitt 262, the world's first twin-engined jet fighter (with engines based upon patented work by the British engineer Frank Whittle). With a top speed of up to 540 miles per hour, the ME-262 could fly one hundred miles per hour faster than its nearest American rival, the piston-powered Mustang P-51 (itself powered by a British Rolls-Royce engine).

GM's president Alfred Sloan, and his vice presidents James B. Mooney, John T. Smith, and Graeme K. Howard, remained on the board of General Motors-Opel throughout the Second World War. In spite of the loss of life in the Japanese air raid on Pearl Harbor and the carnage in the Pacific at Okinawa and Iwo Jima, GM also maintained its operations in Japan.

At the end of the war, unlike such reluctant participants as Hans Ledwinka of Tatra, the Americans were able to walk away from the conflict. GM, like Ford, asked the American government for compensation for damage done by Allied bombing to their plants in Axis countries.

In 1947, GM was subjected to considerable criticism after the U.S. Secret Service revealed its wartime role in the dark workshops of the Reich.

In 1967, the year of Ledwinka's death and the year after Sloan's death at the age of ninety, General Motors received $33 million in tax exemptions for "troubles and destruction occasioned to its airplane and motorized vehicle factories in Germany, Austria, Poland, and China."

By the early 1950s, Sloan had driven GM from 10 percent of the market to a dominant position in America and a powerful position around the world. The GM slogan was "a car for every purse and purpose." GM's Charles Erwin "Engine Charlie" Wilson declared to the Senate Armed Forces Committee, "What is good for the country is good for General Motors, and what's good for General Motors is good for the country."

The "GM Five" catered to all the rungs on the ladder. The young, upwardly mobile first-time buyer would opt for the moderately priced Chevrolet. When he was promoted and earned a few dollars more, the first thing he did after buying a bigger house was to buy an Oldsmobile. The next step up the ladder brought a Pontiac. The next step brought a Buick. He was at the top of the ladder, when he acquired a Cadillac.

Sloan's inventiveness extended to pricing. The five main automobile divisions could have corresponded to five different market levels, where the top price in one division stopped short of the bottom price of the next one up the ladder. Sloan encouraged overlap at each end; as a customer approached the top of one division, the next division up was already competing at the same price for the same customer.

Sloan opposed corporate protectionism, even in an empire as successful as General Motors. GM component manufacturers had to sell to GM on an equal footing with everybody else. If they could not compete successfully, they were eliminated from future contracting.

Sloan saw the danger that lurked at the very top of his empire in separating long-term strategy and the management of day-to-day operations. He established a system of regular meetings between the heads of the GM Five and his own four-man executive committee. No decisions were ever made at these meetings; their purpose was to enable those who were planning the future to gauge the mood of those who were managing the present.

This was a lesson Sloan had learned and practiced to vast effect by the time he retired in 1956, at the age of eighty. In the 1980s, the failure of his successors to remember this lesson would lead to a downslide on a correspondingly imperial scale.

Foreigners like Toyoda, Agnelli, and Giacosa might have frowned at the inflexibility of the production lines. They might have derided the huge, gull-winged gas-guzzlers from Detroit. But the revolutionary management techniques of Alfred Sloan and the increasing affluence of the customer made the GM Five a huge commercial success.

GM also diversified into trucks and other commercial vehicles, and manufactured most of its own components. By the early 1950s the United States made more than 80 percent of the world's automobiles. By 1957 it was producing 6 million cars a year, three times the output of Germany and the United Kingdom together, many in the luxury high-profit end of the market.

The first inroads into the American market by foreigners took place in the middle 1960s, when the Volkswagen, Datsun, Toyota, and, to a lesser extent, the Renault Dauphine, became popular with college students and hippies — a growing population that needed economical basic transportation. This was a market overlooked by the big American manufacturers until the end of the decade. The dawn of the 1970s saw the introduction of the Vega by Chevrolet and the Pinto by Ford, both small four-cylinder cars designed specifically to compete with Volkswagen, Datsun, and Toyota. Chrysler, with no small cars in development, imported cars from England and Japan. These sold poorly, with the U.K. models containing all the negatives of a British car industry that was committing collective suicide, and the Japanese models being technically outdated. This only confirmed the giant American manufacturers in the opinion that imports were of limited value.

Meanwhile, the GM Five were beginning to look more and more like each other. Up to half of the cost differences were in the optional "extras."

The 1973 Yom Kippur War sent oil prices soaring, and lines at gas stations traumatized the American car owner. Still, GM saw the passing of the oil shocks and the stabilizing of gas prices as proof that the small-car fashion was a transient phenomenon of the minority. GM was still bigger than pitiful international squabbles.

Like the deterioration of Detroit, the men in Motown ignored what was happening outside, not least because they chose not to see. The fifteen-story headquarters stood amid, but aloof from, the streets of a city that had by now earned the sobriquet "Murder City, U.S.A." The management and staff went to and fro via secured entrances and exits and covered walkways that bypassed the mean streets and led them to their enclosed garages and the GM Five.

The Germans and the Japanese — GM's World War II partners — continued their penetration of the West Coast of America.

Meanwhile, the men at the top of the empire in Motown saw only the profits, and carried on business as usual. Arrogant, sheltered, complacent, entrenched, and blinkered, they would soon discover that Charlie Wilson was right: what would be bad for America would be very bad for them indeed. But, as yet, nobody in Detroit was prepared to risk saying the wrong thing.

(Above) The Tatra V570, designed and built two years before the first Volkswagen and misappropriated by Hitler and Dr. Porsche in circumstances about which the German company remains intensely sensitive to this day.

(Left) Adolf Hitler and the Volkswagen "Strength-Through-Joy" car at the opening of the People's Car Factory in KdF-Stadt. Sixty years later, Germany had died and been reborn and "the people's car" was a worldwide phenomenon. *(Photo © Hulton Deutsch Collection Limited)*

(Left) Hans Ledwinka. The brilliant Czech designer became a tragic casualty of history and the forgotten man of motoring. *(Photo © Ludvigsen Libary)*

(Opposite abou
The revolutionary Mi
outdid the Italians on their ov
ground and became
world-beater—yet never made
penny in profit. *(Photo © The Rona
Grant Archi*

(Opposite below) The drive-
movie. By the 1950s, 40 percent
American marriages we
proposed in automobiles. *(Photo
Range/Bettmannn/UI*

(Below) The FIAT Cinquecento brought freedom to postwar Italians. *(Photo © Rod Shone)*

PARAMOUNT PICTURES presents
AN OAKHURST PRODUCTION **MICHAEL CAINE & NOËL COWARD** DO **THE ITALIAN JOB** (U)

(Left) Ford Europe finally chose the name of this small town in the Dolomites for its first people's car: the Cortina *(Photo © Rex Features Limited)*

(Left) Four-cylinder power. BMW's towering Munich headquarters was built to reinforce its image as a maker of highperformance cars. *(Photo © BMW AG)*

(Below) George Turnbull and Alec Issigonis: two knights of the road during the lost heyday of British Leyland. *(Photo © Lady Turnbull)*

The ultimate car chase. Steve McQueen's 1968 movie *Bullitt* marked a new high for the car as a phenomenon of popular culture. *(Photo © Kobal Collection)*

When he lowered the top, you knew he meant business. In *Day of the Jackal,* the Alfa-Romeo convertible was the perfect screen vehicle. *(Photo © Kobal Collection)*

Gianni Agnelli at the helm. In spite of the Soviet deals, by the late 1970s the Communist Red Brigades had declared war on FIAT and the Agnellis were the most heavily guarded family in the industry. *(Photo courtesy of Rex Features Limited)*

"Even if I were to live again, I would still drive a Mercedes": such was brand loyalty in the Arabian Peninsula. *(Photo © Barry Lewis, Camera Press London)*

Lockout. In the 1980s it was France's turn to face mass unrest, and Peugeot fought the "Battle of Poissy." *(Photo © Popperfoto)*

General Motors headquarters in Detroit became a monument to corporate malaise in a no-man's-land of mean streets and crack dealers. *(Photo © The Independent/ Simon Calder)*

Facing facts at Nissan in Sunderland, England. The British may have destroyed their own auto industry, but they welcomed the Japanese investment, if only to keep the Americans out. *(Photo © David Modell)*

George Turnbull and Margaret Thatcher. The British prime minister stopped the government's blank checks to British Leyland, but not before "that lad" had gone into self-imposed exile. *(Photo © Lady Turnbull)*

13

Auto da Fé

Snapshots from the Suicide of the British Auto Industry

I~N~ 1968, the leading French newspaper, *Le Monde*, declared, "The automobile is a symbol, whether its owner is an individual or a nation, of power, independence, and renown."

In 1968, British Leyland, the new British car conglomerate, was the eighth-largest car manufacturer in Europe. Volkswagenwerk was seventh in Europe, FIAT was eleventh, and the state-owned French Renault company was seventeenth. Citroën was in fifty-second place.

Ten years later, British Leyland would be in terminal decline. By the criteria of *Le Monde*, Britain's car industry would leave the nation powerless, dependent, and embarrassed — wanting on all three counts.

It is questionable whether modern British governments have ever understood the British car industry. Bad management, bad labor relations, deteriorating competitiveness, and interfering politicians have, at one time or another, threatened most of the car industries of Europe. All have threatened FIAT, Renault, and

Peugeot. Yet only in the tormented Britain of the 1970s would the combination prove fatal and the recriminations last for years to come.

Longbridge, England, 1968

The British Leyland Motor Corporation was the product of the merger of Leyland Motors and the British Motor Corporation (BMC).

By the mid-1960s, BMC was in financial difficulties and looking for a rescuer. The company had failed to reinvest properly the postwar profits it had made in a seller's market. Leyland was a successful truck maker with ambitions to become the manufacturer of a line of trucks and cars to rival Daimler-Benz. Leyland had already absorbed two of Britain's most prestigious car companies: Standard Triumph, which made a wide range of high-quality sedans and high performance sports cars, and Rover, which made the four-wheel-drive Land-Rover, a direct descendant of the American wartime jeep, with an identical layout down to the four-wheel-drive controls mounted next to the stick shift. Rover also made a line of high-quality sedans with a reputation for comfort and speed that was to deteriorate in quality in the 1970s.

The merger of Leyland and BMC, two large private companies and major employers, was strongly encouraged by the British Labor government, and in particular by the minister of technology, Tony Benn. Benn and the Labor government promised the management of BLMC substantial financial support and anticipated taking the political credit for a rosy future.

The merger meant BLMC had a workforce of 200,000 people, forty-eight factories, and names such as Austin, Morris, Rover, Jaguar, Standard Triumph, MG, and Austin-Healey. BLMC had 40 percent of the British market and was one of the leading car companies in the world.

The managing director of the new British Leyland Motor Corporation was the dynamic engineer and salesman who had headed Leyland, Donald Stokes. The two men who worked most closely with Stokes were John Barber and George Turnbull.

Barber had come from Ford, where he had helped develop the Cortina. He was the finance director who wanted BLMC to move upmarket. Turnbull, a hands-on motivator who had proved himself at Standard Triumph, became managing director of the Austin Morris division of BLMC.

Austin Morris was the largest and weakest division of BLMC, suffering from a spiral of falling profitability and lack of investment. This spiral deepened in the face of foreign competition. Turnbull understood the problems Austin Morris faced. He understood volume production. He also understood the quirky character of the legendary technical director of the Austin Morris division, Alec Issigonis.

Issigonis and his managers had almost no idea of how to calculate costs as a car was designed. The ultimate example of this was the Mini. The best small getaway car in the world and the most revolutionary design in automotive history lost BLMC forty-five dollars for every car built.

BLMC factories such as Longbridge were theoretically run by management, but in reality they were controlled by trade union shop stewards. At Triumph, the shop steward hired, fired, and set production levels. The unions worked at piecework rates, which meant a man simply did his daily quota and went home. The quality of work deteriorated, and many factories were half deserted by 2:00 P.M. Engines disappeared out of the gates in car trunks because the unions had negotiated a "no search" policy.

Turnbull began by assembling a younger, more able team of executives. He attacked the problems of labor relations and poor quality of manufacturing and design. He excelled at communication with both management and employees. But it was going to be a long road, and uphill all the way.

Elsewhere, the struggle at first had been even harder.

Ulsan, South Korea, 1968

Ulsan, until the 1960s, was a tiny fishing village on the southeast coast of the Republic of Korea. The Republic of Korea was still a largely agricultural country that had been dominated by foreigners, especially the Chinese and Japanese, since the thirteenth century. All this began to change with the coming of the *chaebol*.

Hyundai was founded by Chung Ju Yung. Chung was born in

poverty in what became North Korea. His first job was as a rice delivery boy. In the last years of the hated Japanese occupation of Korea, he ran a truck company and a car-repair company. After the defeat of the Japanese and the end of the Second World War, he worked for the American forces as an automobile mechanic.

Shortly afterwards, Chung founded Hyundai Engineering. *Hyundai* means "modern."

Hyundai flourished with orders from the Americans during the Korean War of 1950–53. After the war, companies like Hyundai were given soft loans by the South Korean military government. Hyundai, like Kia, Daewoo, and Samsung, grew into one of the *chaebol*, the diversified conglomerates that dominated the South Korean economy from electronics to shipbuilding — and cars.

In 1967, Chung set up Hyundai Motors. Ulsan, the tiny fishing village, became the site of a small factory. The year that saw the formation of the mighty British Leyland Motor Corporation also saw Chung's little Hyundai Motor factory begin to assemble Ford Cortinas imported in kit form from Britain.

Cowley, England, 1971

In 1971, George Turnbull and his team at BLMC produced the new company's first new car, the Morris Marina. The car was aimed at the market for the Ford Cortina. In the circumstances that surrounded volume production, it was a miracle that the car appeared at all.

In 1970, Austin Morris enjoyed only two weeks without industrial action throughout the entire year. The piecework system of the trade unions meant that any modification or production-line equivalent became a negotiator's nightmare. Even moving the cigarette lighter from left to right resulted in the unions demanding to renegotiate rates for building the entire car.

Two decades after their Japanese competitors had instigated lean production and "just in time" parts procedures, the management at BLMC was still forced by the constant threat of strikes to maintain two suppliers for everything down to radiators and exhausts.

Turnbull began to despair. His wife, Marion, dreaded reading press reports that British Leyland had made profits, because these would inevitably be followed by the next round of union demands, and strikes when these demands were not immediately accommodated.

In 1973, Turnbull and the technical director of BLMC, Harry Webster, produced the Austin Allegro. This was meant to replace the Issigonis-designed 1100 and 1300. The car failed to meet expectations, and BLMC's star waned further in the worsening economic and political climate.

Donald Stokes was on the brink of retirement. A power struggle began for the position of his successor. The two men directly below Stokes became the two poles of the wider struggle for the future of the company.

George Turnbull believed BLMC could and should solve the problem of successful volume production. This would be best achieved by decentralizing the group and delegating power to autonomous divisions.

John Barber believed that BLMC should go upmarket, and that the company should be recentralized along the lines of Ford and General Motors.

Barber and the centralizers won the day — or so they thought. In May 1973, Barber was appointed Stokes's deputy and de facto successor. Six months later, Turnbull resigned as managing director of Austin Morris.

Turnbull's resignation shocked many in the industry. But he had always stood by his ideals, and he was not about to abandon them. He did not even have another job to cushion the blow.

His former colleagues were even more surprised when they heard where he had eventually gone.

Ulsan, South Korea, 1974

Hyundai and Ulsan had grown in the six years since the factory began assembling kit-form Cortinas. Chung Ju Yung and Hyundai Motors had pushed forward the automobile operation with the vigor and drive that characterized the rest of his *chaebol*.

Chung knew that the next leap forward would require the presence of a foreigner. In a country where foreigners had wrought such havoc for so many years, this would be tricky. But this foreigner would be here on Korean terms. The foreigner whom Chung chose was George Turnbull.

Turnbull arrived at Hyundai headquarters in the South Korean capital, Seoul, in early 1974. His assignment was to establish a car manufacturing facility at Ulsan and put the first car into production within two years. In a country that had no automobile manufacturing infrastructure, this was a formidable task.

On his first visit to Ulsan, Turnbull was escorted around the new factory by Chung Ju Yung personally.

"Where is the heating?" Turnbull asked.

"When we make profits," retorted Chung, "they get heating."

Winters in South Korea were bitterly cold. Turnbull eventually persuaded Chung to install heating equipment, ready for use when the profits came.

They named the car the Hyundai Pony. Its styling was agreed on in the spring of 1974. The technology for the first car made by the "modern" company came secondhand from Mitsubishi of Japan. Two years later, the Hyundai Pony was triumphantly launched as the first South Korean people's car. Hyundai — and a Briton — had put South Koreans on the roads.

Turnbull stayed in South Korea for three years. He saw how the volume production that had been thwarted at BLMC in Britain could still be achieved by a privately owned conglomerate with government help in a developing country. The Koreans hated the Japanese, and were a match for them in terms of the work ethic. The question was whether Chung and Hyundai had the drive and determination to export this combination abroad.

Longbridge, England, 1974

In 1974, the year Turnbull had gone to start up the automobile manufacturing arm of the South Korean *chaebol*, the British government nationalized the British Leyland Motor Corporation. This was to prove a commercial and political disaster, further compounded by the effect of the oil-price shocks on the spending power of the domestic consumer. North Sea oil revenues drove up the pound against other currencies, making export-dependent goods such as

BLMC cars uncompetitive abroad. BLMC, the fifth-largest car company in the world, was fast turning into a liability for the government.

The British prime minister, Harold Wilson, turned to his adviser, the businessman Sir Don Ryder.

The Ryder Plan, as it was known, was a makeshift blueprint for the expansion of the state-owned indigenous British car industry. It did not distinguish between one make or brand of car and another. It threw the latest book of management and marketing fashions at an industry that was unlike any other. Ryder did not consult BLMC directors, yet tried to appease disenchanted trade unions that had lost control of their most militant members. He involved them in the very same management process that those militant members had abused for the past decade.

Under state ownership and the Ryder Plan, BLMC became a national joke, a byword for poor quality, endless strikes, lost productivity, and spiraling wage demands. The government poured North Sea oil revenues and taxpayers' money into the company. Proud names like Austin, Morris, Rover, Jaguar, and Mini were dragged down in the mire. Individual divisions lost the reputation for excellence without which they had no hope against America, Japan, and mainland Europe.

In 1977 the new chairman of BLMC was Michael Edwardes. Edwardes took over the company at an all-time production low of four cars per man per year. He was a political appointee of the embarrassed Labor government of Prime Minister James Callaghan. The new deputy chairman was the tough Scots-American, Ian MacGregor. Edwardes and MacGregor proved themselves in many battles with the trade unions over the following two years — but BLMC continued to consume vast amounts of state money.

In 1979 the BLMC board extended a luncheon invitation to the leader of the opposition, Margaret Thatcher.

Mrs. Thatcher was preparing for power. She had scarcely taken her seat before, as Edwardes recalled, she fired "the first salvo." "Well, Michael Edwardes, and why should we pour further funds into British Leyland?"

Margaret Thatcher and the Conservative Party were elected to government the same year. One of the principles underpinning the first Thatcher government was that the solution to the problems of the British economy lay in the monetarist approach. Decentraliza-

tion and privatization were the way ahead. There would be no turning back.

British Leyland Motor Corporation became the most frequently
cited example. In 1980, Industry Minister Keith Joseph bailed out
BLMC with $700 million only because the alternative — insolv-
ency — was still deemed too costly in political terms of unemployment. The government subsequently poured a further $1.5 billion
into BLMC. The prime minister resented every penny. The government was by this time more secure, and its price was uncompromising: decentralization, privatization, breakup.

By 1982, Edwardes had sold off nineteen BLMC businesses, reduced
the workforce from 196,000 to 104,000, and shut down Triumph and
the MG sports-car works. He had instigated the Rover linkup with
Honda. He also presided over the introduction of new models such
as Metro, Maestro, and Montego.

In 1986, Sir Graham Day took over from Edwardes at BLMC.
Day changed the name of the company to Rover and took it upmarket. The British government announced its intention to sell
Rover to General Motors. In a Commons rebellion that became a
symbol of Conservative unease at the excesses of privatization,
thirty Conservative MPs voted with Labor against the sale. Rover
was privatized as part of British Aerospace.

Instrumental in the psychology of the rebels was the indelible
association of Land-Rover, the company's famous four-wheel-drive
vehicle, with the Union Jack. The suggestion that such a potent
national symbol should be allowed to fall into American hands was
unthinkable. Land-Rover became the subject of a management
buyout, still within the Rover Group, organized by David Andrews, a
former colleague of George Turnbull.

In 1994, British Aerospace sold Rover to BMW, the company
whose fear of competition from the old Rover line had fired the
renaissance of the pride of Bavaria in the first place. Rover, although
becoming profitable once more, was no longer in British ownership.
Although the last true Rover sedans had been marvels of modern
design, clever engineering, and abysmal manufacturing quality, and
subsequent Rover cars had been little more than thinly disguised
Hondas, this still rankled in some British minds — including many
who had been responsible for the debacle in the first place. The

German company owned the Rover, the Land-Rover, the MG, and the Mini.

BMW's takeover of Rover, like the Honda plant at Swindon and Toyota at Derby, would become synonymous with the death of the British auto industry. But although the BLMC era had been a chapter of disaster, the story of the British auto industry continued, albeit under the direction of Munich, Detroit, Yokohama, Nagoya, and Seoul.

Pessimists portrayed this as a further indignity: having assisted at the *auto-da-fé* of the indigenous British car industry, the Americans, Germans, Japanese, and South Koreans were taking their pick, unopposed, of its skill centers and supply networks. Optimists pointed out that, by the summer of 1995, foreign investment in Britain by global car companies was at an all-time high, driven by the fall in sterling, and sustained by better industrial relations and high standards of quality. The indigenous British-based, foreign-owned operations became profitable. They shrugged off accusations that they were no more than aircraft on a carrier for Japanese and German assaults on mainland Europe.

In 1994, Samsung, one of the South Korean *chaebol* with automotive ambitions, announced it was to set up an electronics plant in northeast England. In early 1995, Daewoo too announced it was building a U.K. car plant.

The Germans, Japanese, and South Koreans had come to Britain. Were the coming of BMW, Toyota, and Daewoo the final nails in the coffin of the British car industry, or the prediction come true of a vehicle visionary who saw the beginning of a brave new era? Only time would tell.

14

The Last of the Line Leaves Wolfsburg

ONE OF ITS PREDECESSORS IN GERMANY had recorded over a quarter of a million miles and never failed a road test. Another would become the first functioning production car in the Antarctic. Another would log over 1,402,000 miles in California. Another started on the first turn of the ignition key, after lying partially buried for five months in the Libyan desert. It went straight to the museum.

The date was January 19, 1978. The car was Volkswagen Beetle number 16,255,500 — the last of the line. The Volkswagen had overtaken its mentor, the Model T Ford, six years earlier, to become, at 15,007,034, the best-selling car in history. Ford later announced that they had revised their arithmetic. They had made 16.5 million Model Ts between 1908 and 1927. By the time they made the announcement, the Volkswagen had overtaken that figure, too. "King" Nordhoff, "the cat who liked to walk alone," appointed by Major Hirst, had presided over the rise of the most famous car on earth. He had also been criticized for not working toward a successor.

As early as 1957, industry observers had declared themselves unhappy that the company still relied on a prewar design. Nordhoff's reply was uncompromising: "Can anybody seriously believe that we will change this car, which has scored so many successes?" he said. "You can rest assured that I will not make this mistake."

Herr Generaldirektor Nordhoff continued, with Germanic certainty, "We shall concentrate on eradicating, gradually and positively, all those small and large design errors, inevitable in any car, and this is what we are doing."

Nordhoff's critics accused him of creating, in Volkswagenwerk, the "sleeping giant of Wolfsburg." Porsche engineers had in fact been working on a replacement since 1953. The problem was that, for the Beetle, every time Nordhoff contemplated production, he had only to look at the Volkswagen's continuing sales figures to find an excuse to delay for another year.

In 1961, Nordhoff introduced the Volkswagen Type 3. This was a new car with a rear-mounted engine and a new body shape. Sales would never threaten those of the Volkswagen Beetle. By 1968, the year of Nordhoff's death, Volkswagenwerk was still looking for a replacement for the people's car. The financial position of Volkswagenwerk was so precarious that the company faced its greatest crisis since the months after the end of the Second World War.

Ferry Porsche, son of Dr. Ferdinand, spent four years working on Project EA 266. This was a mid-engined, water-cooled attempt at a successor, with the engine located under the rear seat. The project was clever, but was abandoned in 1971.

Kurt Lotz, who succeeded Nordhoff, developed new models. Rudolph Leiding, who took over in 1971, pushed through the next generation of Volkswagens. These included the Passat, the Scirocco, and the Polo.

By 1974 the list also included the acknowledged successor to the original Volkswagen, the Volkswagen Golf. Giorgetto Giugaro's work on the Golf made him the successor to Dr. Porsche as the world's most successful volume car designer in the 1970s.

The first million Golfs were sold in only thirty-one months. The car went to the top of the German sales statistics and stayed there. In 1975, Volkswagenwerk launched the Golf in the United States, calling it the Rabbit.

In 1983, the year after Carl Hahn became chairman, Volkswagenwerk stopped production of the Golf after making over 6 million in Germany, the United States, South America, and South Africa.

In 1984, however, Volkswagenwerk launched the Golf II. The Golf had rescued the fortunes of the sleeping giant of Wolfsburg, whose future had looked so doubtful at the beginning of the decade.

Meanwhile, the original people's car simply would not go away.

In 1954, production of the Volkswagen had begun at Clayton, near Melbourne, Australia. In 1959, production had begun in São Paulo, Brazil. In 1967, President Salinas of Mexico had asked Volkswagenwerk to build the Mexican people's car.

There were 80 million Mexicans. At the factory in Puebla, Mexico, seventy miles southeast of Mexico City, in the shadow of the great volcano Popocatépetl, every two minutes, another people's car came bumping off the production line.

Mexican dealers also bought new Volkswagens from the Puebla plant and sold them to their own directors, who exported them privately to individual directors of dealerships in Britain and elsewhere. These British dealers sold them on to enthusiasts. The people's car, commissioned in Germany and built in Mexico, became a collector's item in these and other countries.

In 1975 the Nigerian government was tired of discovering top-of-the-line Mercedes-Benz cars wrapped in giant plastic bags and concealed in containers of molasses unloaded at Lagos harbor. It was determined to thwart the march of the *Wabenzi* and standardize its employees' automobiles. In 1975, production of the Volkswagen began in Lagos.

Nigeria, like Australia and Brazil, initially imported Volkswagens in kit form from Brazil, Peru, and Uruguay. The Volkswagen soon became known as "the car of the masses" in Nigeria.

In an attempt to control traffic congestion in Lagos, a city of 7 million people, the authorities dictated that vehicles with even-numbered license plates should travel on certain days of the week, and vehicles with odd numbers should travel on the other days of the week. The Nigerian masses responded by buying two Volkswagens: one for the odd and one for the even days of the week.

The Lagos plant manufactured more than 135,000 Volkswagens and exported many of these back to Germany where demand exceeded supply.

The last of the line might have left Wolfsburg, but the Beetle had become the vehicle of freedom and mobility for races whom Hitler and Speer would have damned as *Untermenschen* and consigned to

Nacht und Nebel. The Thousand Year Reich had lasted only a few short years. The *Volkswagen* would never die.

Wolfsburg, West Germany, 1978

Major Hirst had left Wolfsburg thirty years earlier, after they started making the Volkswagen. The year they stopped making the Volkswagen, Major Hirst came back. There were many familiar faces. Helmut Amtenbrink, who had arrived here at KdF-Stadt as a sixteen-year-old, was plant manager. The man Hirst had hired as a secretary, Toni Schmuecker, was *Herr Generaldirektor.*

The Volkswagenwerk top brass did not know quite what to do with Major Hirst. He had so much history. They sent him off to watch a demonstration in which a Volkswagen truck pulled a trailer over a series of thrashing metal blades. The inference was that the Volkswagen could still hold the road.

Major Hirst was sitting in an armchair on a podium. The only other people there were a group of Chinese. Nobody seemed to be paying any attention to them.

China had recently embraced capitalism. Deng Xiaoping, once condemned by Madame Mao and her Gang of Four as a "capitalist roader," had declared, "It doesn't matter whether a cat is black or white, as long as it catches mice."

Major Hirst got up from his armchair. He signaled to his German interpreter. Through the German, the Englishman and the Chinese engaged in dialogue.

"Who are you?" asked Major Hirst.

"I, sir," said the first Chinese, "am the head of the Chinese national car plant."

"I, sir," said the second Chinese, "am the head of the automotive section of the Chinese civil service."

"I, sir," said the third Chinese, "am the assistant to the head of the automotive section of the Chinese civil service."

"Nobody wants to talk to us," said all three Chinese, "except you."

Major Hirst did not want to impose too much upon the hospitality of his German hosts. On the other hand, he had had a certain amount of influence in the progress of this enterprise to date.

Besides, who knew what possibilities lay ahead for Volkswagen in a country as vast as China?

He alerted the attention of the management to the presence of these visitors. Hirst thought no more about this at the time. But later, as momentous events unfolded, he did wonder whether or not he had just witnessed the birth of Volkswagen Shanghai.

15

Collision

The Autocrat and the Commissars

B Y THE END OF THE 1960s, Gianni Agnelli was certain of only one thing: there were uncertain times ahead. "The institutions are being challenged," he said, "and rightly so. We'll have to spend more on our public institutions, even if it means overheating the economy and even if our national income doesn't justify the expenditure."

Some found it impossible to tell whether he was speaking for FIAT or for Italy. "I'm afraid of losing time," Agnelli said. "I want to get everything done and have everything in its place."

The truth was, he was speaking for both. He feared the failure of the center-left Christian Democrat government to meet the needs of the Italian people. He knew this would result in the implosion of the center, and violent swings to both left and right.

Agnelli was a man for all seasons, the old and the new, the right and the left.

It is true that the old guard of conservative Turin regarded the Agnellis with suspicion and envy, and dismissed them as *arrivistes*. After all, they had only had big money for seventy years. Agnelli's wife was a Neapolitan princess, but she was also half American. The

Agnellis did little entertaining, and an evening in their thirty-room palazzo often meant a movie in the private cinema, where thirty or forty were screened a year.

And the charm that some found so persuasive, others suspected. Who else but *L'Avvocato* could have described as "an aesthetic problem" the 10-percent stake in FIAT held by Muammar Ghaddafi's Libya? Did this mean a terrorist owned 10 percent of Italy? Of course not. Yet the militant left regarded the Agnellis and FIAT as suspiciously as did the old guard. Agnelli would be one of the first targets, if *Il Boom* — *Il Miracolo* — backfired. If Italy was ultimately ungovernable, FIAT was a multinational corporation beyond government.

But Gianni Agnelli and his younger brother, Umberto, were men who commuted with apparent ease between capitalism and communism, conservatism and collectivism, New York, Rome, Paris, Tripoli, Turin and Moscow. Right and left, north and south, rich and poor all distrusted but acknowledged the power and intentions of *i fratelli d'Italia* — "the Italy brothers" — Gianni and Umberto Agnelli.

For Agnelli, there were other activities more worrisome than how many Italians and their *bambini* were taking off in their FIATs for *Il Weekend* on the *autostrada*. By the early 1970s, FIAT was heading for trouble, and what was bad for FIAT was bad for Italy. Labor relations had deteriorated sharply since the "hot autumn" of 1969. Agnelli had bought peace from the trade unions, but his concessions only brought spiraling wage demands. Dialogue broke down, and ideological differences were polarized between militant left and right. The focus tightened on the 120,000 FIAT employees in Turin.

During the economic crisis of 1972, FIAT invested heavily in new plants and technology, but the wisdom of such long-term investment was lost on disaffected workers on the production line. Managers and foremen were the obvious targets for militant anger; but the climate of terror spread.

When office staff at the Mirafiori plant refused to join a blue-collar strike, they were forced out of their offices on pain of physical violence. Once they had emerged, they were still forced to run the gauntlet of four thousand jeering workers, who spat at, jostled, kicked, and physically assaulted terrified secretaries.

In 1973 and 1974, the OPEC oil shocks quadrupled the price of oil. FIAT was left with 300,000 unsold cars. The company diversified into buses and coaches. These failed to generate revenue, starved the car side of capital and hindered the development of new models.

The Marxist/Maoist *Brigadi Rossi* — Red Brigades — began a campaign of kidnapping and murder. Their role models were the urban guerrillas of Latin America. Their bible was the two volumes published on this subject by the rich left-wing publisher Giangiacomo Feltrinelli. He was obsessed with the notion of a right-wing coup in Italy. The greater threat to him, however, came from himself. In 1972, at Segrate, near Milan, he blew himself up while attempting to attach a bomb to a power-line tower.

The Red Brigades' "targets" were the wealthy bourgeoisie, the liberal center-left, the right, and FIAT and the Agnellis. They terrorized an entire faculty out of the university. They kneecapped teachers and abducted the children of the rich. But they reserved their full hatred for FIAT.

On April 18, 1974, Gianni Agnelli became president of the national employers' association of Italy, Confindustria. Agnelli would bring a prudence to the position unmatched by his predecessors, but this did not placate the *Brigadi Rossi*.

The Red Brigades announced that his appointment was "the beginning of a Gaullist-style coup in Italy" and kidnapped a judge. The kidnapping brought them the nationwide publicity they wanted; the judge was released, unharmed, thirty-five days later.

Between 1973 and 1979, the *Brigadi Rossi* murdered four FIAT managers and shot and wounded twenty-seven others. Many managers were simply unable to reach their offices. Red Brigade members and sympathizers infiltrated the production line.

All this time, FIAT employees were turning out eleven cars each a year. Toyota employees were turning out forty-three.

FIATS came off the Mirafiori production line with screws all over the carpet, and the mirrors fell off after a few hundred miles on the *autostrada*.

FIATs were falling apart.

FIAT was falling apart.

Turin was falling apart.

"It's like *gnocchi*," said the mayor of Turin, Diego Novelli. "The flour, the potatoes, the eggs, and the water may all be better in Turin.

In Naples, everything's bad, but somehow the dough holds together better. The trouble with Turin," the mayor went on, "is the problem of hopeless individualism. You don't know who lives above you, or who lives below."

Novelli had grown up in Turin, near the Lancia plant. "The greatest ambition is to have a car. The Torinese doesn't mind if you pinch his wife's bottom. But if you scratch his car, he'll crack your skull."

In 1978, the *Brigadi Rossi* kidnapped the Italian prime minister, Aldo Moro. They held him for fifty-five days, murdered him, and dumped his body in the center of Rome in the trunk of a Renault Five. The Agnellis became among the most closely guarded families in the world.

By the summer of 1979, relations between FIAT and the militants in the trade unions were at the breaking point. Two hundred thousand cars were lost in that year through strikes. Absenteeism was running at 20 percent. The factories were riddled with prostitution and protection rackets.

Organized crime hovered at the side of the *Brigadi Rossi* and the violent group *Autonomia Operaia*. The attacks on managers worsened. Foremen were beaten up: "Do you want to finish your days in a wheelchair?" was a frequent threat.

FIAT had had enough. It fired sixty-one workers on suspicion of terrorist connections and upheld its case in the courts. The tide was turning against *Autonomia Operaia* and its bully-boy tactics. In 1980, Agnelli felt strong enough to take the hard-line advice of his younger brother, Umberto. He made him deputy chairman and brought in Cesare Romiti, a tough *Romano* who had turned around the Italian national airline, Alitalia, as managing director. He also appointed the diminutive, dynamic Vittorio Ghidella, a man in the mold of Dr. Valletta, to run the car business.

Romiti began by announcing that because of falling world car sales, he was placing 24,000 workers on redundancy for fifteen months. At the end of that time, half would be allowed back to work at FIAT; the other half would have to find work elsewhere. Three days later, Romiti announced he was also firing fourteen thousand workers.

The moves shocked Italy, but Romiti and Agnelli knew that

under the *Casa Integrazione* state compensation system, the government would pay 90 percent of the redundancy costs. The trade unions called a total strike with picketing of the FIAT factories.

On September 25, 1980, the Italian Communist leader Enrico Berlinguer arrived at the gates of Mirafiori. He promised the strikers support "so as to enable you to last one hour longer than the *padroni.*"

Two days later, Romiti announced the suspension of the sackings and the reduction of layoff time from fifteen to three months. The workers were divided, especially when Berlinguer's promise began to look hollow. But the strike dragged on. One evening, Romiti decided to see for himself at closer quarters what was happening.

Romiti sent his bodyguard home early and, with only a friend for company, set out by car for Mirafiori. This was a dangerous undertaking for FIAT's managing director. But Romiti wanted to prove to himself that he was right.

They drove all the way around the outside of Mirafiori. Romiti was struck by one thing in particular:

> I saw that the pickets were made up of people who were cheerful, who were singing and laughing . . . and then I understood. These weren't FIAT workers, because FIAT workers at that moment could only have been worried, tormented, and anguished . . . These were the usual two thousand trade union professionals; they were playing a political part, the hard men, but it was still a part. So I returned home a little encouraged . . .

The strike had lasted thirty-three days. It ended on the thirty-fourth day, and in a way that changed the political and industrial climate of the country.

The March of the Forty Thousand, Turin, Italy, 1980

On the thirty-fourth day of the strike, something extraordinary happened, even by the standards of modern Italy: forty thousand FIAT foremen, managers, office staff, secretaries, and production line workers took to the streets of Turin.

They marched in silent demonstration and let their placards

speak their message. *Novelli, Novelli, fai aprire i cancelli ...* "Novelli, Novelli, open up the factory gates."

The mayor of Turin was as surprised as anybody at what he saw. But, as one moderate union leader realized, what he was seeing was evidence of the inability of the unions to represent the people.

The broad masses — not the two thousand trade union professionals or the imaginary army cited by *Autonomia Operaia* — had spoken. They included many thousands of blue-collar workers traditionally alienated from the sentiments of the middle levels of the workforce. After nearly a decade of murder, intimidation and extortion ... *basta*. These people, like the management of FIAT, had had enough. They wanted to go to work.

The next day, they did. On the same day, in the Smeraldo cinema in Turin, the workers who made up the FIAT factory council met the trade union leaders, and they signed an agreement with FIAT. It was the end of the long, twisting, and increasingly dangerous road that had begun in the "hot autumn" of 1969. The trade unions' stranglehold on FIAT — and on Italy — was gone forever.

After the March of the Forty Thousand, industrial relations stabilized at Mirafiori and other plants. Management, staff, and workers developed their own labor organizations and broke up the collective political base exploited by militants, both inside and outside the plant, for over a decade. By 1990, fewer than one in three FIAT employees would belong to a trade union.

In 1982, Italy won the World Cup, not least with players from Juventus, the club owned by the Agnellis. FIAT was back on the road to recovery. In 1983, the FIAT *Uno* was successfully launched, and voted European car of the year.

In 1985, FIAT and Ford began merger negotiations, but, although the coalition would have brought unprecedented savings to both companies, *L'Avvocato* said no. If he could not retain control — too much, said the Americans — then he preferred to stay as a rival instead of as a partner.

Agnelli and the fortunes of Italy were inseparable in the Italian mind: "Agnelli has become a talisman," said one observer, "he has assumed an aura of immortality."

But no one — not even Agnelli — could live forever. In 1993, FIAT was caught in Europe's worst postwar recession, and Agnelli, who was seventy-two years old and planning to retire, was compelled to stay on as chairman in return for a massive injection of capital by key shareholders. Agnelli's brother, Umberto, who had been designated heir apparent, was sidelined on the grounds of his indifferent managerial record. The company produced a string of best-selling cars and returned to profit.

But the issue of succession, however taboo a subject to journalists in the presence of *L'Avvocato*, would not go away. In 1996, Agnelli, whose own son Edoardo was unstable and addicted to drugs, finally announced that he was handing over day-to-day control of FIAT to Cesare Romiti, in the hope that by 1998 the reins would be passed to Umberto's son Giovanni Junior, known as Giovannino, who ran the Piaggio scooter subsidiary. The responses of the key players were striking.

Romiti's reaction was typical of the man who had broken the strike of 1980: "Here at FIAT we have one boss at a time."

Umberto Agnelli, sidelined once and for all by the prospect of his bitter enemy Romiti and his own son, said tersely, "I believe the age of the family firm is over."

"At least he is a normal person," retorted a journalist of Giovannino, "which in the context of the Agnelli dynasty is saying a lot."

And *L'Avvocato* himself?

"Romiti's younger than me, but not by much," he mused, *"L'e pi' nen 'na musna."* ("He's not a child.") He refused to be drawn out on the subject of the young Giovannino. Like the *Nuova Cinquecento* that he had helped launch forty years earlier, the saga of FIAT and the Agnellis would run and run.

16

The Coming of Age of the Samurai Sedan

In 1975, Toyota overtook Volkswagen and sold 800,000 cars in America. The country whose car industry had been saved in the 1950s by America's military spending for the Korean War was about to take the American auto market by storm — again with the help of a war in Asia, this time in Vietnam.

Japanese cars had traditionally been small, low-powered, two-cylinder models, built for Japan's narrow island roads. By 1960 the cars were bigger and better designed in an international style. The four-cylinder 1.5-liter Prince Skyline Deluxe and the Toyopet Crown Deluxe were nonetheless still a perplexing amalgam of the worst in Western styling, in a size the Japanese government allowed.

Western journalists of the time remarked, however, on the professional styling — and individualism — of the 1.5-liter, seventy horsepower Cedric Deluxe from Nissan of Yokohama.

Nissan, known previously as Datsun, had modeled its first car on the British Austin Seven in 1930. In 1952, Datsun had assembled the British Austin Somerset, imported in kit form from Britain. In 1960 the quality of these new indigenous Japanese cars surprised

Western engineers who remembered the poor finish of Japanese prewar consumer goods.

Yet at the popular level the prewar image endured, perhaps because people could not associate such a momentous transformation with so alien a country and so familiar a commodity as the automobile. To many in the West, Japan was still synonymous with wartime atrocities, and the Japanese visitor was still President de Gaulle's "little transistor salesman."

This momentous transformation was the product of tremendous forces below and beyond popular understanding. In the 1950s no one had predicted developments of such far-reaching significance for Japan and the rest of the world. Japan was still dependent on American postwar aid, and this situation was perceived as a drain on the economies of both countries.

Japanese sovereignty was restored in 1952. In 1953 the Korean War ended. But the popular perception of Japanese subservience remained. In Washington, however, there was mounting anxiety about the Communist threat to East Asia.

President Eisenhower's new secretary of state was John Foster Dulles. On January 27, 1953, Dulles made a national radio and television broadcast to the American people, in which he said:

> The Soviet Russians are making a drive to get Japan, not only through what they are doing in the northern areas of the islands and in Korea but also through what they are doing in Indochina. If they could get this peninsula of Indochina, Siam, Burma, Malaya, they would have what is called the rice bowl of Asia. That's the area from which the great peoples of Asia, great countries of Asia such as Japan and India, get a large measure of their food. And you can see that, if the Soviet Union had control of the rice bowl of Asia, that would be another weapon which would tend to expand their control into Japan and into India. That is a growing danger.

The American people digested this scenario, delivered as it was with such homespun authority. The following day, Dulles chaired a meeting of leading diplomats and military and intelligence officials.

General Omar Bradley declared that a French defeat in Indochina would "lead to the loss of all Southeast Asia."

Dulles added, "If Southeast Asia were lost, this would lead to the loss of Japan." The problem, as far as America was concerned, lay with "China being Commie."

China might not annex Japan straightaway, but "from there on out the Japs would be thinking on how to get on the other side."

This perception of Japan as the prize in the war between the free West and Soviet and Chinese Communism maintained and fueled the momentous transformation of Japan, of which the Japanese auto industry would become the most conspicuous manifestation.

As had been the case in the Korean War, the cost of this strategy in financial terms would be colossal. Between 1945 and 1955, America spent $2 billion in economic aid and $4 billion in military procurements in Japan. Between 1955 and 1960 — the year the Western journalists began remarking on the Nissan Cedric — American spending on military procurements in Japan rose by a further one and a half billion dollars.

Between 1965 and 1970, American spending on the Vietnam War accelerated. American military orders placed in Japan rose by a further $3 billion.

The total was around $10 billion. This was equivalent to an average annual American subsidy for Japan of $500 million a year over twenty years.

This was the Japanese *Wirtschaftswunder.*

The human cost of America's strategy was unquantifiable. The Vietnam War would leave a tragic legacy across Vietnam and the United States long after President Nixon announced the withdrawal of American troops from Vietnam and began the policy of reconciliation with the Soviet Union and China.

In cruel ironies appropriate to the scale of these events, Nixon and America would also pay a high personal and economic price. Nixon's career would end in disgrace after Watergate. Japan, after all of America's efforts to isolate Communism in the region, would become the major trading partner with Vietnam, Southeast Asia — and China.

By 1968, Japan was producing over 4 million cars a year, and exporting 600,000. By the early 1970s the Japanese had set up a network of dealerships across America. They built on their early success in California, the American state nearest Japan and most susceptible to new ideas. The car that put Datsun on the map in America was the four-seat Datsun 510 sedan, named the Bluebird in Japan. Mimicking the engine, suspension layout, and chassis of the German BMW 1600, with a body designed by the Italian firm Pininfarina, assembled by Japanese workers, the Datsun 510 was multinational in engineering and design. Datsun's contract with Pininfarina demanded that Pininfarina keep silent about designing the body of the 510.

These and other Japanese cars with funny names like Camry and Cherry and Sunny, made by companies with funny names like Toyota, Nissan, Suzuki, and Honda, were the first to land on the beach, and became the bridgehead for the main assault.

The effect of the 1973 Yom Kippur War on the price of oil may not have been taken seriously enough in Detroit or Washington, but it was observed and noted in Tokyo and Yokohama. As the OPEC oil shocks of 1973 and 1974 died away, gas prices stabilized. But Americans continued to buy Japanese cars.

The same thing happened in Britain. Japanese cars were perceived as being cheaper to run and better made than cars made by the British Leyland Motor Corporation.

In 1979 the second OPEC oil shock took place. In the same year, Toyota sold 1,800,000 cars in the United States. America wanted low-mileage automobiles. Japanese companies already had 20 percent of the American market. Yet the great American automobile manufacturers in Detroit still seemed unable or unwilling to acknowledge this demand.

In Tokyo and Yokohama, the Japanese saw this demand as more than a passing phenomenon. They also conceded to themselves that they could not rely on a supply of wars and oil shocks to sustain their phenomenal growth. The Japanese decided to open their first auto plants in America and Britain.

4

The Battle for World Domination

17

Brand Loyalty and the Bedouin

Mercedes-Benz and General Motors in the Middle East

AT THE BEGINNING OF THE 1980s, America and Europe were joined by Japan as world car powers. The Japanese achieved this in exactly the same way the Americans and the Europeans had done, by satisfying the fundamental desire of people for freedom through the automobile.

In the battle for world domination that followed, even the strongest would feel the pressure, and the weak would fall by the roadside. This was the decade in which international capital would begin to undermine the traditional distinctions between capitalism and communism, Christianity and Islam, East and West.

As the national and international consequences of these forces deep at work beneath the surface began to be felt, there were exotic manifestations in the markets of the developing world. This was especially true of the lands whose oil shocks had first helped launch the Japanese assault overseas and had resounded throughout the developed world for three decades since Suez, whose oil revenues had created a valuable new kind of market: the lands of the Middle East and the Arabian Peninsula.

The Great Bitter Lake, Suez Canal, 1945

During the Second World War, ARAMCO, the Arabian American Oil Company, had left fewer than one hundred oilmen in Saudi Arabia. But President Roosevelt realized that Saudi Arabian oil was too important to remain within the sphere of British influence.

The President decided to meet secretly with Abdul Aziz Ibn Saud, King of Saudi Arabia, on the way back from his historic meeting with Churchill and Stalin at Yalta. The secret meeting took place in February 1945, on board the USS *Quincy* on the Great Bitter Lake in the Suez Canal, midway between the Mediterranean and the Red Sea.

Roosevelt, a dying man, charmed and impressed the legendary desert monarch. The chain-smoking president resisted the temptation to light up in the king's presence out of deference to his religious feelings, and slipped out to the ship's elevator for a quick cigarette when he could no longer do without. Ibn Saud mentioned that he was crippled with arthritis and could only walk with a stick, and showed a keen interest in Roosevelt's wheelchair. The president made him a gift of his spare wheelchair on the spot.

The King of Saudi Arabia was impressed by the President of the United States. Roosevelt was unable to spare the time to enjoy an Arab dinner. The king insisted that coffee be brewed and served by his men on the *Quincy* as the minimum permitted gesture of Arab hospitality. This was a gesture of respect from a leader whose own authority was forged in Bedouin protocol and desert war.

The British prime minister, Winston Churchill, by contrast, although a great wartime leader steeped in the tribal protocol of the British Empire, could do nothing right when he tried to outdo Roosevelt's overtures. Churchill met Ibn Saud three days later, in the raffish atmosphere of the Grand Hotel du Lac, fifty miles south of Cairo. Ibn Saud had already asked Roosevelt if he had any objection to his meeting the British prime minister. Roosevelt's magnanimous lack of objections to this meeting must have sent a strong signal to the king.

Churchill did not see the need to match Roosevelt's famous charm in dealing with the monarch who presided over the world's largest known oil reserves. "If it was the religion of His Majesty to deprive himself of smoking and alcohol," he declared, "I must point out that my rule of life prescribed as an absolutely sacred rite smoking cigars and also the drinking of alcohol before, after, and, if need be, during all meals and in the intervals between them."

The King of Saudi Arabia went home on a British cruiser — intended to impress him by contrast with the smaller destroyer placed at his disposal by the Americans.

He was not impressed. "The food was tasteless," he told the first permanent U.S. envoy to Saudi Arabia, Colonel William A. Eddy. "There were no demonstrations of armament; no tent was pitched on the deck; the crew did not fraternize with the Arabs; and altogether I preferred the small and more friendly U.S. destroyer."

The King of Saudi Arabia and his retinue had enjoyed all these and more diversions on board the American destroyer which brought them to the Great Bitter Lake.

The king had showered both leaders with gifts of jewels, gold daggers, swords, and clothes worth many thousands of dollars. Roosevelt's gifts to the king, besides the aforementioned wheelchair, included a Douglas DC-3 airliner with an American crew on free loan for a year.

Churchill, not to be outdone, had promised the King "the finest motorcar in the world."

Riyadh, Saudi Arabia, 1946

By the time of the meeting between the British prime minister and the Saudi Arabian monarch, the Rolls-Royce had been out of production for nearly six years. A prewar model in mint condition was eventually discovered in a dealer's garage by the British Ministry of Supply. It was fitted with a special throne and dispatched to Saudi Arabia, taking a year to arrive.

Two members of the British legation and one of Ibn Saud's former drivers drove the Rolls-Royce from the Saudi Arabian port of Jeddah on the Red Sea four hundred miles across the desert to the Saudi capital, Riyadh. They parked it in the courtyard of the Murabba Palace and had it cleaned and polished, ready for the official presentation the following day.

The king graciously accepted the Rolls-Royce from the two

members of the British legation. Then he ordered the car taken away.

The problem was simple: the steering wheel was on the right. The king, who liked to sit in front, especially when hunting, would be on the left of the driver. The Arab place of honor was on the right. The best car in the world was not good enough for the King of Saudi Arabia.

By the time Churchill's Rolls-Royce arrived, Roosevelt's DC-3 had been flying the king and his family around the kingdom for months. Churchill was out of office and Roosevelt was dead. Thirty years later, the Rolls-Royce would be discovered rusting in a royal garage during the search for exhibits for an Ibn Saud museum. TWA would still be in business with Saudi Arabian Airlines, running some of the Middle East's most profitable air routes. And America would have the concessions to Saudi Arabia's oil.

In the boom years of the 1960s, when Ford and Austin fell afoul of the Arab blacklist of companies that invested in Israel, Saudi Arabia and Kuwait became gold mines for General Motors. The GM Five — Chevrolet, Pontiac, Oldsmobile, Buick, and Cadillac — especially Cadillac — found favor in the lands where oil and gas were cheaper than water and the customer did not have to climb the conventional career ladder.

Germany found favor of a darker kind through its combination of engineering values and anti-Zionist sentiment. The rulers of the Arabian Peninsula remained distressed by the Israeli displacement of Arabs from Palestine, and saw the European war of the infidels from a different point of view. Hitler, although the loser, was perceived in many an Arab mind as a man who knew how to deal with the Jews. Britain, on the other hand, although the nominal victor, was the imperial power that had divided and ruled the Arabian Gulf in order to protect its trade route to India. "My enemy's enemy is my friend" ran the Bedouin proverb — and in such dark corners of the Arab heart were durable loyalties born.

Mercedes-Benz had found its agent in Saudi Arabia in the 1950s. The Juffali brothers had made their name by winning the contract for the Mecca electricity supply. At first the Mercedes-Benz agency proved an average proposition; what propelled it to wealth was the OPEC oil shock of the 1970s.

Saudi Arabia was the trucking country to beat all others, with a scattered population and a huge land area, one quarter the size of the United States. It also had only one railway. In the 1970s and early 1980s, Saudi Arabia was undergoing the biggest building boom in history.

The Juffalis soon mastered the art of winning the heart of the Bedouin trucker. The Bedouin liked the Mercedes-Benz trucks because they were strong and fast and their bodies rode high off the ground and thus were easy to repair. They called them *Umm al-Awlad* — the mother of their children. The Bedouin and their children could sleep under them in their desert encampments.

The Bedouin decorated parts of their trucks, such as the fuel tanks, with Alpine scenes reminiscent of the Muslim picture of Paradise. But the overall color had to be gray-green. They liked Mercedes-Benzes because everybody else had them. The truck would not have been acceptable to them if it hadn't had the hood sticking out in front in the 1960s style. The Bedouin doubted whether any other model in any other color was really a Mercedes-Benz.

A similar brand loyalty impervious to marketing characterized the Al Ghanim agency for General Motors in Kuwait. Whenever a drop in sales led the agency to diversify, the automotive division recovered and the Al Ghanims were forced back to dependency on their General Motors agency. Even Mercedes-Benz could not break the domination of General Motors, even though the higher price of the Mercedes-Benz was no obstacle to the Kuwaitis.

Cars' lives, like those of humans, were shorter in the Arabian Gulf than elsewhere. The fashion-conscious Kuwaitis preferred the annual changes of style of the Cadillac. The wealth of the Kuwaitis meant that they saw no virtue in the cheapness of Japanese competitors. Kuwaitis bought Japanese cars for their wives and servants.

The head of the wealthy Kuwaiti family still wanted a powerful, large, comfortable, quiet American car. The Chrysler New Yorker might have been obsolete in New York, but in Kuwait it meant a cool, calm, quiet journey to and from the office. Even the taxi drivers in Kuwait City drove Chevrolets.

So it happened that Saudi Arabia and Kuwait, the two richest petroleum producers in the world, who had done so much damage with their oil shocks, drove up the profits of Mercedes-Benz by their demand for German trucks assembled by Turkish migrant workers in Saudi Arabia, and boosted the flagging fortunes of General Motors by their demand for the GM Five.

In the early 1990s, the oil shock would backfire on Kuwait when Saddam Hussein of Iraq invaded the country and set fire to the Kuwaiti oilfields. But this was how the man who electrified Mecca made his country into the biggest market for Mercedes-Benz commercial vehicles outside Germany, and how a single Kuwaiti became the biggest General Motors dealer outside the United States.

The psychological makeup behind the brand loyalty of the Arabian Gulf consumer extended beyond Saudi Arabia and Kuwait and the leading car companies of Germany and America. In the small, wealthy Gulf state of Qatar, Omar Almana, a member of an old established Qatari merchant family, acquired the Peugeot agency.

Almana swiftly discovered that French cars such as Peugeot and Renault and Citroën were all equally difficult to market in Qatar because of popular resentment at the French colonial war in Algeria. The sympathies of many an otherwise moderate-minded Muslim lay not with President de Gaulle, but with the would-be assassins of the OAS. This resentment, like the resentment against the British, was reinforced by the memory of France's role in the arbitrary admission of "non-Muslims" to the predominantly Muslim Palestine at the end of the First World War.

The Qatari market was dominated by Austin and Opel. In the early 1960s, however, Austin fell afoul of the Arab boycott of Western companies that invested in Israel. Almana saw his chance. He employed mechanics trained in Europe, built up a vast spare-parts facility, and devised novel incentive schemes, personalized and backed with cash, to sell Peugeots to middle-range car owners and particularly taxi drivers.

By 1970, Almana and Peugeot had 30 percent of the Qatari car market. Peugeot in Qatar survived the Japanese assault on the Middle Eastern middle-range market.

Peugeot and Almana benefited from the Arab boycott and the freewheeling commercial climate of the 1960s in the same way as Mercedes-Benz and the Juffalis in Saudi Arabia and General Motors and the Al Ghanims in Kuwait. A further advantage to the rulers and commercial elites of these remote desert autarchies was the absence of workers' rights and the right to strike, and their access to a passive pool of disenfranchised migrant labor.

In France, the same French car companies — and their pool of disenfranchised migrant labor — became the epicenter of industrial and political unrest on an Italian scale well into the 1980s.

18

Marx, Mao, and Motoring

Internal Combustion at Renault and Peugeot-Citroën

To the French government, Renault has always been a mixed blessing.

On September 7, 1914, seven hundred taxis built at the Renault factory at Billancourt on the Ile Séguin in the Seine had assembled in the square in front of the Hôtel des Invalides. The majority were small Renault *Coupés*. To General Gallieni, the *commandant de Paris* and officer in charge of the city's defense force, this was their moment of glory.

General Gallieni allotted five reservists to each *Coupé*. Overnight, and without lights, the taxi drivers transported nearly four thousand infantrymen to reinforce General Maunory's hard-pressed army, forty miles away on the Marne. This forerunner of the motorized column swung the balance of the first great battle of the First World War. A Renault *Coupé* stands to this day outside the Hôtel des Invalides.

They called it "the miracle of the Marne" and spoke lyrically of "the epic song of the taxis which saved Paris." The slaughter of reservists was terrible. So was the fare. The French taxi drivers kept their meters running, both ways.

By 1938, 42,000 people worked in the Renault factories. Renault had built a modern assembly line, a mile long, at Billancourt. Louis Renault, the founder, was a true autocrat for whom the sole priority was the manufacture of automobiles.

At the outbreak of World War II, Renault, who was in America on business, rushed back to Paris. When the Germans marched into Paris in 1940, Renault, like Pierre Boulanger, the designer of the Citroën 2CV, knew exactly what to do. He used his factory at Billancourt to make vehicles for the Germans.

Renault's many defenders after his death insisted that his motives were to preserve his company in the hope of an Allied victory, and to protect his workers and plant from being transported to the Third Reich. And he paid a heavy price. Billancourt was repeatedly bombed by the Allies. After the Liberation and the change of government that brought the arrests of the architects of the Strength-Through-Joy car, Dr. Porsche and Anton Piech, Renault too was arrested and accused of collaboration with the Nazis.

Dr. Porsche, who had joined the Nazi Party and the SS, and his son-in-law, who with *Herr Doktor Ingenieur* had overseen the slave labor force at KdF-Stadt, were released. Louis Renault was not so lucky. He died in detention.

His company's punishment was to be nationalized. *Renault Frères* became *Regie Renault*. The decision was to haunt successive French governments for decades.

In the 1960s, Billancourt was still regarded as a model car plant. One British newspaper wrote:

> The Renault factory of France can be placed in the same industrial category as the Ford and Morris of this world. Like them, it was founded by one man, and kept going through any number of difficulties by his drive, energy, and single-mindedness to become one of the largest industrial complexes in its country.
>
> Today it is owned by the State, and remains one of the most successful examples of nationalization in the world . . .

In 1968, nationalized car industries were not yet a poisoned chalice for Western European governments. British Leyland was the eighth-largest car manufacturer in Europe. Renault was nine places behind, in seventeenth place. Renault's successful small cars, the Dauphine, the Caravelle, and the Renault Four, were the most popular cars in France and were exported to more than one hundred countries.

But the late 1960s were a time of growing political turbulence. The *autunno caldo* of industrial unrest was spreading across Europe, and in France, as in Italy, Communist influence within the trade unions grew. The automobile industry became the focus of terror and militant discontent.

The French Communist-led CGT union saw itself in the vanguard of the international class struggle. The events of Paris in 1968 brought revolutionary alliances between students and workers, and strikes that paralyzed the city and threatened to topple President Charles de Gaulle.

Renault workers at Billancourt at first refused to back the strikes. The CGT drew many of them into the imbroglio. There followed bizarre and violent scenes. The philosopher Jean-Paul Sartre appeared at the towering old factory on the island in the Seine and lectured workers from an upturned trash can. There were strikes, sit-ins, and speeches. Pierre Overney, a Maoist militant demonstrator, was shot dead at the gates of the factory by a Renault security guard. The guard himself was murdered a few years later.

It would not be long before such methods of class warfare would spread from nationalized Renault to the private sphere of France's premier maker of quality cars — Peugeot-Citroën.

By the 1970s, Levallois, the Peugeot-Citroën plant in the former Victorian bicycle factory a mile from the Eiffel Tower, employed four thousand people. These were mainly poor immigrants recruited as cheap labor from the former French colonial possessions in North Africa, the French equivalent of the euphemistically named German *Gastarbeiter;* "guest workers" from Arab countries doubly blighted by their French colonial heritage and their lack of oil.

Levallois was a dark, dirty, noisy place, off limits to journalists. It was a crucial part of the Communist "red belt" that ringed Paris. In the early 1980s the Communist CGT agitated for Peugeot-Citroën to be nationalized. Levallois, where a heterogeneous North African immigrant workforce still hand-assembled the so-called *pur sang* 2CV, embodied the many problems of the French automobile industry and, indeed, of France.

Oil-shock-driven recessions, strikes, and spiraling wage demands bedeviled management, forced cuts in the workforce, and antagonized the French trade unions, as they had their comrades in Italy and Britain.

By 1983, Peugeot-Citroën was facing bankruptcy. In spite of the effects of the recession on its power base, the trade unions made strenuous efforts to resist further job cuts. In the same year, at Poissy, Peugeot-Citroën's huge Talbot plant outside Paris, workers decided to take the law into their own hands.

The Battle of Poissy, Paris, 1983

Poissy was one of the biggest repositories of the potentially explosive mix of forces within the French car industry. More than half of its seventeen thousand workers were from North Africa or from former French colonial possessions in sub-Saharan Africa. Racial tensions fueled the overheating climate on and around the great production line.

Jacques Calvet was in charge of day-to-day operations. Calvet was a tough, short-tempered man who had been chairman of Banque Nationale de Paris (BNP), France's leading nationalized bank. But Calvet was no Socialist.

Calvet's rise at Peugeot-Citroën had been rapid and effective. He had announced a job cut of 7,500, or 10 percent, a record for a French company. Nearly three thousand of these layoffs were to be at Poissy.

Talbot had been a disaster for Peugeot-Citroën ever since they had bought it from Chrysler. The company was the biggest single money-loser for the Peugeot-Citroën group. The layoffs were to be accompanied by a desperately needed program of investment in new technology. The entire Peugeot-Citroën recovery program was intended to spearhead President Mitterrand's modernization of French industry from cars to chemicals, steel, and shipbuilding.

The French automobile trade unions accepted the proposal for job cuts only in the form of early retirements. They rejected the proposal for layoffs outright. They wanted to be nationalized like Renault.

Calvet's response was to threaten to shut down Poissy for good. The specter of seventeen thousand layoffs shocked France, terrified the French government, and turned Poissy into what a government spokesman described as *un drame*. The trade unions called a strike and occupied the plant. A classic standoff had begun in which there could only be one winner — or could there?

Inside the plant, workers arrived clutching pink slips from the management. A CGT leader who tried to explain the virtues of retraining and transfers to other companies was shouted down. Tensions between strikers and nonstrikers were fueled by the racial unrest that had been simmering for years.

Dialogue broke down and was replaced by the fist and the boot. Militant Communists clashed with the extreme right-wing National Front. The settling of old scores turned into a full-scale riot.

After three days of rioting, even the most militant of the unions realized the situation was out of control. They asked the management to call in the CRS riot police to evacuate the plant. Poissy was closed until further notice. Many feared it was closed forever, just as Calvet had threatened it would be.

Eventually they reached a compromise that *Le Monde* described as "a typically French affair."

There would be layoffs, but there would also be compensation and retraining. There would be no nationalization, but the compensation and retraining would be at government expense. The CGT could claim that it had saved jobs and that "nobody will be thrown onto the street." Peugeot-Citroën somehow still had to finance a top-heavy labor force from the slender resources of the company. The Mitterrand government could claim that its industrial modernization program was intact.

The "Battle of Poissy" exposed the racial tensions inside French car plants and became a test case for relations between organized labor and the Socialist Mitterrand government. Jacques Calvet continued to walk a tightrope between tortuous progress and the collapse of Peugeot-Citroën throughout the rest of the 1980s.

While the Poissy plant survived, Peugeot-Citroën closed the Levallois plant after nearly forty years' production in 1988. With the plant died the Citroën 2CV, even though the Middle Eastern oil shocks had given a new lease on life to the fuel-efficient *deuche*. There were many who lamented its passing. No other car, not even the Volkswagen, had been produced at the same plant for so long, or ever would be again. A few 2CVs would be manufactured during the next two years at Mangualde, in Portugal.

Jacques Ravenel had started work in the paint shop at Levallois forty years earlier. In 1988 he was managing director of Citroën and president of the French car manufacturers' association. "You can't help feeling sentimental about Levallois," Ravenel said. "But you can no longer produce cars in an urban environment where supplies have to be brought through the narrow streets by truck."

The North African workers at Levallois were not so sentimental. Marooned in what had been the "red belt" but was now a white, middle-class Gaullist suburb, they were caught in the path of a re-surgent, racist right. Many had settled here with their families and were reluctant to return home.

The chances of retraining were slight for many older workers with language difficulties. The offer of "repatriation grants" was insufficient to tempt many back to North Africa.

As a North African worker from Poissy put it, "We are at the root of all the problem. No one wants or needs us anymore. Neither the Government nor the unions nor anyone else in France is really going to fight for our rights and dignities. They hope the problem will go away and that we will go away."

The outcome of the labor disputes of the seventies was no different at state-owned Renault. Renault expanded its plants in the provinces and wound down operations at Billancourt. Billancourt, as had been the case at Levallois, was no longer the center of the company.

In 1985, Georges Besse became chairman and concentrated on a cost-cutting program. The following year, Besse was murdered by the terrorists of *Action Directe*. The leader of a nationalized industry could not expect protection merely because he was the servant of a Socialist state. But by this time the CGT had lost its grip, and the killing was seen as an isolated incident rather than as the symptom of a national — or nationalized — malaise.

Besse was succeeded by Raymond Levy. Levy was a risk-taker who was not afraid to delay the launch of a new car at a cost of $150 million; he was the driving force who developed the links with the Swedish car and truck giant Volvo, and who backed Renault's brilliantly successful new small car, the Twingo.

In 1989, Levy and Renault closed Billancourt for good — over the objections of the unions. "We do not accept the end of production at Billancourt," said a CGT leader. Renault, he added, "wanted to wipe the part played by Billancourt in social struggles from our consciences."

The CGT at Peugeot-Citroën in Levallois, at Talbot in Poissy, and at Renault in Billancourt had suffered a reversal comparable to that of their comrades at FIAT in Turin. Marx and Mao were going out of fashion in France, as in the Soviet Union and China.

The French car industry in the 1980s was a potent example of the effects of recession and the waning grip of the trade unions in the struggle between governments and organized labor. Renault, the most important company in the industry, proved an embarrassment, as a nationalized company, to a Socialist government racked by recession yet pledged to the goals of competitiveness and public ownership.

Ultimately the government found a way to resolve the denationalization issue with positive commercial results. It privatized Renault, but retained a majority shareholding. This appeased the trade unions and defused the left as it was gearing up for the presidential elections.

Full privatization of Renault would remain contingent upon economic rather than short-term political factors. Meanwhile, the Renault corporation share offer closed in November 1994. The following day, the French Economy Ministry announced with some satisfaction that the offer had been more than fifteen times oversubscribed.

19

Toyota, Mazda, Datsun, and the Drive Upmarket

THE MAJORITY OF CARS made by the Japanese in Japan — and in America and Britain — continued to be for the mass market. But ever since Eiji Toyoda's visit to Detroit in 1950 and the evolution of the Toyota Production System, Toyota and other companies had been aware that they could, in theory, make any kind of car for any kind of market anywhere on earth.

The success of their mass-market cars in the international markets had given them the resources and incentive to take on the American and European sports-car makers. There was a little-known precedent. It involved Datsun in Japan and an exiled German aristocrat car stylist in New York.

Count Albrecht Goertz had moved to New York from Hitler's Germany in 1937. He trained under the great American designer, Raymond Loewy, and the following year, Goertz designed his first car, for himself. (Loewy was famed for his designs for Studebaker, and had many of his designs copied by European manufacturers, from Alfa-Romeo to Citroën. His "Targa" roll bar was appropriated by Porsche in the 1960s. Nevertheless, his talents were never fully utilized by the American companies.) Goertz spent five years during the Second World War in the U.S. Army, where he served against the Japanese in the Pacific. After the war, he returned to New York, traveling to Germany several times a year to help his wife manage her family estates near Hanover. But he remained a designer at heart who believed that car manufacturers above all others should resist the danger of loss of identity in the rush for corporate growth.

Goertz was an automotive milestone designer. In 1959 he designed the 507 sports car for BMW, a sensation when introduced and now considered one of the most beautiful cars ever produced. The detail design from the fenders of the 507 can be seen today in the new BMW sports car being produced in America. But the failure of the count's German refugee friend Maxie Hoffman, the baron of Park Avenue, to compete with the Corvette and Thunderbird and successfully market the 507 in America brought BMW to the brink of bankruptcy.

Early attempts by the Japanese to emulate British sports cars resulted in copies of cars that existed already, and sold poorly; the Datsun 1600 sports cars emulated the British MGs and Triumphs so slavishly that they included not just the worthy features, but the design flaws of the originals. In 1969, Count Goertz designed another sports car, this time for Datsun.

The Datsun 240Z, a closed grand touring car with a hatchback, swiftly became a classic and a commercial success. As with Pininfarina, Goertz was contractually restricted by Datsun from taking any public credit for the design of the 240Z (called My Fair Lady in Japan). Like Datsun's earlier sports cars, the 240Z was a copy in general layout, this time of the E-Type Jaguar. It also borrowed the design for its rear suspension from the 1963 Lotus Elan. But it was light and reliable when Jaguars were becoming heavy and troublesome, and it was affordable and easy to repair. By combining the best of British engineering, Japanese low-cost labor, and the talent of a German-American designer, the Japanese had succeeded in producing a "Japanese" sports car that could rival the best.

It sold like wildfire. Japanese manufacturers understood not only how to borrow from the best, but how to create a market, something that the Americans had mastered with the Ford Mustang.

The Japanese domestic market for its own sports cars was small in the late 1960s and 1970s. The Japanese elite, like elites all over the world, preferred prestigious foreign imports. But the Japanese realized that the decline in the traditional sports cars manufactured by British companies, such as Triumph, MG, and Jaguar, was not the result of a decline in demand. The decline of the British models in particular was caused by unfavorable currency movements between Britain and America, poor quality, poor marketing, and the collective suicide of the British car industry.

In the 1980s the Japanese hired more German and Italian stylists to work with their designers. The results were the Toyota MR-2 and the Mazda MX-3, the first two Japanese sports cars to match the style and performance of the classic European sports car.

The Toyota MR-2 was a Japanese copy of the ill-fated Pontiac Fiero, with a transverse mid-mounted engine and two seats. The Mazda MX-3, produced by the company that had begun life as a lightbulb manufacturer and is now over 25 percent owned by Ford, revived the front-engined sports car and created a vogue for the British originals.

The Japanese design process still began with the traditional sketch by the designer, which was then converted into computer data and fed into a clay modeling machine that took eight hours to make a model of a kind that had taken forty hours to sculpture by hand. Such reductions in time meant the Japanese companies could profitably design for niche markets.

The results in Japan were cars like the Suzuki Cue and the Nissan Figaro, the limited edition "retro" style concept car for which 400,000 people applied to buy the twenty thousand manufactured; the decision was made by lottery. The Figaro became an instant classic and starred in the Japanese youth movie *Library Love*.

Mazda would go further and develop new models in California. The result here was the Mazda Miata (in Europe the MX-5), another "instant classic." It was also an updated copy of the 1963 Lotus Elan, albeit reliable and inexpensive where the exciting but temperamental Lotus (unofficially and widely accepted as the acronym for "lots of trouble, usually serious") was not. Mazda, like Datsun before them, created a market by rehashing and modernizing what the British felt was expendable.

Thus it was that a German count, who had fled from Hitler to New York City and fought for the Americans against the Japanese in the Pacific, first put the Japanese in the fast lanes of the freeways, *autostradas*, and autobahns. But many who bought the latest Italian-designed Japanese best-seller could not help wondering what might have been, if only the indigenous European car industry had kept its dominance in the sports-car market. And by the time the British MG did return, in 1995, its success was ensured by the fact that it was designed by an international consortium and styled to look like a Mazda.

20

Inside Castle Volvo

PG, ET, and the Company That Outgrew a Country

THEY CALLED IT "CASTLE VOLVO" — the marble-corridored head-quarters atop a rocky, rainy outcrop outside Gothenburg in Sweden. Volvo watchers sometimes suspected it was easier to get into the Kremlin. If the car was the company, then it was no wonder that Volvo built their cars like tanks. Volvos did not just have doors, they had "side impact protection systems."

In the 1980s, Volvo's only problem was so unusual, so exquisite, that, instead of hiding it, the company's CEO, Pehr Gyllenhammar, might have felt justified in thrusting it into the public eye. Gyllenhammar — P.G. as he was known — was only fifty in 1986, but he had been in charge since 1971. He was part of the problem — indeed, he was its author. Volvo had grown so big that Sweden, as the polite way of putting it went, "was a nation too small for its major company."

Gyllenhammar could recite the figures. Volvo accounted for 11 percent of Sweden's gross national product. Volvo accounted for 12 percent of Sweden's sales of goods overseas. Volvo dominated the domestic car market and had to be politely restrained from wiping out its fellow Swedish manufacturer, SAAB, until SAAB was rescued by General Motors.

It did not seem to matter that Volvo made the civilian equivalent of the tank rather than something more stylish, such as the SAAB Turbo. Volvo drivers were like Mercedes-Benz drivers; 95 percent repeated the purchase. In brand loyalty, they were rivals of the Saudi Arabian Bedouin.

Volvo was a Swedish *zaibatsu*, a Scandinavian *chaebol*. But the car operations of the company were not making as much money as people thought. Then a foreigner came to the gates of the castle — and, in the tradition of Scandinavian fairy tales, all sorts of creatures flew out when Volvo unlocked the door.

Pehr Gyllenhammar had married the boss's daughter.

He took over from his father-in-law, and — or so he thought — pursued a quest for diversification happily ever after, away from the automobile business. He said he was motivated by what had happened to other middle-sized groups such as Rover, Citroën, and Alfa-Romeo, all of which had been gobbled up or merged with varying results.

Gyllenhammar's wife said he was motivated by a well-meaning but impulsive naïveté.

A British merchant banker said, "The real reason for his relative neglect of Volvo's automobile business is that somewhere in his psyche there's a deep dislike of making cars . . . perhaps he was simply trying to get out of the shadow of his father-in-law."

The 20-percent cross-shareholding between Volvo of Sweden and Renault of France was a manifestation of Gyllenhammar's Francophilia. PG spoke fluent French and sported the lapel button that signified his membership in the *Légion d'honneur*. He was close to Renault chairman Raymond Levy, and to Levy's successor, Louis Schweitzer — whom Prime Minister Edith Cresson of France had called "ET" because she claimed he looked like the creature from the Spielberg movie.

P.G. and ET got along well, but the news that the close links between Volvo and Renault were turning into a full-scale merger brought the Volvo watchers hammering on Gyllenhammar's door.

Who really owned Volvo? How much of the earnings would be

coming back to Sweden? What was the relationship between Renault and the Swedish government? If Volvo was so profitable, why was there going to be a merger? Was the new company really to be run from Paris and known as Revolvo?

The merger of Volvo and Renault was announced in the summer of 1993. This was followed by an autumn chill and a winter of discontent in Sweden. The new company, whatever it was called, would be worth $42 billion, employ 100,000 people, make 2 million cars a year, and be the fourth-largest vehicle manufacturer in Europe and the sixth-largest in the world.

Industry analysts — never a reliable barometer of the wider constituency — suggested that the car companies were beginning to understand they would fall all the harder on their own, rather than together.

But the new company *would* be called Renault-Volvo. Renault and French shareholders *would* effectively control 65 percent of the shares. The French government *would* hold 46 percent. The French government *would* also hold the golden share enabling it to block future takeovers. The headquarters *would* be in Paris.

The new company would not be called Revolvo. But it was called this, all the same, in Paris and Gothenburg.

In Paris, a Renault insider said, "This is a Renault-owned company and will be directed from Paris."

In Paris, Industry Minister Gerard Longuet said that Renault would be the "driving force" in the partnership. Longuet described Volvo as "the minority partner."

In Gothenburg, these remarks were widely read in the Swedish press. The Swedish government forced the French government to backtrack and make soothing noises, but the damage was done. Volvo, and Gyllenhammar, were on the rack.

Stockholm, 1993

Volvo directors met in Stockholm only five days before an extraordinary shareholders' meeting in Gothenburg. There was only one significant item on the agenda.

The big shareholders, such as the insurance group Skandia and several other institutions, voiced their doubts at the wisdom of the merger. The spectacle loomed of a similar reaction from individual shareholders in five days' time. The share price, which was already depressed, would fall further in the event of a public show of confidence in the company that was supposed to be bigger than Sweden.

Of the political consequences, no one liked to speak.

Gyllenhammar and three other directors resigned from the board. Among them was Raymond Levy, the former chairman of Renault who had initiated the merger in the first place. Three months later, Renault and Volvo dissolved the cross-shareholding that began in 1990.

A source close to both companies attributed the breakdown of the merger to a combination of "Swedish stupidity and French arrogance."

The departure of Gyllenhammar from Volvo did not diminish his popularity with the Swedish people, who had regularly voted him their favorite businessman. Volvo did not crash and bring down the Swedish economy. Volvo shares even rose in the aftermath. The Renault share offer, too, was fifteen and a half times oversubscribed, as the French government was only too happy to repeat.

Yet the breakdown of the alliance revealed the vulnerability of the Swedish automotive giant that had seemed as indestructible as the cars and the rocky outcrop on which stood its headquarters. Volvo shareholders — and the Swedish government — had received a warning from the breakdown of the merger. In 1995, Volvo began radical new marketing campaigns to update its image and launch a "younger" range of cars in the international markets. It also negotiated a supply of engines from Audi in Germany.

The French company was vulnerable as well. Louis Schweitzer had been appointed to Renault's chairmanship by the architect of the merger, Raymond Levy. Schweitzer had said that the merger was essential if the two companies were to counter the threat posed by Japanese operations in Europe. With the merger on the rocks, Renault had to come up with a new answer to the Japanese challenge.

In 1995, Renault responded by forming an alliance with Mercedes-Benz to manufacture the small "C" class Mercedes and the Renault Twingo at a new plant in Brazil. The French company already produced 100,000 cars a year in Argentina and had for some time set its sights on the potentially lucrative markets in South America.

The alliance with Mercedes-Benz was no merger on the scale of Renault-Volvo. But in the dawn of the global market an alliance no longer needed to be a marriage — just an affair between like minds trying to manage an ever-widening agenda.

21

Radial Chic

The Coming of Age of Four-Wheel Drive

THE FIRST FOUR-WHEEL-DRIVE VEHICLE is widely believed to be the wartime U.S. Army Willys Jeep. In fact, many manufacturers preceded it, albeit on a much smaller scale, from Stryker to Bugatti. Furthermore, like Volkswagen, Willys appropriated the design of the vehicle — with the encouragement of the highest authority — from a competitor, the Bantam company. It did so with the blessing of the United States government. The vehicle that introduced reliable everyday four-wheel drive to the world was thus manufactured by a competitor of the original manufacturer, as Bantam went out of business.

The first commercial four-wheel-drive vehicle was based on the Jeep, with a body made of iron girders and aluminum panels. It was conceived on the farm of a Briton, Maurice Wilks. Wilks was the chairman of the British Rover Motor Company. In the early postwar years, Rover needed to boost production and win overseas sales. Wilks decided the company should produce a utility vehicle based on the Jeep. Wilks's own Jeep was wearing out. He intended the replacement to emulate the design philosophy popularly believed to be behind the American name: Just Every Essential Part.

Wilks's aim was to design and produce the vehicle as quickly as possible, and phase it out when demand returned for the quality sedans Rover had made before the Second World War.

Gordon Bashford was the thirty-two-year-old charged with the initial design of new postwar Rover cars. Bashford was also given the job of designing the new four-wheel-drive vehicle for Rover. He took Jeep components, a new frame, and reconfiguring the body slightly, used the four-wheel-drive layout of the Jeep. Bashford had the prototype on the road in six months — not a short development time when major mechanical systems not only already existed but were utilized. For Bashford, this was just another job, in this case of borrowing engineering from another designer — who had in turn appropriated the design in the first place.

They called it the Land-Rover.

The Land-Rover was unveiled at the 1948 Amsterdam Motor Show. It cost 495 British pounds, but seat cushions, side screens, and doors were extra.

Over the next two and a half decades, the Land-Rover became established as the world's leading four-wheel-drive vehicle. By the 1960s it was assembled in more than thirty countries. Off-road, across deserts, through swamps and far-flung villages and distant oases, the Land-Rover was the definitive developing people's car.

This had not escaped the notice of the Japanese.

The first serious competitor was the Toyota Land Cruiser. It was more comfortable and more fuel-efficient than the Land-Rover, and it cost less. Toyota adopted the traditional Japanese strategy of investing in what they believed to be a new long-term market. The Toyota Land Cruiser's competitiveness was boosted by the deterioration in availability and quality and increase in price of the Land-Rover, caused yet again by the suicide of the British Leyland Motor Corporation.

By 1981, Land-Rover was seeing its Third World markets wiped out by Toyota, Mitsubishi, Nissan, Isuzu, and even the Lada Niva, from far-flung Togliattigrad. In 1981, Britain almost lost Land-Rover when the British government tried to sell the parent company to General Motors.

The head of Land-Rover was David Andrews. Andrews had been a colleague of George Turnbull at BLMC, and had survived the nationalization of the company and the purges initiated by Michael Edwardes. In 1986 Andrews organized a management buyout and saved the company.

Land-Rover took heed of its second chance. The company took the four-wheel-drive wars to the Japanese. The Land-Rover was already used by one hundred armies and two hundred police forces around the world. In the 1990s Land-Rover and Range Rover moved upmarket, found new and profitable niches, and enjoyed success in the United States. The Land-Rover's descendant, the Defender, would be named "four-wheeler of the year" at the 1994 Detroit Automobile Show.

In the same year, the new Range Rover was launched. Its six-year development had involved three hundred people and cost $500 million. An $8 million global television linkup showed famous explorers, Gulf War commanders, astronauts, and minor members of the British royal family driving the new vehicle through the English countryside, the Botswana bush, the woods of Vermont, the terrain of South Argentina, and the foothills of Mount Fuji.

The designer of the original Range Rover attended the launch. "In 1970 the marketing people told us we must be mad to build a four-wheel-drive car that would sell for $3,000," he said. "But engineers could look forward then . . . they are not allowed to anymore."

The Range Rover was notable in that it possessed full-time four-wheel drive, which, unlike the Land-Rover and Jeep, allowed it to use four-wheel drive on conventional pavement. At the same time in America, Jeep marketed the Wagoneer, a full-time four-wheel-drive vehicle remarkably similar to the Range Rover technically, but lacking the style and cachet. Ironically, the Range Rover, the most British of cars, is powered by an American-designed engine. Purchased by Rover from General Motors, this aluminum V8 was one of the best deals Rover ever made. General Motors tried to buy the engine back, but found it was not for sale.

Land Cruiser . . . Trooper . . . Shogun . . . Patrol . . . Cherokee . . . Range Rover . . . Defender . . . Discovery. These descendants of primitive forerunners were no longer just means of transport for wizened tribal patriarchs to carry their wives and goats to the Saturday market and park by the fortified walls of the *souk*. These were vehicles for sophisticated people who lived in the gilded cages of

Western cities. For these people, life was circumscribed by routine, but it was still implicitly adventurous. This imaginary capability required a high degree of organization and endurance over long distances, possibly even off roads. For these people, without these machines, their adventurous spirits would have remained socially unfulfilled.

Most traveled no farther than the few miles from Beverly Hills to Malibu, or from the *troisième arrondissement* to the avenue Foch. Occasionally they ventured down the highway or *route nationale* to their weekend homes and *maisons secondaires*. The crucial inference — true or false — was that these four-wheel-drivers were two-home families, a rung up on the ladder above their one-home, two-wheel-drive neighbors.

But, in spite of the layers of social snobbery and sophistication and marketing, the ghost of the once-free spirit, the residue of the nomadic ancestry of all settled peoples — sprayed with sixteen layers of paint, soothed by stereo sound, and secured with seatbelts — was still there in the machine, all the same.

22

"How Much of Your Garden Are You Going to Give to the Japanese?"

Roger Smith and the New Ghost Towns of the Midwest

I N 1980, it finally happened. General Motors, the biggest automobile manufacturer in the world, the barometer of American industry on Wall Street, posted a loss of $760 million — the first in its history.

The maker of the "GM Five" was paying the price for indifferent quality and failure to learn the lesson of the most recent oil shock. The men in Motown were worried. GM and Ford were the biggest domestic producers, but the Japanese were here, making cars, in mainland America.

In 1979, Honda had opened the first Japanese automotive plant in the United States at Marysville, Ohio. Marysville cost $250 million and began by making motorcycles. By 1983 it would be assembling fifty thousand Honda Accords a year.

By 1984 the figure would triple. Honda would spend another $240 million on another plant in America to build the Honda Civic. By this time, Honda would have built twice as many cars in America as Volkswagenwerk, which had been there a lot longer.

Nissan had also started work on a plant to make pickup trucks at Smyrna, Tennessee. Smyrna was an area of high unemployment and low wages. One hundred twenty thousand American men and women applied for two thousand jobs. Applicants were subjected to aptitude tests and pre-employment training. Four hundred were transported to Japan to acquire the "Nissan style."

This included the "3P" movement, or "Productivity through Participation of Workers in Prosperity." After a bitter fight with the United Automobile Workers union, before whom American car companies had traditionally taken a supine position, Nissan imposed its own trade union style.

This maintained power and privilege in the hands of management, but it also made sure workers who conformed were promoted, and it made life uncomfortable for those who stepped out of line. "We will devote all our labor," went the Nissan company song, "the result of sweat and toil, to prosperity and happiness in this world."

The Japanese had come to the poor, white, rural backwaters of America. Americans were not required to sing this song, but they still appeared to be happy. Were they really happy, or did they have no choice in the matter? Suddenly, when Mazda started to build a new plant at Flat Rock, Michigan, it no longer seemed like a long drive from Detroit, Michigan, to Marysville, Ohio, and Smyrna, Tennessee.

The men in Detroit estimated it would not be long before Japan had the capacity to supply 5 percent of total U.S. car sales from their plants inside the United States. "How much of your garden are you going to give to the Japanese, even if they do grow better flowers?" asked Walter Hayes, vice chairman of Ford Europe. Hayes was a cultivated man in an industry dominated by motorheads from Michigan. Ford had worked hard in the 1970s to consolidate its position in Europe and America.

Roger Smith, the new chairman of General Motors, preferred the frontal approach. "What did the Japanese invent in cars?" he demanded. "The only thing I can think of is that little coin holder. I think there's a dedication," Smith went on, "inherent in the Japanese people's outlook and attitude which means they do better at repetitive tasks. I think the American mind does not like repetitive types of assignment. With the Japanese, the reverse is true. They don't like to be shifted around."

Alfred Warren Jr. was GM's Vice President for Industrial Relations: "The Japanese have a different discipline," he declared. "Any time the top boss comes in, everybody clicks their heels and bows." In the U.S., he went on, things were different: "We don't have a culture that bows to the boss."

The men in Motown were making these remarks over forty years after the boss of the Japanese manufacturer they feared most had returned to Japan determined not to imitate exactly the "repetitive types of assignment" he had seen in Detroit.

Honda workers in Marysville did not bow to the boss. Nor did Nissan workers in Smyrna. Nor would Mazda workers at Flat Rock, Michigan. General Motors workers, by contrast, were demoralized after long months of being laid off, only to be called out of the blue and told to report for work at 6:00 A.M. the following day.

Attempts by workers to introduce new ideas and make better and cheaper cars were crushed by bureaucracy. Efforts by management to motivate workers met with a similar fate. At one GM plant, messages such as "Squeezing Rivets Is Fun!" were displayed electronically on a giant board.

A GM worker recalled, "We had no idea whether this was some kind of big-bro Orwellian brain-dunk or just some lowly office jerk's idea of a joke. Whatever it was, we didn't think it was funny."

GM struggled through the early 1980s. The company lowered the prices of the GM Five and produced economy cars. The critics called them "cookie cutters." The company offered low-interest financing to would-be purchasers. This helped the would-be purchasers, but did not help General Motors. By the time the recession had deepened in the late 1980s, GM was the third-largest home-loan lender in the United States.

Motown itself was falling apart. The area around GM headquarters had turned into a no-man's-land of crazed predators and crack addicts. People locked their cars and drove through at top speed without looking from side to side. Detroit had gone from Motor City to Murder City, U.S.A.

In his first couple of years, Roger Smith had closed plants and laid off 200,000 workers. He also opened a joint-venture plant with Toyota in Fremont, California. At the same time, he had tried to diversify the giant company so that the emphasis was less on the "Motors" and more on the "General."

In 1984, Smith bought Electronic Data Systems (EDS) of Dallas, a computer service company, for $2.5 billion. With the company, he bought the founder of EDS, the buccaneering billionaire H. Ross Perot.

Perot had funded the search for American soldiers missing in Vietnam. He had funded the mission to spring two EDS employees from an Iranian prison. Perot came on the General Motors board. He saw no reason to toe the company line.

If an EDS employee saw a snake, said Perot, he would kill it. But at General Motors, "First thing you do is organize a committee on snakes. Then you bring in a consultant who knows a lot about snakes. Third thing you do is talk about it for a year."

After a year, Perot was still philosophical about the culture of the Motown giant: "Revitalizing GM," he said, "is like teaching an elephant to tapdance. You find the sensitive spots and start poking."

After two years, Perot was becoming desperate. "This place cries out for engineers with greasy hands, who know how to make cars, to be making the policy," he cried.

Perot ridiculed the practice of giving GM directors a new car every three months. He refused to accept a car at all. "This company could do a number of things to signal a new day at GM," he said. "For example, I'd get rid of the fourteenth floor. I'd get rid of the executive dining rooms; I would urge the senior executives to locate their offices where real people are doing real work."

By 1986, Perot had been on the board of General Motors for two and a half years. Roger Smith could stand Perot's witticisms and criticisms no longer. The clash of personalities and lack of common cultures were terminal. Perot could not stomach the new cars given to GM executives every three months. Smith could not understand why Perot had expensive paintings by Frederic Remington and Gilbert Stuart on the walls of his office.

Smith persuaded the GM board to pay Perot $750 million for his shares. Perot resigned, and General Motors kept EDS. Under the deal, Perot also had to hand back 1 percent of his payoff if he criticized General Motors in public. To a billionaire, $750 million was hardly hush money — especially to a billionaire like H. Ross Perot.

Smith continued the program he had begun with the plant closures. He pursued the joint venture with Toyota. He spent $80 million on automation. This had worked wonders for FIAT. One day the GM robots went berserk. They fitted the wrong parts; they sprayed the wrong colors; they destroyed the Cadillacs they had been designed to build.

In 1988, GM made more profits in Europe than it did in America. *The Wall Street Journal* gave Smith the title of "Management Turkey of the Decade": "He roared into the 1980s with an overflowing bank vault, two dead-duck competitors and quota protection from the Japanese, but sputtered out of the decade with a deflated market share . . . and tens of billions of spending frittered away on high-tech gizmos . . ."

In 1989, the documentary movie *Roger & Me* brilliantly illustrated the gulf between the chairman of General Motors and the devastation wrought by plant closures and unemployment lines in Midwest car towns like Flint, Michigan.

The Japanese continued their advance. General Motors' market share continued to slide.

This was becoming serious.

Detroit, 1989

Roger Smith admired the new car in the downtown parking lot.

"What's that?" he asked the attendant. "The new Mercedes-Benz?"

"No, sir," the attendant replied, "that's one of the new Japanese models."

Later Smith could still not believe it. He knew his cars. He was chairman of General Motors. But it was true . . . here in a downtown parking lot . . . here in the heart of Motor City . . . he thought it was German . . . *and it was made by the Japanese.*

General Motors continued to close plants in one place and open them in another, and to invest in technology on a scale appropriate to the world's largest automaker.

Roger Smith had joined General Motors as an accounting clerk in 1949. Forty years later, as chairman, he was coming up for retirement.

Smith drove in at 6:30 A.M. each day from the suburb of Bloomfield Hills. He arrived at the fifteen-story fortress with the shops that did not open onto the streets, and the enclosed parking garage.

Smith took the elevator up to the fourteenth floor. He passed through two locked entranceways on the way to his walnut-paneled office. If he went anywhere within the GM complex, he did so by the covered walkway that connected it to four other buildings. Otherwise he did not have to go anywhere until it was time to go home.

The average age of General Motors' employees was forty-two. The number of retired employees drawing company benefits meant that $170 was added to the cost of making every GM vehicle by the cost of health care alone.

Perot had taken the money and gone from the GM board. EDS remained, and the purchase was proving expensive in terms of both money and cultural differences. GM staff complained that EDS staff lacked training and experience. One analyst doubted the wisdom of GM's massive investment in technology as a means of driving itself back into the fast lane. He claimed that GM "bought EDS in the belief that EDS had more knowledge about automating manufacturing than it actually did."

In 1990, Roger Smith retired as chairman of General Motors. His successor was an engineer, the company's president and chief operating officer, Robert Stempel.

In 1991, H. Ross Perot ran for President of the United States. Perot lost, but won a reputation as a popular hero. One of the first questions he asked the winner, Bill Clinton, was what he was going to do about the Japanese attempt to destroy the American automobile industry.

President Clinton was devoted to his '64 Ford Mustang, but he was unable to give the answer Perot — or the people — wanted to hear. In 1995, however, an embattled Clinton approved in principle the imposition of $6 billion worth of tariffs on Japanese luxury cars imported into the United States.

"We're going to drop the bomb on them!" an exultant Mickey

Kantor, U.S. Trade Representative, told Jack Smith of General Motors.

"We can't sweep this under the rug any longer," Clinton said. He was referring to the need to appease the key Democratic vote among organized labor at home, as well as to send an uncompromising signal to the Japanese.

23

Fallen by the Roadside

Trabant and Zil in a Disintegrating Europe

THEY CAME TO SYMBOLIZE THE HYPOCRISIES of social engineering and the irresistible potency of the automobile. The one was for the proletariat, in whose hands, theoretically, lay their own destiny and the means of production. The other was for those with whom the power truly lay.

Jean-Paul Sartre, astride his trash can at Billancourt, had had a shrewd feeling for the short-term susceptibility of the striking auto workers. But when it came to the real roads to freedom, he had no idea.

The Trabant and the Zil were the Communist world's equivalent of the Model T Ford and the Cadillac. The irony was that they existed at the same time in history. One looked like a collision between a mailbox and a lawnmower, the other like a cross between a hearse and a 1960s shark-finned gas-guzzler. They made three million of one and several thousand of the other. The waiting lists for both ran into decades. But at last the waiting was over.

Berlin, 1989

The thousands of Trabants that poured across the border came to symbolize the new freedom that followed the fall of the Berlin Wall. The East Germans, or "Ossis," voted the Trabant "Car of the Year" simply for helping thousands of them to escape to freedom from Czechoslovakia and Hungary. Many families crossed the old border and simply abandoned their vehicles, disassociating themselves from the grotesque parody that had been the other German people's car.

Others drove in convoy up the autobahns to new jobs in places such as Stuttgart. Their new employer drove in front, in second gear in a Porsche; they drove behind, straining to keep up in their Trabants. The first thing Trabant drivers bought was an Opel or a Volkswagen Golf.

Six hundred thousand "Wessis" and "Ossis" flocked to see the movie *Go Trabi Go*, in which an East German family took advantage of the fall of the Berlin Wall to undertake a journey by car to visit relations in Italy. For part of the journey, the Trabant was taken on an auto transport. The transport driver proceeded to tell no fewer than 118 Trabi jokes — beating the number of jokes told about the Skoda, and a world record for a car.

"How does a Porsche engine feel inside a Trabi? Like a pacemaker in a mummy." "Why does a Trabi have only one exhaust? So you won't mistake it for a wheelbarrow." "What did the cowpie say to the Trabi that had just run over it?" . . .

Before the fall of the Berlin Wall, a Trabi cost the equivalent of a year's salary. By 1990 you could buy a Trabant for the equivalent of fifty cents. By 1991 the six thousand Trabant workers were out of a job. Zwickau was a servicing center for Volkswagenwerk.

As for the Trabants on the junk heap, burning would release dioxins into the air. If buried, the car would taint the soil with the same carcinogens.

In time, the Trabant would become a cult object in a Berlin racked by the cost of reunification. One dealer would parade his pink "stretch" Trabi, eighteen feet long, with sun roof, quadruple exhausts, and stereo. Another would have his lined with fur — on the outside. Another would drive his Trabi across the United States, and organize the first Trabi rally from Berlin to Marrakesh and back.

Meanwhile, unlike the regime that spawned it, there seemed to be no way this deadly little dinosaur would auto-destruct. Scientists were looking for a microbe that would eat it.

Moscow, 1989

The Zil had been manufactured since 1962 by more than 100,000 workers at seventeen sites across Russia. The most notorious was the gigantic plant on a bend of the river Volga in the south of Moscow. *Zavod Imeni Likhacheva* (ZIL), as the plant was known after its first director, Ivan Alekseevich Likhachev, was described by occasional Western observers as "an ecological inferno." Visitors were discouraged on the grounds of commercial sensitivity.

The murderous black shark-finned Communist Cadillac had become synonymous with Stalin, Khrushchev, and the Politburo. Likhachev himself had been a model Soviet citizen who had run the main plant when it was known by its previous name, *Zavod Imeni Stalina* (ZIS), and was awarded five orders of Lenin and buried in the Kremlin Wall for his services.

Cavalcades of Zils swept in and out of Red Square and attended the ministries around the Kremlin. The chauffeurs — on pain of death if they failed — reported the conversations of their masters to the KGB.

The Soviet foreign minister Andrei Gromyko did not even notice when an elderly woman stepped out in front of his Zil. The 3.35-ton vehicle was already too heavy to need armor-plating, and too little was left of her to enable identification by relatives.

The Zil did not fade away with the coming of *glasnost, perestroika,* and Mikhail Gorbachev. In 1985, when Gorbachev visited London, his convoy of Zils looming out of the early-morning mists on the way down Fleet Street to Buckingham Palace, the Soviet leader was barely visible between enormous bodyguards.

On Gorbachev's only visit as Soviet leader to the Caucasus — a day trip to Armenia after the earthquake — he had his Zils flown down to Yerevan for the occasion. The prime minister, Nikolai Ryzhkov, aware of local sensibilities, persuaded him to leave them at the airport and use a bus.

Then came Boris Yeltsin, and the Zil still did not fade away.

When Vice President Rutskoi criticized him in a speech, Yeltsin took away his Zil. Yeltsin had grown up in appalling poverty, and liked to denounce privileges in his own speeches, but he found it difficult to give them up himself. When Gorbachev had demoted him from first secretary of the Communist Party to first deputy chairman of the State Committee for Construction, the hardest thing Yeltsin had found to bear was the loss of his Zil.

The Zil still carried President Yeltsin and his bodyguards at high speed through the streets of Moscow. The Zil was also increasingly popular with smart young Russian bankers and *biznismeni*, on the journeys to and from their offices and their dachas. The armor plating and thick curtains gave them a degree of security from random attack and the attentions of the Moscow Mafia.

The hard-liners of the Communist old guard schemed to destabilize Yeltsin. One day, if they had their way, his Zil would give way to a lowly Moskvich, just like theirs. Other Zils remained in government garages, short of gas, unattended, in mothballs.

The Zil plants remained open for the time being. Attempts were made to attract Western investors. A scheme was hatched to sell them to Albania, but foundered with the Albanian government. For the time being, the Zils remained. Like the Tupolev bombers in their hangars and the missiles in their silos, they waited, in case Yeltsin and *glasnost* and *perestroika* went and the Cold War returned.

Eisenach, Germany, 1990

Albert Siedler, the American GI who had witnessed his loss of freedom, and the Russian soldier who had held him, had long since vanished into the ether of history.

The Siedlers themselves had vanished to West Germany in 1950. In the same year, BMW had won a court case against Avtovelo for copyright infringement. Avtovelo would make no more German cars in Eisenach under Soviet false pretenses.

The Russians had changed the name to *Eisenacher Motoren Werk* or EMW. Eisenach made three-cylinder, two-cycle Wartburgs, named after the castle that overlooked the town. For the next forty years, the factory that had once made the magnificent Auto Union racing cars manufactured cars for the career Communist, the middle-management Marxist, and the opportunistic Ossi. The remaining two and a half million had to make do with the Trabant.

Then came the fall of the Wall. Middle-management Marxism, and Wartburg, fell soon afterwards.

In 1990, BMW came back to Eisenach — not to rewind the clock, or repair the damage done by history, but there was a certain poignancy as the Federal Commerce Minister laid the foundation stone for the "new" BMW works, here at Eisenach.

The new BMW plant at Eisenach opened for production of large pressing tools and small body parts in 1992. BMW management noted with particular pleasure that, from the outset, efficient work structures and high production quality were achieved through project management and group work.

If this smacked of a captive local labor force, it was surely a coincidence. So, for that matter, was the fact that one of its major customers, among many "non-BMW" companies, was Porsche.

General Motors had had a long relationship with Germany. This was merely the latest chapter. At the outbreak of the Second World War, GM had declared itself to be above "petty international squabbles." Throughout the war, the company had exploited its profit centers inside the Third Reich. In the 1960s, the company had exacted compensation for the inconvenience it had experienced in so doing.

With the fall of the Wall, General Motors saw an opportunity to cash in on the peace dividend in Germany and offset its huge losses in America. In 1990, General Motors' Opel subsidiary began producing cars at a new plant. The location of the plant was Eisenach. GM began assembling cars at Eisenach in kit form. But the plant's manager, Tom LaSorda, had encountered Japanese methods in the GM joint venture with Suzuki. LaSorda was determined to give GM's Opel employees at Eisenach flexibility and incentives, and to push forward the Japanese way.

By the autumn of 1994, General Motors' Opel plant at Eisenach was the most productive of its operations in Germany. The Eisenach plant was held up as an example to General Motors' Opel plants in the west of Germany at Bochum, Kaiserslautern, and Rüsselsheim.

Ossi employees at Eisenach made more cost-saving suggestions per month, and more of these suggestions were put into practice, than their "Wessi" counterparts. The president of GM Europe, Louis

Hughes, announced that GM would spend $2 billion over the coming year bringing Bochum, Kaiserslautern, and Rüsselsheim up to the standard of Eisenach.

For Ossis at Eisenach, the fall of the Wall meant economic freedom through the American company that had once collaborated with the Third Reich and thus contributed to the creation of the Iron Curtain. A further irony was that the success of Eisenach in Germany in the 1990s was based on principles of production established over forty years earlier by General Motors' other World War II partner — the Japanese.

5

The End of History and the Beginning of the Global Market

24

Contenders

Malaysia and South Korea

Bᴀ ᴛʜᴇ ʙᴇɢɪɴɴɪɴɢ ᴏꜰ ᴛʜᴇ 1990s, more and more car companies had grown from independent organizations operating within their national economies into supranational corporations that transcended national and international frontiers. The traditional components of history no longer applied to them; they were players in the first truly global marketplace in the history of the world.

All the players in this new global marketplace were as competitive as they were interdependent. As Europe had been to America, and Japan had been to America and Europe, the latest contenders were the emerging nations of the Far East. Of these, Malaysia, and particularly South Korea, were using cheap labor and the latest technology to produce mass-market cars. But beneath the industrial ambitions of these new participants lay all the old forces of nationalism in their most combustible form.

Kuala Lumpur, Malaysia, 1993

"It's tough now, and it's going to get a lot tougher," said Mohamad Nadzmi Mohamad Salleh. "Proton is the cornerstone of the country's industrialization program. It's daunting to take on such a job." Salleh was thirty-nine years old. He was the latest head of Proton — *Perusahaan Otomobil Nasional Bhd* or "the National Automobile Enterprise" — Malaysia's national car company.

Proton was the brainchild of the fiercely nationalistic Malaysian prime minister, Dr. Mahathir Mohamad. In 1985, Mahathir had opened the Shah Alam factory. "The Proton Saga," he declared of the first model, "is more than just a quality automobile. It is a symbol of Malaysians as a dignified people."

The Proton Saga (the name was derived from an indigenous, resilient Malaysian tree) was voted Malaysia's 1985 "Man of the Year." Malaysia was the first country ever to extend such an honor to a car. The Proton plant, installed by the Japanese company Mitsubishi, was in fact obsolete, and the car was assembled from thinly disguised kits of the Japanese Mitsubishi Lancer Fiore.

By 1986, Malaysia was in recession and the government was losing 35,000 *ringgit* (fifteen thousand dollars) on each Proton sold.

In the same year, Dr. Mahathir had announced that the Proton Saga would go on sale in the United States.

The first car was dispatched to America. The entire management team had assembled at Kuala Lumpur's international airport. An Islamic cleric offered a prayer, and the managing director sprinkled blessed water on the white Proton Saga, over which was draped a banner reading "On to the U.S.A."

Dr. Mahathir had been impressed by the American automobile entrepreneur Malcolm Bricklin. Bricklin had arrived in Kuala Lumpur clutching a letter of recommendation from the former U.S. secretary of state, Dr. Henry Kissinger, who had taught Dr. Mahathir as a student at Harvard.

But, unknown to Dr. Mahathir, and possibly to Dr. Kissinger, Bricklin had a checkered history. On the one hand, he had successfully launched the low-cost Yugoslav Yugo and the Japanese Subaru in the United States. On the other hand, he had failed with his gull-winged car, the Bricklin, in the mid-1970s.

Shortly after Bricklin imported the first Protons to the United States, he revealed that he had not bothered to secure the proper permissions from the authorities. He promptly sold his company in the middle of negotiations with the Malaysians. The result was a massive financial loss and a major embarrassment for Dr. Mahathir.

Three years after the glorious launch, the Malaysian management was thrown out and replaced by an all-Japanese management team. The unfortunate Malaysian management was berated for the Bricklin fiasco by the Malaysian finance minister. "If that happens to a Japanese," he told them with a meaningful look, "he commits hara-kiri."

In the early 1990s, Proton began to penetrate the export markets of Europe. But it remained little more than a symbol of a nation's need to fulfill its industrial vision. And now, in 1993, Mohamad Nadzmi Mohamad Salleh and a Malaysian team had taken back the management of Proton from the Japanese. Salleh was speaking for himself, but he could equally have been speaking for his authoritarian prime minister and Dr. Mahathir's one-party, fundamentalist Malaysia: "If things go wrong, then that's the end of my career. There's no turning back. We have to succeed."

Ulsan, South Korea, 1994

Ulsan, once a tiny fishing village in South Korea, had become the largest vehicle manufacturing complex in the world.

Giant seagoing supertransporters, made by Hyundai and insured by Hyundai companies, towered over the dockside where thousands of Hyundai cars were parked, destined for the United States, Europe, Australia, Mongolia, and Ecuador. The cars had been built by Hyundai robots and electronics in a factory built by Hyundai. Components arrived here by train in Hyundai rolling stock and in containers on Hyundai trucks. Hyundai workers arrived here in Hyundai buses. These Hyundai workers relaxed in Hyundai hotels, shopped in Hyundai department stores, and recuperated in Hyundai hospitals.

The company, started up by Chung Ju Yung and the exile from the British car industry, George Turnbull, had grown into the biggest automotive *chaebol* in Korea. Hyundai made more than a million cars and trucks a year, made half the cars on Korean roads, and exported half a million cars a year. Hyundai had opened a Canadian assembly plant to export cars to North America. Hyundai was the first Korean car maker to become a contender in the new global marketplace.

∾

In 1981 the South Korean government had decreed that passenger cars should, for the time being, be made by only two companies. These were Hyundai and Daewoo ("Universe"). Japanese cars were banned from Korea, and other foreign cars carried prohibitive import tariffs. Koreans who were prepared to pay these tariffs were targeted by the income tax authorities on the instructions of the Korean government.

The Koreans hated the Japanese with the atavistic loathing of the occupied for the occupier that transcends time and the healing of old wounds. In the sixteenth century, the Japanese warlord Hideyoshi Toyotomi marched through Korea with 100,000 troops, slicing off the nose of any Korean who protested. During the Japanese occupation of Korea between 1910 and 1945, Koreans were forbidden to speak their own language, and saw their shrines and royal palaces razed to the ground.

Thousands of Koreans were transported to Japan during those years, and put to work at heavy manual labor. After the 1923 Tokyo earthquake, the Japanese blamed the Koreans for the fires that consumed all the wooden houses in the city, and lynched them by the thousands. During the Pacific War, the Japanese forced 200,000 Korean women and girls, many as young as twelve, to serve Japanese soldiers as sex slaves in frontline "comfort stations."

In 1993, some twenty thousand of the noses in question were discovered in a stone tomb in Japan, and repatriated with due solemnity to Korea. This made no difference. On August 15, 1995, the fiftieth anniversary of the Japanese surrender in the Second World War, the Korean government still planned to bulldoze the pretty National Museum in Seoul, on the grounds that it was once the headquarters of the Japanese colonial government. The bulldozer would doubtless be a Hyundai.

Several hundred types of Japanese goods were banned in Korea, as well as cars. The reason, as one South Korean diplomat put it, was simple: "We hate them."

Yet this hatred of the Japanese was matched by the Koreans' respect for the Japanese work ethic, and the way they too had plucked their country from the ashes of war. This combination ensured that the Koreans had more than enough drive and determination to export their car industry abroad.

Hyundai was protected by the government ban on Japanese

imports, but it had rival *chaebol* at home, including Daewoo, Kia Ssang Yong, and Samsung. Hyundai's Chung Ju Yung harbored political ambitions and handed over control of the company to his younger brother, concentrating his energies on the South Korean presidential campaign. Chung, however, also had rivals. When he fought and lost the campaign, the new government of Kim Yung Sam accused him of financing his campaign through illegally diverting $65 million in Hyundai funds.

They put him on trial, found him guilty, and sentenced him to three years in prison.

The seventy-eight-year-old who had begun his career as a rice delivery boy was granted bail. "We expected that the sentence would be suspended, given all that the honorary chairman did for the national economy," said a Hyundai spokesman.

By 1995, Hyundai was investing $390 million a year in research and development, introducing a new model every year, and was capable of making more cars than the whole of Italy. Daewoo, already Korea's largest company and the thirty-third biggest corporation in the world, was aiming to raise production from 700,000 to 2 million vehicles a year by the year 2000. Daewoo was building a global network of facilities in Germany, China, India, Vietnam, the Czech Republic, the Philippines, Iran, Indonesia, Uzbekistan, and Britain. It was also penetrating mainland Europe through innovative sales and marketing techniques.

In 1995, both Washington and the European Union announced they would investigate the South Korean car market. Only 1,800 cars from the European Union had been sold in South Korea the previous year, representing 0.1 percent. At the same time, Korean car sales in the European Union had risen to over 100,000, almost 1 percent of the market.

But the stakes for these heavily protected companies were high in more than the commercial sense. In Malaysia, the national car was the vehicle for the political ambition of the prime minister. In South Korea, a car had put the founder of Hyundai on a presidential road that ended in a jail sentence. The ambitious strategies of these nations and their leaders had a downside that was not only economic. Political repercussions, also, awaited every country that tried to weather a recession by intertwining its fortunes with those of a car.

25

"This Is an Economic Pearl Harbor"

General Motors and the Downsizing of Detroit

GENERAL MOTORS HAD ENDED THE 1980s with 35 percent of the North American automobile market, down from 42 percent at the beginning of the decade. The world's largest corporation and biggest automaker had spent $40 billion on new models in five years, closed or mothballed seventeen obsolete plants, rebuilt others, and constructed more from scratch. GM had spent $1.5 billion retraining its workers to handle the new technology, and had made a deal with the United Automobile Workers Union. GM had acquired Electronic Data Systems and Hughes Aircraft.

GM had launched the $5-billion Saturn project in Tennessee. This was not many miles from Nissan at Smyrna, and the aim was to turn out the world's most advanced small car. The Saturn styling was firmly in the General Motors school; but if the car succeeded, it was because the methods of management, the manufacturing processes, and the configuration of the cars were all equal to the standards of the Japanese.

The Motown giant had only come out of the 1980s with a profit as a result of its diversification away from automobiles. But automobiles were its business. Its divisions in America and Europe, where GM had ambitions to secure a bigger share of the market, were under increasingly heavy attack from the Japanese.

Robert Stempel, the GM chairman, believed there was no alternative to his predecessor Roger Smith's strategy of plant closures and openings and massive investment in new technology. But, at the same time, there would be no moratorium on the onslaught by the Japanese. In 1991, the U.S. car industry as a whole lost $8 billion. For the third year running, the Japanese Honda Accord was America's best-selling car.

GM posted a loss in that year of $4.5 billion. GM's North American car division was losing $15 million a day. GM accounted for a large chunk of America's manufacturing industry, and, directly or indirectly, employed more than 1 million people. The only way the huge GM investment could work — if it worked — was for the company to implement a ruthless program of cuts and closures at plants across America.

They gave it a brave new euphemism: "downsizing."

In late 1991, Stempel announced the closure of twenty-one factories and laid off 74,000 workers, nearly one fifth of the total workforce. By 1995 the GM workforce would be only half the size it had been at the beginning of the new decade.

Across the Midwest, the result was abandoned plants and lines for welfare checks. Automobile towns of the Midwest were devastated. Here and there, laid-off GM employees and their families held on to the hope that their abandoned plants might be acquired and reopened by a foreign automaker. They were not too fussy about who this might be. There was no point in blaming foreigners for America's industrial deficiencies when foreigners could pay the rent.

Moreover, they were beginning to hear differently from what they had always heard: favorable tales about how the Japanese had won the hearts and minds of people like them at American-staffed, Japanese-owned car plants in places like Marysville, Ohio, and Smyrna, Tennessee.

The Senate, Washington, D.C., 1991

Democratic Senator Donald Riegle was in no doubt. "This," he said, "is an economic Pearl Harbor."

The heads of General Motors, Ford, and Chrysler lobbied President Bush for protection. In 1992, President Bush, a World War II navy pilot, visited Japan. He took with him the three heads of the automobile companies. Bush, like his challenger Bill Clinton, had his eyes on the coming reelection campaign. The Americans spent much of the visit pressing their Japanese counterparts to buy more American automobiles.

The visit is remembered for the president's dramatic collapse at a state banquet given by Prime Minister Miyazawa in full view of the world's television cameras. But a worse gaffe was caused by his appearance in the self-appointed role as automobile salesman.

"President Bush's visit has produced much confusion and distress among the Japanese people," observed a Japanese management consultant in *The Wall Street Journal.* "Most of us don't understand why the President of the United States has taken up issues usually handled by assistants to Carla Hills [the U.S. trade representative]."

The visit did nothing to improve trade relations between the two countries. As a vote-winner, too, it was a failure.

Lee Iacocca's success in persuading the U.S. government to rescue Chrysler in 1980, and his self-congratulatory autobiography, *Iacocca,* had made him an American hero. "Ideologically," he said, "I've always been a free-enterpriser, a believer in survival of the fittest."

Iacocca had accompanied President Bush on the visit to Tokyo. Once he was back in America, however, he wasted no time in criticizing the Japanese government for helping its own auto industry and in telling Americans what he thought they wanted to hear about the Japanese. "We ship them food and chemicals and raw materials, just like a colony," he declared. "And they ship us value-added cars and machine tools and electronics, just like a mother country."

Iacocca's comments infuriated Yutaka Kume, president of Nissan and chairman of the Japan Automobile Manufacturers Association. "Mr. Iacocca's behavior and remarks were outrageous and insulting to us," he said, and swore never to meet the three Americans again.

The aftermath of the Japanese visit soon proved who were the losers. Within a short time, all four Americans would lose their jobs. President Bush would lose his campaign for reelection; the president of Ford would retire; Iacocca and Stempel, too, would be fired.

At General Motors, the downsizing and the losses went on. Marryann Kellner was a leading automobile analyst on Wall Street. "If GM continues to weaken," Kellner said, "and the market share it gives up is taken by overseas competitors, it will have an enormous impact on the United States. Apart from direct job losses, dealers will close and suppliers will also have to cut back. Cities like Detroit, Michigan, which rely heavily on GM, will be devastated."

In 1992, Stempel himself was downsized in a boardroom coup engineered by external directors worried that he was not doing enough to turn the company around. Other executive heads rolled in the same dust. One man rose to the top.

John F. "Jack" Smith Jr. had started work as a boy in his family ice-cream-parlor business in Worcester, Massachusetts. Smith had started at GM counting metal stampings and body parts in a Fisher Body plant. At fifty-six he was the new president and chief executive officer of the largest industrial corporation in the world.

Smith was of average height, slightly overweight, and wore button-down shirts and shapeless suits. He occasionally skipped lunch with the intention of taking exercise in the company gym, but usually just ended up skipping lunch. His friends said his widow's-peak hairline made him look like the 1960s TV sitcom character Eddie Munster. Like Eddie Munster, appearances in Smith's case were deceptive. In addition to his own considerable and modestly concealed talents, Jack Smith had a secret weapon.

The Return of Alfred P. Sloan, Detroit, 1994

One of the first things Jack Smith did when he became top man at General Motors was to form a president's council. This small, fluid, tightly knit group of friends oversaw a worldwide workforce of nearly 1 million people, over half of whom worked in automobile and truck operations in the U.S.A. and Canada.

There were six men on Jack Smith's president's council. Five of them were alive and one of them was dead.

The five alive were Jack Smith, Bill Hoglund, Harry Pearce, Rick Wagoner, and Louis Hughes.

The dead man was Alfred P. Sloan. "We're focused on Sloan," Smith said. "He came in when the place was upside down and got it straightened out."

The shade of Sloan haunted the fourteenth floor and the meetings of the president's council. But this was a more benign presence than the austere autocrat who kept GM above pitiful international squabbles. In the new global market, Sloan's autocratic vision and xenophobia were as obsolete as the Chevrolet Caprice Classic and the Oldsmobile Cutlass Supreme. Smith and his colleagues were focused on the managerial and technical visionary who had turned GM around at the lowest point in its history.

Over the two years after Jack Smith's appointment, they abolished time-honored corporate accounting practices, headquarters bureaucracy, self-defeating competition between divisions, uncoordinated purchasing policies, and discounts to car rental fleets.

They synchronized the divisions all the way along the process from the drawing board to the arrival at the dealership. They reduced the number of platforms on which the cars were built, and increased the technological ability of the platforms that remained. They set in motion programs to design and build better cars.

In 1991, GM had lost $4.5 billion. In 1992 the company posted a loss of $23.5 billion. Nearly $21 billion of this was due to an accounting change that required companies to include future liabilities for retired employees' health benefits. But with three thousand dollars lost on every car sold, this was still technically the biggest loss in corporate history.

In three years, GM had lost $17 billion in its operations in North America alone. Standard & Poor, the world's leading credit rating agency, downgraded GM from "stable" to "uncertain." But Smith and his colleagues were aware that they had no choice but to press ahead, and that, if they succeeded, they would do so on an epic scale.

As one observer put it, while GM was sinking, its size weighed it down like an anchor. In 1994 the company would make an overall profit and break even in North America. Now that it had stopped

Turnbull's legacy: Hyundai at Ulsan, South Korea, the tiny fishing village that became the world's biggest automobile plant. *(Photo © Hyundai)*

Rally at Spartanburg. The arrival of BMW in South Carolina in 1992 was the climax of an extraordinary relationship between big European companies and a small town in America. *(Photo © BMW AG)*

(Above) "Nothing could be finer than to be in Carolina . . ." BMW became the first company to drop the "Made in Germany" tag and yet keep its hard-won reputation at home and abroad. (Photo © BMW AG)

(Left) Pehr Gyllen-hammar was the King of Castle Volvo, until the attempt to merge with Renault swept him from office in a wave of patriotic resentment. (Photo © Pressens Bild AB)

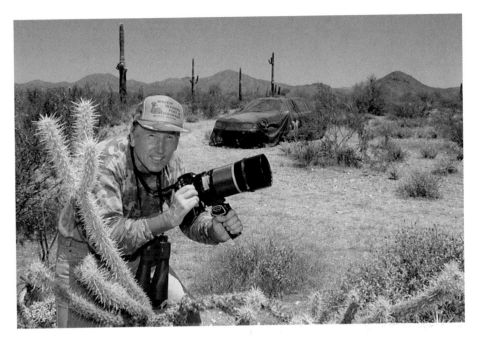

The legendary Hans-Georg Lehmann on assignment. The covert car wars are fought every bit as fiercely as the public campaigns. *(Photo © Hans-Georg Lehmann)*

Superlopez. The boy from the Basque country was the hero of General Motors until the biggest industrial espionage scandal in history. *(Photo © Yates/Saba/Katz Pictures Limited)*

Jack Smith of General Motors was a "motorhead" through and through, but just in case he needed advice, there was the ghost of former CEO Alfred P. Sloan Jr. at his elbow. *(Photo © Chris Buck, Alexander Griffin Photography)*

Ferdinand Piech. The VW chief faced down the Superlopez charges with all the steel of a Prussian aristocrat and grandson of Dr. Porsche. *(Photo © Associated Press)*

The mere rumor that GM might be opening a plant near Toronto brought thousands of job-hungry Canadians out into the cold. *(Photo © Popperfoto/Reuter)*

The ultimate Soviet status symbol. To lose your Zil, as Gorbachev did this one, was to lose everything, except your life. *(Photo © The Independent/Keith Dobney)*

(Above left) A Moscow car dealer survived this Russian Mafia bomb attack; his chauffeur was decapitated. *(Photo © Popperfoto/Reuter)*

(Above right) Nicholas Hayek. The flamboyant Lebanese émigré spearheaded the Swiss watch industry's fight back against the Japanese with the Swatch; now he intended to do the same for Europe's car industry with the Mercedes-Benz Swatchmobile. *(Photo © SMH SA)*

The Swatchmobile. A revolution in motoring or just another fashion accessory? Either way, the outcome was crucial to the world's oldest surviving automobile manufacturer. *(Photo © Mercedes-Benz-Foto)*

Shanghai, the center of the growing Chinese car industry. China and the Far East will pose the same threat to Japan in the twenty-first century that Japan posed to the United States and Europe in the twentieth. *(Photo © Tony Stone Images, David E. Myers)*

Night flight by *tai fei*. The waters between Hong Kong and southern China became the busiest smuggling lanes in the world. *(Photo © Alan Crowther)*

Freeway madness. The legacy of General Motors' success in shutting down the railroads is damage to the ozone layer and California's "zero-emissions" legislation. *(Photo © Rex Features Limited)*

The Volkswagen Concept 1. The car of the future? But however "interactive" and environmentally friendly the car, the driver will never surrender the freedom to drive, and the internal combustion engine will continue to dominate. *(Photo © Volkswagen Press)*

sinking and was beginning to rise, the same mass could be used as an offensive weapon to achieve real economies of scale.

On the fourteenth floor in Detroit, Jack Smith and the men at GM had reason to congratulate themselves on achieving the beginnings of the biggest corporate turnaround in American history.

After the real attack at Pearl Harbor, America had reluctantly entered a pitiful international squabble and emerged confirmed as the most powerful nation on earth. Over half a century later, General Motors had similarly been forced to fight back, and stood a chance of victory in the conflict that had begun with the traumatic "downsizing" forced on it by the Japanese.

Jack Smith and the men at GM had a further secret weapon, as well as the ghost of Alfred P. Sloan. This man was very much alive and, in an American industry still populated by motorheads from Michigan, he was an exotic and rare specimen.

He was an energetic, charismatic, messianically minded Spaniard from the Basque country. Smith had worked with him in Europe. He had worked wonders there, and here in America too, his was a name to conjure with, and his works were a wonder to behold. His name was José Ignacio Lopez de Arriortua.

26

Supermodels and "Superlopez"

The Catwalk and the Covert Car Wars

IN THE SPRING OF 1993, Europe was the battleground for the auto-makers' spring offensive.

The British took out full-page advertisements for the Rover 600: "Cars built this well are few and far between," read the caption, and it was true that the 20-percent stake taken in Rover by Honda had brought technical and managerial improvements and revived the health of the company.

The Swedes dazzled the driver with science: "1978 . . . SAAB was first with a pollen-fine ventilation air filter system . . . 1993 . . . SAAB is first with Trionic, an engine management system that can actually clean city air . . ."

The Germans were firing on all cylinders: "Discover the fragrance of *Umwelt*. By Volkswagen." (The "fragrance" was in fact clean air, the supposed product of the Umwelt diesel's turbocharger and catalytic converter.)

"Why is the Mercedes at the bottom of this table? Because it's at the top of this table . . ." (The first table listed cost per mile over three years, and the second listed retained value.)

The Japanese adopted their familiar confident approach: "The car in front of the BMW and Volvo is a Toyota Camry . . ."

This was not enough for Mitsubishi: "BMW, Mercedes-Benz, Citroën, Volkswagen, Volvo. Make room for the new Mitsubishi Sigma wagon . . ." The Japanese did not appear to compete openly against each other — only against the rest of the world.

The Italians felt the FIAT Tempra was above overt comparisons: "At last. A wagon worth looking at . . ."

The French were comparing the Peugeot 405 station wagon with a toy car for flexibility: *Now you can handle 57 cubic feet, the way you handled 1 cubic inch . . .*

The Americans used the background of an active volcano: "Contour from Ford. Everything we do is driven by you . . ."

General Motors wanted a piece of the action. The car they chose for the job was their Opel subsidiary's new small car, the Corsa: "Christy has concrete proof no rival beats the Corsa for interior space . . . Linda christens this Corsa the most environmentally sound car in its class . . . Tatjana can't wait to test the Corsa's all around safety cage . . ."

Christy, Linda, and Tatjana were the fashion world's "supermodels." One filled the car with liquid concrete; another covered it with green paint; another stood atop an upturned car with a sledgehammer.

For this TV commercial, which ran in England, the supermodels were paid $250,000 each a day by Opel and its advertising agency, Lowe Howard-Spink. The eighty-second ad cost $4 million.

In the commercial, the supermodels fail to tempt red-blooded males away from the new car. Beneath the sophisticated execution lay a breathtakingly crude message: men were expected to fall for the charms of a small car over those of Christy Turlington; women were expected to accept unfavorable comparison with a two-door sedan.

Many people remembered the commercial but forgot to buy the car. Car advertising in America and Europe in particular was still a decade or so behind that of Japan.

In the following year, 1994, many advertising campaigns reverted to the less sexy but more potent values of low cost and high fuel economy. In some cases the effect seemed to achieve the opposite of the aim of the exercise: "I'd buy a new Mercedes but I haven't finished with my old one . . ."

Many automakers failed to realize that the small cars with which the Corsa was expected to compete, such as the Nissan Micra, could be sold successfully without such costly pretension, perhaps because they were not supermodels but people's cars. But advertising was only the overt propaganda arm of the car companies' battles.

Things had changed since BMW obtained a Douglas motorcycle after the First World War and Datsun (later Nissan) got hold of an Austin Seven and stripped it down before developing the first Japanese car.

The car companies went to extraordinary lengths to maintain the secrecy surrounding the development and testing of their latest models, and to equally extraordinary lengths to find out about the latest models being developed and tested by the others.

Prototypes and new models underwent exhaustive development within the secure confines of the auto plants, but they still had to be tested for thousands of miles on the roads. The car companies sent their heavily disguised new models out at dawn and in the middle of the night on remote stretches of autobahn, *autoroute*, and freeway. But there was no way of shaking off the determined observer.

By the 1990s there was a thriving industry within an industry, and the covert car wars were as fiercely fought as the public campaign. Some automobile manufacturers were more offensive-minded than others — they reputedly included Nissan, Toyota, Ford, and BMW — while Mercedes-Benz, General Motors, and Volkswagen were reputedly above such stratagems.

A key figure in all these covert car wars was Hans-Georg Lehmann, a German photographer who stumbled into this lucrative trade reputedly by accident during the 1960s. By the 1990s he was the ultimate *auto-paparazzo* and the world expert on the heavily camouflaged multimillion-dollar prototype. He was also very rich.

Lehmann had grown up near Wolfsburg, and as a boy would wake up in the night to see the latest Volkswagen prototype flash past his house. His career was launched by his illicit photographs of a later model.

Volkswagenwerk's chief, Ferdinand Piech, did not return the compliment. "If he wants to photograph us," said Piech, "then he's risking his life."

In the 1970s, Volkswagenwerk tried to have Lehmann's driver's license revoked, claiming he had driven dangerously and blocked the road while photographing a prototype on test. Lehmann's pictures of the episode proved that the VW test driver had blocked the road. The case against him was dismissed before it came to trial.

Lehmann was rumored to have a string of informants inside the major car companies, as well as in Finnish gas stations and hotels in North Africa, the two climatic extremes in which cars were routinely and exhaustively tested. He revealed:

> BMW and some other companies go to Morocco, but Porsche and Audi always go to Algeria. They won't take prototypes to the north coast, because Audi doesn't go where there are German tourists. They have to go south — into the Sahara.
>
> Now, there are only a certain number of places they can stay. They need a good hotel for their testing team — with running water, a restaurant, a little bit of comfort — and a gas station for the cars. And Audi always flies in Piech and its top engineers for the tests, so they need an airfield.
>
> You can see cars a long way off in the desert. We saw three coming towards us — they weren't close together, like prototypes usually are. Then we saw the big sideview mirrors . . . Then the dark-blue color, very unusual for the desert, but the color Audi has been using for the past two years. "That's it," I said, "that's the new one . . ."
>
> In our lousy hire car we had no chance to catch them — that Audi is very, very fast. But we turned around to follow. The cars went up a little hill, down a little hill — and stopped. It was fantastic luck. We drove past them, stopped, jumped out of the car, and with two cameras — click! click! click!

Nobody knew the extent to which Lehmann was commissioned by the car companies, and how far he operated on the open market to sell his pictures to the highest bidder. Even to be rumored to have obtained his services was interpreted as a sign of weakness. But the car companies knew that new-car-watching was the name of the game in the new and fabulously valuable global market where a mistake would be on a correspondingly disastrous scale.

Everyone knew this, but nobody liked to say so, until the energetic, charismatic Spaniard whom Jack Smith had liked to think of as his secret weapon suddenly turned into the bizarre Basque, and prompted the biggest industrial espionage scandal in history.

Amorebieta, Spain, 1993

In the little town in the Basque country on the road between Bilbao and Guernica, he could do no wrong. *El Tarta* — the stammerer — they called him at school, because of his speech impediment. "Josein" was what they called him in everyday conversation, and he was called "Superlopez" in the biography they sold on the streetcorners of Amorebieta. He was the son of a factory worker, and he had risen to be a vice president of General Motors . . . they of the supermodels and the Opel Corsa.

Lopez had grown up a studious, religious boy, uninterested in soccer or girls until he met his wife at a local dance. He had studied engineering and specialized in production techniques, before working in Spain for Westinghouse and Firestone.

Amorebieta was a typical small industrial town in a frustrated car country. Spain had had little to show for itself since the magnificent Pegaso sports cars had ceased to appear at international automobile shows many years earlier. By the 1960s, living standards were still so low that few Spaniards could afford more than primitive miniature cars such as the TZ and the Autonacional Biscuter. Spanish factories began to assemble American and European cars, and Spanish FIAT clones were made by SEAT, later the troubled subsidiary of Volkswagenwerk, in an upmarket Iberian Togliattigrad.

José Ignacio Lopez de Arriortua was going to change this. He had a dream for his hometown, and the whole town knew about it. He was going to build an auto plant here — not just any auto plant, but the most advanced and revolutionary auto plant in the world. General Motors was going to lease the site from the local consortium that would build the plant. Amorebieta would be thrust into the front line against the Japanese.

Lopez was possessed with missionary zeal when it came to beating the Japanese. He said:

> The battle for the European automobile industry is the final struggle. If we lose it, we shall become second-class citizens of second-class countries.
>
> We can win this battle because the third industrial revolution will be driven by creation, and there is more creativity in Europe than in Japan.

The Japanese are not creative. No inventions, no Nobel prizes. Cars are a European discovery, especially German. We must learn to walk tall again.

By the time he made these remarks at a press conference in Hanover in June 1993, Lopez was no longer working for General Motors. He would cite as the main reason for his defection the fact that GM did not want to build his revolutionary new auto plant in his hometown in Spain. He was confident that his dream would be realized with the help of his new employer, Volkswagenwerk.

Volkswagenwerk's Ferdinand Piech had been courting the eccentric genius for some time in the hope that he would bring his dazzling skills to Wolfsburg, where losses were so great that one industry analyst had called the plant an "industrial dinosaur."

All along, Lopez had assured Jack Smith of General Motors he would stay in Detroit. Smith had even called a press conference to this effect.

Just minutes before the conference, Smith was handed a note from Lopez: "Sorry. I have changed my mind."

Smith was still shaking with rage when he addressed the press a few minutes later.

"It is not clear to me," he said, "what his intentions are or where he is at the present time."

Lopez was on board an executive jet bound for Chicago. There he would board the Lufthansa flight that would take him to Germany. A number of his closest associates would follow. The following day, he was triumphantly presented in Wolfsburg as the new board member in charge of improving production.

The day after, in Detroit, General Motors executives frantically searched Lopez's office. They were looking for the large amount of secret information Lopez and his lieutenants were known to have amassed in Detroit. They found none. "In their last months at GM," said David Herman, president of GM's European subsidiary Adam Opel, "Lopez and his colleagues got a lot of information. After they left, we could no longer find it. The question is, where the hell is it?"

The allegation was that Lopez and his colleagues had taken secret information with them to Volkswagenwerk, including details of Adam Opel's new small car, code-named "O," a revolutionary vehicle that could be built in record time and at maximum efficiency.

The allegation, like the missing documents, remained secret until May 1993. In the same month, Adam Opel leaked the story. It was published under the heading "The Unscrupulous One" in *Der Spiegel*. "This could be the industrial equivalent of Watergate," said GM's Louis Hughes, "a case of industrial espionage of unbelievable proportions."

German Chancellor Helmut Kohl said the matter was "extremely distasteful." The German minister for the economy said he wanted to "make sure that no conflict arises between America and Germany."

In Amorebieta, people were in no doubt. "He would not need to do such a thing," said one. "He carries all he needs to know in his head."

Der Spiegel alleged that Volkswagenwerk was in possession of secret construction plans, internal cost calculations, and purchasing lists for sixty thousand parts used by Opel. To carry such information in his head would quite simply be an impossible feat . . . even for "Superlopez."

For the boy from the Basque country, this was an extraordinary journey.

Lopez's career began in 1980, when he joined General Motors España. In 1987 he was moved from Saragossa to Rüsselsheim. There he made his reputation. They called him "the Butcher." Lopez squeezed suppliers until they screamed, and then squeezed some more. Opel became one of the most efficient manufacturers in Europe.

In 1990, Jack Smith brought him to Detroit.

At the headquarters of GM, they called him the Grand Inquisitor. Lopez called his executives "centurions" and his cost-cutters "warriors." His hero was St. Ignatius Loyola, the founder of the Jesuits. He might equally have been Machiavelli, for whom the end justified the means.

Lopez neither smoked nor drank. He exhorted his centurions and warriors to follow his caffeine-free, high-fruit diet. He persuaded them to wear their watches on their right wrists until GM was back in profit. Even Jack Smith had taken up the practice.

Now they were calling Lopez by other names. The Butcher of Rüsselsheim and the Grand Inquisitor of Detroit was facing an investigation worthy of his own merciless standards.

In July 1993, the Darmstadt prosecutor, Dorothea Holland, let it be known that there was sufficient evidence to justify the issuing of search warrants. Her investigators raided offices and apartments belonging to VW employees. In an apartment in Wiesbaden occupied by two Spaniards formerly employed by GM, and now working with Lopez at VW, they found four boxes of documents. The documents closely resembled those missing from GM.

Ferdinand Piech, grandson of Dr. Porsche, had been brought in to save Volkswagenwerk. Piech had hired Lopez on a five-year contract worth $22 million, to help him to this end. Piech gave a press conference. In a flat voice, his normally cold eyes blazing, the third-generation Austrian autocrat who had fathered twelve children by four marriages denied all the allegations and accused GM of waging a vendetta against Lopez and Volkswagenwerk.

Piech treated the questions of reporters from all over the world with a dismissiveness bordering on contempt. He suggested the documents found by the investigators acting for the state prosecutor had been planted. The press conference was a PR disaster.

In the same month, Piech told *Die Welt* that there was "no question" of Volkswagenwerk building a revolutionary new auto plant in the Basque country.

In August 1993, *Der Spiegel* revealed that soon after Lopez had arrived in Wolfsburg, Volkswagenwerk employees at certain outlying offices had punched GM/Opel data into the company computer.

Warning lights flashed at the Frankfurt stock exchange. "It looks increasingly as if Lopez did take the documents when he left GM," said one trader, "and the question we must ask ourselves is whether Ferdinand Piech knew about it."

VW shares fell sharply. The government of Lower Saxony, which held 20 percent of these, was forced to leap to the defense of its investment and the company.

Ferdinand Piech and Jack Smith tried to talk. But the atmosphere between the two men, their two companies, and their two countries, was too poisoned for dialogue to survive. Piech returned to the counterattack, again with catastrophic results. In the spiral of attack and counterattack, the German company only looked and acted more guilty.

Piech continued to make defiant statements while under fire from his supervisory board. Volkswagenwerk claimed that documents had come with employees from GM. Volkswagenwerk employees had destroyed these documents in order "to avoid the danger of their being distributed within Volkswagen."

GM's reaction was simple: "Haven't they heard of the mail?"

By August 1993, Piech's future was believed by many to be as intertwined with that of Lopez as that of Volkswagenwerk was with Lower Saxony. The FBI asked GM for copies of documents.

In Detroit, the mood remained one of revenge. As a senior executive put it: "We're going to nail the bastard." But the "Superlopez" scandal, like the automobile industry, was beyond the control of companies, countries, or governments.

At every level in these strata, however, there were those who saw in the Lopez affair the opportunity for professional and political gain.

Gerhard Schroder was the flamboyant, ambitious prime minister of Lower Saxony. Schroder, many of whose voters were Wolfsburg workers, saw the GM/Opel campaign against Volkswagen as a U.S.-inspired war against Germany, and said so.

In Wolfsburg, the supervisory board commissioned an independent report by the auditing firm KPMG Deutschland. The report cleared Volkswagenwerk of any illegality — but paradoxically addressed no illegality that may have been committed by Lopez and his colleagues when they left GM.

In early 1994, neither Piech nor Lopez was to be seen at the Detroit Motor Show in the United States, where a new car from Volkswagenwerk would cause a sensation for the German company. The investigations dragged on in Germany and America. But the situation within Volkswagenwerk was by this time too serious for the supervisory board to contemplate the departure of the two men.

In 1993 the company had lost over a billion dollars. Wolfsburg was on a four-day week. Piech had no alternative but to encourage Lopez to administer the medicine he had brought him here to administer. Lopez, his centurions, and his warriors set about the task with undiminished zeal. But the same forces were ranged against them as had defended Germany against the trade warriors of America.

Volkswagenwerk was the major employer in Lower Saxony. Unemployment in Lower Saxony was already running at 14 percent, six points above the national average. "The situation at VW is serious and getting more serious," said an industry observer. "Unless Lopez and Piech can get around the Lower Saxony political bloc and the excess labor force, all their best efforts on the shop floor may be undermined."

Whatever happened to José Ignacio Lopez de Arriortua, he would go down in the history of the global market.

At the headquarters of GM in Detroit, they reviled him as a thief and a traitor. In the spring of 1996, GM filed a civil complaint in the federal district court of Detroit against Lopez, seven other former GM executives, and Volkswagen, alleging theft of company secrets and implicitly demanding compensation estimated in the German media at up to $1 billion. The previous year, at the 1995 Geneva Motor Show, GM had unveiled its revolutionary small Opel Maxx, a car that could be built in six man-hours to the individual customer's specifications, and the plans for which were believed to have been taken by Lopez to Volkswagenwerk at Wolfsburg.

On the production lines at Wolfsburg, they greeted his reappearance with applause. Ferdinand Piech cited Lopez as the essential component in his plan to build 5 million cars a year — in some cases in as few as seven man-hours a car — by the end of the century.

In the Parliament of Lower Saxony, they feared for their shareholding if he failed, and for the votes of the laid-off auto workers if he succeeded. In a small town in Spain, too, in the bars and on the streetcorners, they knew their hero would one day return.

27

How the Rise of Japan and the Fall of the Wall Brought the Germans to South Carolina

IF MERCEDES-BENZ EVER EXPERIENCED DIFFICULTIES, Germany must be in trouble . . .

Germany had been in trouble since 1989 and the fall of the Berlin Wall. The euphoria brought about by reunification of the two Germanies only temporarily masked the fact that other European countries and America were heading into a deepening recession.

The recession hit Germany later and more deeply, and by the time it did so, the honeymoon period of reunification was over. At times such as this, East and West were as far apart as ever.

Wessis accused Ossis of being ungrateful, lazy, good-for-nothing products of a dependency culture. Ossis accused Wessis of being selfish, overbearing, and dismissive of everything and everyone who had the misfortune to come from behind the Iron Curtain. Germany was at war with itself — for a change.

Wessis, unlike Ossis, were ill-equipped by experience to cope with the traumas of the deepening recession.

In Stuttgart, the hometown of Mercedes-Benz, an engineer returned from a holiday in the Congo infatuated with the simple pre-industrial village life and disillusioned with suburbia. He decided to build a mud hut in his living room.

His wife watched as he emptied the buckets of mud onto the living-room carpet. He stripped off his clothes, donned his wife's apron, and performed a fertility dance. He pretended — quite convincingly — to sacrifice the family hamsters.

At this point his wife ran screaming from the house. Somehow, and she could not work out why, the values of the "Three Ks," *Kinder, Küche, Kirche* — children, kitchen, church — would never be the same again.

Then she filed for divorce.

Unemployment rose and production fell. The German automakers were the first to feel the chill.

Volkswagenwerk was the worst affected. In José Ignacio Lopez de Arriortua, Ferdinand Piech had found a man capable of killing or curing the company. The company also linked its name to the world tour of the rock group Pink Floyd, itself noted for overmanned productions and expensive attempts to maintain its position in the market. Later, Volkswagenwerk transferred its loyalties to the 1995 Voodoo Lounge tour of the Rolling Stones, with noticeably better results, and culminating in a concert in the Wolfsburg parking lot.

Mercedes-Benz was next on the firing line. In 1992 the company was outsold by BMW for the first time, and shed 22,000 workers. In 1993 the company announced the loss of a further 14,700 jobs. The main Mercedes-Benz plant in Stuttgart and the plant in Bremen were placed on short time. Christmas and holiday bonuses were cut. The company was even considering abolishing the charitable payments it made to staff whose children made their first communion. The workforce went into collective shock. "Mercedes-Benz never did this kind of thing," said a member of the works council. "It is a break with the old corporate culture." "We can't accept this," moaned another. "The fat's really in the fire."

BMW was the least badly affected. The pride of Bavaria was the thirteenth-biggest company in Germany and the thirty-fifth-biggest in Europe. BMW high-performance sedans had captured the yuppie market of the late 1980s, just as they had done in the late 1930s.

BMW employed 71,000 people. In 1986 it had become the first car company in the world to put research, development, logistics, and quality control under one roof — including six thousand engineers.

In the first half of 1993, BMW's net profits fell by 40 percent to 255 million marks ($155 million). The working week was cut to thirty-six hours. Demand continued to rise, sales continued to rise, but so did costs, and profits continued to fall. BMW workers, the highest-paid auto workers in the world, were put on a four-day week. The Munich factory was shedding seven hundred jobs. The company was shedding three thousand.

BMW already assembled cars with local partners in Latin America and in Malaysia, Thailand, Indonesia, Laos, and the Philippines. The company was signing a similar agreement to assemble cars in Vietnam. But these small operations in Asian-Pacific markets generated only a modest addition to the revenue stream.

Somewhere out there, there had to be a workforce which could build BMWs to the same standard as Germany. The question was where.

Spartanburg, South Carolina, 1995

The sirens sounded, the music played, the crowd cheered. The first car — a BMW 318i sedan — came off the production line.

This was the first BMW made outside Bavaria — discounting the bogus EMWs illicitly made by the Russians at Eisenach after the Second World War. BMW's brand-new American plant covered a 1,039-acre green field site. Sixty thousand people had applied for the first five hundred jobs. The winners had undergone sixty-six hours of test-taking and training, organized and funded by the state of South Carolina.

The state of South Carolina and the town of Spartanburg had also paid $40 million for the site. They had laid on tax breaks, loans, and subsidies worth an estimated $135 million.

The critics said this was Marshall Aid all over again. But big companies such as Hewlett-Packard were already planning to move nearby and lend credence to BMW's pledge to do its best to attract suppliers to South Carolina.

Spartanburg would occupy a unique place in the unwritten annals of the industrial history of small-town America. The town straddles Interstate 85, which links Atlanta and Charlotte, has an airport, and is only three hours away from the deepwater port of Charleston . . . but this is only the beginning.

Spartanburg's links with the industrial giants of faraway Europe date back to the 1950s, when a textile firm moved its research-and-development facility down here from New England. Textile technology was a specialist field of close-knit Swiss and German manufacturers. Soon, Spartanburg was a center for overseas investment in manufacturing. In the 1960s, the town's reputation grew overseas with the efforts of the larger-than-life director of its chamber of commerce, the late Dick Tukey.

Tukey was a big, enthusiastic, cigar-chomping character who would do anything to promote foreign investment in his hometown. He flew the flag for Spartanburg in 1967 at Basle in Switzerland at the International Textile Machinery Show, and dressed up in traditional German costume and threw parties for foreign newcomers and their families.

Tukey had forged links between the town and successive governors of South Carolina. One of these, Carroll Campbell, had appointed Paul Forster, the former manager of a big overseas company in Spartanburg, as Honorary Ambassador for the State of South Carolina in Europe. Forster had persuaded the heads of forty top German companies to write letters extolling the virtues of Spartanburg to BMW in Munich.

There was no other Southern city like Spartanburg, South Carolina. The story of the city read like the mergers-and-acquisitions list of an international corporation. There was no other Southern city where the best restaurant in town was called the Café Vienna. The city carried a range of German beers, wines, and sausages second to none, celebrated Swiss national day with fervor, and laid on a terrific *Oktoberfest*. Spartanburg was the closest place to Germany outside Germany and inside the United States.

Eberhard von Kuenheim, managing director of BMW, had visited the city secretly on a number of occasions. Von Kuenheim conceived a special fondness for the place. BMW spies checked out the town's social and political suitability. They noted its Protestant work ethic and lack of racial tensions; blacks numbered fewer than one in five of the population.

They also noted its lack of trade-union militancy of the kind that had plagued Volkswagenwerk when it bought a former General Motors plant in Pennsylvania. After nearly a decade, all Volkswagenwerk had to show for its investment in America were big losses, low productivity, and a reputation for poor quality. In 1988, Volkswagenwerk had pulled out.

BMW was still nervous. For all its technological strengths and glamorous reputation, the establishment of a new plant so far beyond the frontiers of Bavaria, let alone Germany and Europe, was a traumatic move for the company. The company's motto — "The future belongs to the fastest, not the biggest" — disguised an inner conservatism dating back to the dark days of the late 1950s and early 1960s.

This explained the last-minute change of heart about the site. Spartanburg was happy to buy a site from two locals for a mere $20 million. BMW said *Nein*. The site had to have direct access to an airport. The airport had to have runways big enough for jumbo jets to land laden with engines and drive trains of gearboxes and axles direct from Bavaria. The jumbo jets could then be unloaded in the middle of the plant, just like cars at a railway siding.

Spartanburg bought another site just a mile away. The town paid $40 million to more than one hundred owners, some of whose houses had to be uprooted and transported elsewhere.

This time the town had better luck. In the summer of 1992, Eberhard von Kuenheim announced that BMW was going to spend $400 million on a plant on a green field site at the village of Greer, near Spartanburg. "We have to maintain, secure, and build up the position we have achieved in the American market," said von Kuenheim. "This is becoming increasingly difficult to do from Germany."

Von Kuenheim's successor as managing director of BMW was Bernd Pischetsrieder. Pischetsrieder had joined BMW twenty years earlier, upon graduation from university. He had led the search team that had contemplated 250 sites in ten countries. He was the cool, calm, clear-minded engineer. "For the new, larger Germany," Pischetsrieder said, "1993 marked a decisive change in outlook. The illusion had to stop that all spending could be financed, that Germany could ignore international competition on costs. This illusion had long been cherished, and it was constantly re-created to cope with new burdens . . ."

Spartanburg spelled the end of this illusion, and of the illusion that the BMW driver would only accept a machine labeled "Made in Germany." To the folks of Spartanburg and Greer, this was also the end of the illusion that the South was still America's equivalent of the Far East: "The decision marks a coming of age for the state," said one local resident. "It is proof that the South has made it out of the days when its major attraction was that 'labor was cheap and docile.'"

The deal between the pride of Bavaria and the burghers of Greer and Spartanburg was a triumph for Spartanburg's Chamber of Commerce and South Carolina's Honorary Ambassador in Europe. BMW was the eighty-second foreign company to set up business in these parts, but it generated more excitement than all the others put together. As another local resident put it, BMW was "a pure Hollywood name."

The village of Greer shut down for the day to welcome the motorcade of BMWs to the site of the new plant. Eberhard von Kuenheim broke the ground with Governor Carroll Campbell of South Carolina. The Prussian aristocrat told the blue-collar crowd: "To be successful in the world, a company has to be successful in the U.S.A."

Such was the atmosphere that a tear came to the eye of even the most hardened BMW dealer. To the Germans, Spartanburg seemed like *heimat*, or home.

The first American-made BMW came off the production line in March 1995. The Spartanburg plant aimed to employ two thousand people and produce four hundred cars a day by the end of the century. As well as the 3-Series, these included the 5-Series and a fabulous new BMW sports car, the Z3.

Al Kinzer was the president of BMW Manufacturing at Spartanburg. Kinzer had set up Honda's first assembly plant in America in Marysville, Ohio. Kinzer wore the same white jacket and blue trousers as the floor sweeper. The parking lot had no reserved parking. There was no parking lot at all for unfinished or faulty cars, and no repair bay. If a car came to the end of the production line and was found to be faulty or deficient, they would stop the entire plant and put it right.

Peter Bier had planned BMW plants at Dingolfing and Regensburg in Germany. He had made a revolutionary discovery:

At Regensburg, we relied on robots to produce quality. Since then, we have found out that quality is produced by people.

An open plan plant allows people to be involved in all aspects of production. So if you run into a problem in production, and you have well-educated, intelligent people involved, they will be able to find a solution.

By the end of the decade we would want the ability to fly cars from the factory to customers around the world.

BMW's plan to make cars at Spartanburg and fly them to customers around the world recalled its origins as a maker of high-altitude airplane engines. The difference was that, unlike the First World War engine praised by Lieutenant Udet, the cars would not arrive too late.

The two most important factors in the Spartanburg strategy were the simplest. The first was the realization that people could be motivated to do better than robots. The second was the deployment of the principles of "lean" production pioneered nearly half a century earlier in Japan by Eiji Toyoda.

Honda's Acura, Nissan's Infiniti, and Toyota's Lexus were storming the American luxury market. They had captured over 30 percent of it since the late 1980s. The Japanese would spare no expense in their long-term aim to drive Mercedes-Benz and BMW — and Ford, Chrysler, and General Motors — out of this market in America. General Motors president Roger Smith had mistaken a Lexus for a Mercedes-Benz when he had admired the new model that day in the downtown Detroit parking lot.

Then the Japanese would turn their attention to the same market in Europe. BMW was a prime target. Spartanburg was also a key weapon in anticipating and combating the Japanese in countries closer to Germany.

In 1990 the head of the Mercedes-Benz car division, Jürgen Hubbert, had acknowledged the effects of the Acura, Infiniti, and Lexus: "Our enemy is not BMW in Munich. It is sitting on the other side of the world."

The new head of Mercedes-Benz was Helmut Werner. Werner made a pronouncement that would have been heresy in the Germany of the *Wirtschaftswunder* of the 1950s and 1960s. Mercedes-Benz cars, he declared, were "over-engineered," and their costs were too high: "No one in the world is prepared to pay for German complacency. We will attack the Japanese competition in its market niches by offering our own technologically superior products ... We will bring about a change in the rules of competition with Japanese manufacturers."

That was why, in the spring of 1993, Mercedes-Benz announced that it, too, was setting up in America. Edzard Reuter, the chairman of Daimler-Benz, was the son of a postwar Social Democrat mayor of West Berlin. Reuter's father had fled abroad in the 1930s to escape Nazi persecution. The close association of Daimler-Benz with Hitler and the Nazi Party had not been shared by the Reuter family. "I have a certain aversion against words like Fatherland," Reuter said. "I feel much more at home as a European."

Reuter saw the move to America from a German perspective. He appreciated the turbulence that had come to Germany with the fall of the Berlin Wall: "No one thinks of reunification of the German state. It's a question of lowering the border between East and West Germany."

Mercedes-Benz announced that it would spend $300 million on building a new plant in the United States to manufacture a new kind of four-wheel-drive utility vehicle.

By 1997 the company aimed to produce sixty thousand vehicles a year in the United States. One third would be for the U.S. market and two thirds would be for export. In the U.S. market, the vehicle was intended to compete with the Chrysler Jeep Cherokee and the Ford Explorer.

Mercedes-Benz said the U.S. plant would have production costs 30 percent lower than in Germany. Prominent among possible sites was South Carolina. Eventually they chose Tuscaloosa, Alabama.

There were further reasons why two of Germany's most successful companies were setting up operations in America during the worst recession in Germany for decades.

Currency fluctuations could be circumvented between the dollar and the deutsche mark. Labor costs were still relatively low in America, and higher in Germany than everywhere else. Americans working on American soil could enable Germans to circumvent American protectionism, just as they had done for the Japanese. By 1996, Japan for the first time would be America's number-one car exporter.

The global marketplace had come to Germany, just as it had come to Japan. The rise of the Japanese and the fall of the Berlin Wall had brought the Germans to South Carolina. Above all, building the cars where the most sales were made financial sense. The United States was and is the market. In Germany, the economic miracle was over. In South Carolina, the *Wirtschaftswunder* had only just begun.

28

Send for "Motorhead"

The Empire Strikes Back

IT WAS A SHORT DISTANCE from Spartanburg to Detroit, but a long way from the days when Ford could rule the world with the Model T and conquer Europe by giving a car the name of a small town in Italy like Cortina. But as far as the men in Detroit were concerned, the automobile had started with Ford and it would continue with Ford.

In 1938, Hitler had used Rouge River as a model for his "people's car" plant at KdF-Stadt. In 1939, Agnelli had made the pilgrimage to Detroit from Turin. In 1950, Detroit had been visited by Toyoda, who went on to be the car war leader of Japan.

By 1990, Volkswagenwerk, FIAT, and Toyota had grown out of visits to Ford. Detroit, once the Rome of the automotive world, was on its way to being forgotten.

It was time for the empire to strike back.

But first they had to find the right men.

By the early 1990s, Ford was in better shape than General Motors in North America, but it had skidded into losses in Europe. In 1991–92, these losses, including those of its new Jaguar subsidiary, exceeded $2 billion.

In Australia, the company had climbed back from a loss to a position of profit. Somebody had to be found to do the same job in Britain, Germany, Belgium, and Spain.

The men in Detroit knew that only a committed "motorhead" could halt the advance of the Japanese in Europe.

Dagenham, England, 1993

"If anyone can pull it off," said one Ford veteran, "Jac Nasser can. He's got this company in his blood."

Jacques "Jac" Nasser had pulled Ford out of loss in Australia by shedding nearly half the Australian workforce. Lebanese by birth, Nasser had joined the company in 1968 from the Royal Melbourne Institute of Technology. He had worked in Detroit, Buenos Aires, and Sydney.

He was the new Chairman of Ford of Europe. "Who are the motorheads in your department?" he asked a colleague.

"Motorheads, Jac?" The executive looked confused.

Nasser explained. A motorhead was not just somebody who was a car lover. He was somebody who lived and breathed the automobile. He was someone who knew in his heart of hearts that there was no other industry; he was an autodidact, not an automaton.

Nasser made a note of his colleague's ignorance of the term.

Years before Honda had come to Ohio, Nissan to Tennessee, Toyota to Kentucky and Derby, and Mercedes-Benz and BMW to Alabama and South Carolina, Ford had established its bridgeheads overseas. The Americans and the British might have accepted the coming of the Japanese, but not far beneath the surface, Nasser believed, there were ancient enmities that could work to Ford's advantage.

In Australia, Nasser had concluded that in dealing with the Japanese there was no point in sticking to the rule book. In Europe, too, as far as Nasser was concerned, the Japanese had circumvented "the letter and the spirit" of the deal done between Japan and the European Community. The level of imports of Japanese cars to Europe was set by the Japanese government's industry department and based on Japanese sales projections. "The 6.5 percent reduction in Japanese imports is totally unrealistic," said Nasser. "It should be a minimum of 10 percent and probably over 12 percent; even that could be stretched. There is no incentive for them to be accurate," he said of the Japanese sales estimates. "The fox is minding the chickens."

The Japanese had received disproportionate publicity for their car plants in Britain and operations in Europe: "It's easy to start an assembly plant here and there from a zero base. It sounds like a lot, but it doesn't add up to much. People are looking at a few trees and are missing the forest."

Nasser extended his attack beyond Japan: "The biggest threat to Europe's automobile industry is imported competition, mainly from the Far East, which will replace European jobs with Asian jobs."

Ford was the biggest automobile manufacturer in Britain. It employed more people, exported more cars, bought from more suppliers, and had a bigger presence there than any of its rivals. Ford had to be better than the Japanese and South Koreans at tooting its own horn.

Ford had also lost $1.5 million a day in Britain since 1990.

Ford had to be pulled into profit.

Nasser didn't mince words with the heads of the company's German subsidiary, Ford Werke: their plants at Saarlouis and Cologne were overmanned and underproductive. The German recession had failed to shake them out of their quasi-autonomous complacency. Ford Werke had too long exercised too great an influence on technical and financial resources at the expense of Ford of Britain.

Ford Werke liked to think it was a law unto itself, which was one of the reasons it was skidding into loss. Ford Werke management was stunned by Nasser's outburst. Everybody else in Saarlouis and Cologne and Detroit knew Nasser was right.

"The Germans are losing the battle," said one insider. "Nasser's remit from Detroit is simple: to get Ford of Europe into the same profitable shape as Ford of America. To do that, he must turn Ford of Europe into a genuinely European company. That means bringing the Germans firmly under control. In terms of the internal politics, Nasser has been fortunate. Ford Werke has never been as vulnerable as it is now."

Nasser had three to five years to steer the company through one of the bumpiest periods of its history. Ford, the American company whose new Lebanese-born European head was so outspoken against Japan and the Far East, could and would make and break jobs in Europe every bit as much as the South Koreans and the Japanese.

Detroit, Michigan, 1993

Alex Trotman was a softly-spoken Scot who had worked as a young man with Ford in Britain on the project code-named "Archbishop" that became the Cortina.

At the end of the 1960s, Trotman made an unusual move within the automotive empire. He transferred from Dagenham in England to Dearborn, Michigan. The opposition he encountered was such that he had to buy his own air tickets and start again in a lowly management position.

Trotman was undeterred. He rose swiftly through a series of posts, including that of president of Ford Asia-Pacific, and that of chairman of Ford of Europe, later occupied by Jac Nasser. En route, Trotman saved and successfully relaunched the Mustang, the automobile that had given Ford credibility as a sports car manufacturer and that had become President Clinton's favorite automobile.

Trotman controlled $200 billion worth of assets, 325,000 employees, and plants in thirty countries. He had just become the first non-American to take on one of the most powerful and sought-after corporate jobs in the third-biggest industrial corporation in the world. He was the new chairman and chief executive of the Ford Motor Company. "I doubt all the players can stay in business," he said. "Ultimately, there will be a handful of global players and the rest will either not be there or they will be struggling."

In his office Trotman kept the ornaments from six different car companies that had gone out of business. They were a reminder that the world owed no one a living, not even Ford.

Trotman was a scholarship boy from a poor working-class Scottish family who could not afford to send him to university. Instead he joined the Royal Air Force, where he served a four-year commission as a flying officer and navigator. He saw an advertisement for a job as a management trainee with Ford in Dagenham: "It was the first ad I applied for, and the first job I got. I was looking for a paycheck, not a career in the auto business."

Trotman knew the virtues of discipline, and hated elitism in any form. He still flew back to Scotland two or three times a year to see his brother, who was a bus driver in Edinburgh. He drove himself to work, and was devoted to his family. He found his place in America's classless society.

At Ford in Detroit, he closed executive dining rooms and banned the blue paper used by top managers to distinguish their memos from everyone else's. He introduced a live TV link-up every three months, in which any Ford employee in any Ford plant anywhere could ask him any question they liked. Trotman answered 80 percent of the questions live; he answered the remainder by personal memo within a few days.

Ford under Trotman had spent $6 billion developing a world car. They called it the Contour in America and the Mondeo in Europe. The aim was to sell it in different markets, but to produce it from centrally coordinated manufacturing units. The driver paid a high price in terms of identity for this first manifestation of a global strategy. The Contour/Mondeo was a generalization that passed for a car. The success of the car was proportional to its lack of individuality.

Alfred P. Sloan had come back to haunt the fourteenth floor of General Motors' headquarters in Detroit. The spirit of Henry Ford had returned to Dearborn and Ford. Ford had gone back to basics. The Contour/Mondeo was Ford's "Year Zero." You could have any car you wanted as long as it was the Contour/Mondeo.

The Honda Accord had already been dislodged by American automobiles from the number-one position in the United States. Ford made five of the ten best-selling vehicles in America. But the success of the world car strategy depended upon the ability to make and sell a globally inoffensive car inside and outside its home nation and market. The world car strategy meant a multibillion-dollar investment, so that a Ford could be made anywhere in the world, and nobody would be able to tell what it was, beyond that it was a Ford.

There would be no half measures in the war between the motorheads and the Japanese. Trotman and Nasser were car men, motorheads, as opposed to bottom-line-driven bean counters. If Trotman and Nasser could not pull it off, probably nobody could.

The stakes at this level were stratospheric and stimulating, but the downside was frightening to behold. Trotman and his wife, Valerie, kept their sanity under these insane pressures by backpacking in remote areas of North America, away from all forms of personal transport.

In Detroit and elsewhere, contemporaries and rivals observed Ford's millennial global strategy: "Ford 2000, in a sense, is the largest merger in history," said analyst Scott F. Merlis, of Morgan Stanley. "Ford of Europe and Ford North America together (are) a $94 billion company . . . RJR Nabisco was only $24 billion."

Others were more trenchant: "Why on earth would you want to create these gigantic, earth-spinning organizations?" asked a senior executive at a rival in Detroit. "Why?" echoed Chrysler's president, Bob Lutz. "What's the value of being big?"

Like the name of the new car, the game was global.

29

Capitalist Roads

The Wild East and the New Frontiers

I N THE MID-1990s the pioneers of the new frontiers would include not just the men in Michigan, but French bankers, Swiss watchmakers, and Indian prime ministers.

Calcutta, 1994

Even in 1994, India had only around one vehicle for every 280 people (compared with China's ¹⁄₁₇₀), but its vast population of nearly 1 billion and its 200-million-strong middle class made it extremely attractive to foreign companies. India's biggest car manufacturer was Maruti, owned 50 percent by Suzuki of Japan and 50 percent by the Indian government. The government was unwilling to invest further, and welcomed Suzuki's request to increase the Japanese company's stake to 51 percent. In this way the Japanese company could attract new free-market capital and use cheap local Indian labor to export its Alto micro-car to Japan and Europe. By 1995 the Maruti/Suzuki joint venture was making 350,000 cars a year and controlled 65 percent of the Indian new-car market.

The other big auto manufacturer in India was Hindustan Motors. In 1994 the company signed a $100 million deal with the largest car corporation in the world, General Motors. The aim was to manufacture a competitor to Maruti-Suzuki in the Indian market.

General Motors had come close to a deal with Hindustan Motors four years earlier. GM was deterred by changes in government and civil unrest culminating in the assassination of Rajiv Gandhi. Against these pitiful squabbles, the company had to weigh the fact that India was becoming attractive to foreign investment to a degree that far exceeded GM's operations there between 1928 and 1954. Suzuki was not the only company setting up here with an Indian partner. So were BMW, Daimler-Benz, Hyundai, Daewoo, FIAT, Rover, Peugeot-Citroën, Ford, Honda, Mitsubishi, and Volkswagenwerk.

In Bombay, a rented apartment cost as much as nine thousand dollars a month. It took two hours to cross town because of the heavy traffic. Pirate videos of Disney's *The Lion King* were on the streets before it opened in Europe. The wall of import duties remained as a deterrent to any company intent on exporting here without investing in return. But rampant private enterprise and the gradual deregulation of the markets, reduction of protectionism, and removal of trade tariffs all made India one of the wild new frontiers.

GM and HM — the Indian company's logo already imitated that of its American partner — tied the knot. The two companies would bring to India the Astra sedan made by Adam Opel, GM's German subsidiary. By 1995, General Motors and Hindustan Motors aimed to start manufacturing twenty thousand cars a year at a Hindustan Motors plant at Baroda, in the western state of Gujarat.

The supranational corporation in Detroit and the Indian government in New Delhi made statesmanlike noises. The Indian prime minister, P. V. Narasimha Rao, under pressure to continue economic reform, spoke of "raising the standard of living of the people and bringing the benefits of the modern technological age to our ancient land, while retaining its great moral and spiritual values."

C. K. Birla of Hindustan Motors declared the GM investment "a very positive sign of the world's confidence in India." Birla was particularly pleased that the joint venture would go under the name Birla GM, and not vice versa.

Greg de Yonker was GM's vice president for overseas distribution. "General Motors has been drawn to India by the government's economic liberalization policies," he said. "We hope they will continue carrying them out, as they have said they will."

A few days after he made his remarks, Prime Minister Rao left the heavily guarded offices in Racecourse Road, New Delhi — two of the previous occupants of which had been assassinated — and traveled to Britain. On a cold spring day, Mr. Rao stood and paid his respects before a statue in London's Tavistock Square. The statue was of another murdered man, Mahatma Gandhi.

Once, Gandhi had spoken out for a return to an agrarian idyll and against what he saw as the nightmare of the industrialization brought by the likes of the Birlas to India. Now Gandhi was in many ways a forgotten man, and the industrialization of India was seen as the only hope for the country in the global market.

But the Indian prime minister had not forgotten the lessons of history.

London, 1993

In a twenty-story building near London Bridge, people in suits were talking about revolution. These people were accountants. This building was the headquarters of one of the world's biggest accountancy firms, Price Waterhouse. The revolution was taking place in the countries of the former Soviet Union.

Price Waterhouse had opened its first office in Russia, in St. Petersburg, in 1916. That office had closed shortly afterwards, owing, as one partner put it, to "a little local difficulty." The Bolshevik Revolution meant a gap of seventy-two years and the renaming of St. Petersburg as Leningrad. In 1993, Leningrad was back to being St. Petersburg, and Price Waterhouse was back in Russia, this time in Moscow.

Russia and the countries of the former Soviet Union were the wildest of the wild new frontiers. The largest state economy on earth was being broken up and reinvested as private enterprise. There were fortunes to be made in fees from privatizations, joint ventures, corporate restructurings, and other activities whose anodyne names belied the labyrinthine negotiations, Machiavellian maneuvers, cutthroat calculations, and stupendous numbers that were all part of being one of the world's biggest accountancy firms.

The Price Waterhouse team in Moscow had grown quickly, in keeping with the momentous changes taking place in the largest country on earth. A handful of people in cramped quarters had grown in four years to an organization of four hundred people. Russian-speaking expatriates and local experts staffed the Moscow office. Russian graduates were recruited from the top Russian universities and sent for accountancy training in the West.

These young, ambitious, multilingual Russian sons and daughters of Communist forebears were the true agents of change. Historians would argue whether Communism was merely a transitional phase from monarchy to popular enfranchisement. The reality was that the accountants were already geared up, and Communism was a dead duck. On the Russian road to state-sanctioned capitalism, there was no turning back.

The people in London were discussing last-minute preparations for the big presentation. The competition was not, which was why the people from Price Waterhouse were taking no chances. The World Managing Partner himself was going on the trip.

They came from all corners of the Price Waterhouse world: from London, Birmingham, and Newcastle, England; Hamburg, Germany; Peoria, Illinois; Stockholm, Sweden; Turin, Italy; Warsaw, Poland; and Zurich, Switzerland. They came bearing their credentials of specialist expertise developed in this kind of presentation around the globe.

The team assembled. Visas were authorized. Tickets were issued. Seats were taken in business class. Jackets were hung up, newspapers unfolded. The airplane took off. Drinks were served. They began to relax. The people from Price Waterhouse were going to Togliattigrad.

Watch This Car: Biel, Switzerland, 1993

Price Waterhouse people and other passengers on the Moscow flight wore inexpensive, brightly colored Swiss watches. *Look at me,* they said. *I will not only tell you the time. I will speak your fortune. You are rich enough not to need to flaunt it in the old-fashioned way. No need for you of solid gold, diamonds, and lapis lazuli.*

Nicolas Hayek, a Palestinian born in exile in Beirut, had emigrated to Switzerland in 1953. In the early 1980s, Hayek and his company, SMH, had led the Swiss watch industry's counteroffensive against the Japanese.

Hayek's hatred of invaders and contempt for appeasement in the face of a ruthless enemy may well have been nurtured in the circumstances of his birth. He was no longer prepared to watch Seiko, Casio, and Citizen grab greater and greater shares of the mass market. He refused to retreat into upmarket ghettos from which the dislodgment of the Swiss by the Japanese would have been only a matter of time.

Hayek and SMH took the battle to the enemy in the mass market. "The Japanese thought we would withdraw from there and concentrate on the production of expensive, high-class watches," he recalled. "They were totally flabbergasted when we suddenly started our counterattack in the lower end of the market, and chose a head-on confrontation with their products."

Hayek's marketing brilliance and his outstanding design team had succeeded beyond even his wildest dreams. Between 1983 and 1993, SMH and its "Swatch" watches took the Swiss share of the world watch market from 15 percent to over 50 percent. Swatch's success against the Japanese led to its broadening under Hayek's leadership into plastics, battery innovation, and electronic motor technology. SMH sponsored research engineers at Swiss universities.

But there was one market destiny to which Hayek aspired above all others. This master of marketing in one of the few remaining areas of self-expression could look out the window at the Swiss Alps and still see the equivalent of his Everest unclimbed. Hayek was there in his mind in the summit party. He was there with José Ignacio Lopez de Arriortua and Hayek's fellow Lebanese, Jac Nasser. The final battleground against the Japanese was the car.

Togliattigrad, Russia, 1993

The people from Price Waterhouse touched down in Moscow in midafternoon. Theirs had been a pleasant, uneventful flight. They cleared customs. A car took them across town to the domestic

192 ∞ CAR WARS

terminal. They noted the Cadillacs, Jaguars, BMWs, and Mercedeses; and at least half the cars on the roads were Zhigulis or Ladas.

The domestic terminal stank of sweat and cigarettes. There was nothing to eat or drink. After two hours they boarded the Aeroflot Tupolev bound for Kuybyshev, which, since the collapse of the Soviet Union, was known once more as Samara.

This was an unpleasant, uneventful flight. But they had been told that there was no other way. The problem was not the fact that the trains took two days to cover the six hundred miles. The problem was not that the roads were strewn with giant potholes. The problem was the bandits.

The people from Price Waterhouse touched down, sweaty and dirty, at Samara. Cars took them through the darkness. At midnight they reached Togliattigrad.

The Hotel Zhiguli had cold water only, three days a week. The hotel food was such that, after two days, they gave the staff hard cash to go and buy fresh food in the market. Thereafter, the people from Price Waterhouse ate adequately. The long winter snows had gone, leaving a filthy slush. Around them were miles of beet fields and mining operations. The Zhiguli Mountains were lost in a pollution haze. So were the skyscrapers built to house the 100,000 workers and their families.

They set off to inspect the plant. The two production lines seemed to stretch forever. At least ten people seemed to be working on each car; most were eighteen-year-old girls. Thousands of cars lay at odd angles to the side of the lines, abandoned seemingly because of a minor blemish in the paint or trim. Farther up the lines, perfect, unblemished cars were cannibalized by workers keen to keep their parts of the line working. As a result, the lines stopped altogether until the cannibalized cars, too, were pushed to one side, and the process could start again.

Elderly Russian and Tatar peasant women hawked live chickens, keen to dispatch them on the spot.

The people from Price Waterhouse noted all these things. Then they went back to the Hotel Zhiguli.

Togliattigrad, or Togliatti, as it was known, had initially been hailed as a landmark in automobile production. Even its teething problems were described as hazards of the leading edge. The spectacular deal

Agnelli had cut with the Soviet commissars, so unpopular with the Communist trade unions in Italy, had been the strongest proof yet of the trade thaw gradually permeating the deep frost of the Cold War.

FIAT had finished building the plant at Togliatti in 1970. FIAT had supplied the designs and manufacturing rights for the car. FIAT had trained the management, staff, and engineers. The operation was thereafter owned, managed, and staffed by the Soviet state-owned company AvtoVAZ (VAZ being the acronym for Volga Automobile Works). The Soviet people's car, the Zhiguli, began to come off the production line.

By 1973, thanks to Togliatti, Soviet car production was nearly five times greater than it had been in the first year of the deal between Agnelli and the commissars. Soviet-Italian relations were no longer baffled, but cordial, throughout the 1970s. For Soviet automobile specialists, the Turin connection was a unique opportunity to travel across the Iron Curtain to the West — as it was for the few western automobile specialists who made the journey here to the great plant on the River Volga.

In 1977, AvtoVAZ produced its own first completely new car, the Lada Niva. This was a rugged four-wheel-drive vehicle designed for rural areas. The Niva was also the first completely original Soviet car to achieve popularity in the West.

But all this was achieved against a background of growing political stagnation, economic deterioration, and social unrest. AvtoVAZ complained increasingly about insufficient government funding. Soviet suppliers were unreliable. The Soviet government appeared incapable of putting this right.

In 1981, workers at Togliatti demonstrated in protest over low pay. Nineteen eighty-five marked the coming to power of Mikhail Gorbachev, the former machine operator from Stavropol — before it was renamed Togliattigrad.

By 1988 the Soviet press was describing Togliatti as "pre-crisis." At best, the plant and its 110,000 workers in their high-rise homes devoid of recreational facilities were infected with indifference. At worst, they were bedeviled by embezzlement, drunkenness, and absenteeism: "Who can speak of better quality in these conditions?" asked the Soviet *Literary Gazette*. "Workers at the plant itself should be able to buy their own product much more easily. At a price of nine thousand rubles, it would take an assembly-line worker making two hundred rubles a month nearly four years to get a car . . . if he did not eat or drink."

Yet, somehow, Togliatti was still producing over half of the Soviet Union's cars — most of them still based on the long-obsolete FIAT 124.

The Togliatti management coped heroically in the face of these and many other problems. In the dying years of Communism, AvtoVAZ General Director Kadannikov and Finance Director Gluschkov scoured the West for foreign investment. Twice they had come close to finding it. Twice they had seen the opportunity slip away.

FIAT considered, then declined, a 30-percent stake in AvtoVAZ. Bear Stearns, the U.S. investment bank, valued the company. Deloitte Touche had attempted to render comprehensible to Western investors the company's accounts. This arrangement, too, had collapsed — as, shortly afterwards, had the Soviet Union.

The collapse of the Soviet Union in the winter of 1991 led to the creation of the Russian Federation and the election of Russia's first ever popularly elected leader, Boris Yeltsin. Yeltsin pursued the path of economic reform with the ruthless singlemindedness of a former Communist. The former Soviet peoples of the new Russian Federation suffered accordingly. This hardship spread to Russian industry, to the auto plants around Moscow, and to Togliatti.

In January 1993, the Moskvich auto plant closed down due to lack of funds and shortage of engines from the Ufa plant in the former Soviet republic of Bashkortostan. The Moskvich was named after Lenin's Young Communist League, and was the main rival to the Zhiguli. Four fifths of the Ufa plant's engines had gone to the Soviet military, and the plant had been crippled by cuts in military spending. Ufa faced a deficit of fourteen billion rubles in the first quarter of the year. The management wrote begging for a subsidy to the new Russian prime minister, Victor Chernomyrdin.

In March 1993, the government announced that Zil, the maker of the great, sharklike, black limousines once synonymous with the Politburo, would be sold off. Zil employed 120,000 workers at seventeen sites across Russia, the biggest and most notorious of these being the Likhachyov plant on the Volga in southern Moscow.

The task of privatizing the giant car company was a tall order. But these dinosaurs from the Stalinist era would not easily lie down and die. In the first all-Russian enterprise of its kind, shares were offered for sale at one hundred auction centers across Russia.

At Togliatti, the morale of the workers continued to deteriorate. But hope was at hand for workers and management. Uniquely among Russian automobile makers, AvtoVAZ found itself in the unusual position of being unable to meet demand.

This was not only because of the differences between Togliatti and purely Soviet phenomena like Zil and Moskvich, whose fortunes had been tied to those of the Soviet empire. The saving factor, in the case of the Zhiguli, was the increased demand abroad for its western incarnations, the Lada and the Lada Niva. AvtoVAZ exported 40 percent of all its cars to Europe, South America, North Africa, Asia, and Canada.

General Director Kadannikov and Finance Director Gluschkov knew that this was the attraction for the foreign investment they had so nearly secured in their travels in the West. But this investment would only be possible if AvtoVAZ succeeded in having its accounts rendered comprehensible to western investors.

This process had been successfully carried out by a western accountancy firm for AvtoVAZ Bank in Togliatti and Samara. That firm was Price Waterhouse — which was why the people from Price Waterhouse had returned to Togliatti.

In October 1993 there was another "little local difficulty." T-80 tanks under the command of Boris Yeltsin laid bloody siege to anti-Yeltsin factors inside the Russian White House, or Parliament. To many, this was hardly a political climate conducive to western investment.

Against this background of political unrest and competition from two other accountancy firms, and over a period of several visits, the people from Price Waterhouse gathered their information.

The people from Price Waterhouse — including the World Managing Partner — made their presentation. In November 1993 they were appointed to privatize the flagship of the Russian automobile industry — AvtoVAZ at Togliatti.

Watch This Car 2: Biel, Switzerland, 1994

In the early years of the century, the Swiss had built their own cars, such as the Dufaux and the Pic-Pic. Switzerland had a number of factories assembling American and European cars. In the 1960s, Peter Monteverdi built coupes, and the Enzmann family built futuristic sports cars with plastic bodies and Volkswagen engines.

Volkswagenwerk came on board as partner in Nicolas Hayek's vehicle vision, and invested $4.5 million — a small sum in context — in Hayek's small car. They called it the Swatchmobile. There was much talk of Volkswagenwerk producing the Swatchmobile in Shanghai.

Volkswagenwerk and Hayek were unlikely partners even in the exotic world of automobile alliances. Volkswagenwerk pulled out of the partnership, citing the development of its own "city car" and the cost-cutting strategy that culminated in the arrival of "Superlopez" from Detroit.

Mercedes-Benz was engaged in talks with Hayek even before the departure of Volkswagenwerk. Beneath Hayek's flamboyant self-promotion and marketing pizzazz, there was a synergy between the Swiss seekers on the technological frontiers and the engineering excellence of the most famous German car company.

Mercedes-Benz wanted to make smaller, more fashionable cars. Swatch was sexy and fun, and fun and sex had never been associated with the cars made in Stuttgart. In Swatch they also found a partner who reflected the boldness they had begun to discover in themselves, that had pushed through layoffs at home and begun setting up operations overseas.

Swatch unveiled the Eco-Sprinter and the Eco-Speedster at the home of Mercedes-Benz in Stuttgart in the spring of 1994. The cars were visually and technically revolutionary in a way that had not been seen since Issigonis and BMC unveiled the Mini.

They were just ninety-five inches long and fifty-five inches wide, yet could carry two adults and their shopping through the heaviest city traffic. In the underfloor was a hybrid petro-electric power unit that yielded a range of 350 miles and generated a top speed of ninety miles per hour. The lightweight plastic body was designed by Mercedes-Benz engineers to withstand considerable impact.

Were the Swatchmobiles a gimmick, or was there strength through styling in the first Swiss-watch-inspired people's car?

Hitler would most likely have approved of the road taken by his favorite car company. Mercedes-Benz, for its part, could regard its partnership with Swatch as a way of keeping up with and overtaking the "city cars" of other manufacturers.

Many still questioned the environmental credentials of these small "city cars." The suspicion was that the car companies were merely marketing "second cars" to add to the congestion in cities, when they should be applying their small-car technology to the freeways, *autostradas*, and autobahns.

Ford's "city car," the Ka, was to be manufactured in Spain. The Ka was little more than an add-on tender to its "world" car, the mundane Mondeo or Contour. Hayek and Swatch were the antithesis of *der Fordismus*. You could have any color "Smart Swatch car concept by Mercedes-Benz" you liked, including black.

Hayek planned to launch them at the 1996 Olympic Games in Atlanta. Production would begin in 1997 at Hambach, a small town in France near the German and Swiss borders. The $450-million plant would employ two thousand workers and was expected to produce 200,000 Smart Cars a year by 1997. By the summer of 1995, Mercedes would be swamped by applications from potential dealers in the new "experience center" sales network, which would enable customers to test-drive the car and buy other products, such as Swatch watches.

Thirty-five years earlier, a Middle Eastern émigré, Alec Issigonis, had produced the world's most fashionable small car, the Mini. Thirty-five years later, another Middle Eastern émigré had a vision that he believed would give that crucial spark to the right combination of engineering and design.

Togliatti, Russia, 1994

Price Waterhouse began the complex job of converting the Russian company's accounts to western standards, training local staff, setting up internal audit departments, and rendering them comprehensible to the western investor.

AvtoVAZ management and staff, and 160 million Russian citizens became potential shareholders through the distribution of vouchers to Russian households and the offer of shares to corporate investors. However, the success of these unprecedented ventures into popular capitalism was limited. The real money lay in the West.

Yet all Russian companies were facing increasing problems in raising finance in the western capital markets. Western banks were still rescheduling debts owed to them by the former Soviet Union. They were reluctant to lend directly to Russian companies without guarantees from their own governments.

In November 1993, AvtoVAZ won a $150-million loan from Forus Services, a Swiss-based finance company. Forus said it had raised the money from its own funds and from western banks such as Banque Nationale de Paris, for lending on to AvtoVAZ to modernize Togliatti. Forus said its own guarantees to banks included future revenues from the export of Lada cars to Europe, the Middle East, and Latin America.

The people from Price Waterhouse became used to the short, hot summers and the long, freezing winters. They became used to the plant, with its French-style squatting lavatories and its teeming, chaotic army of workers. They moved out of the Hotel Zhiguli and into their own apartments. These apartments were renovated and equipped with VCRs and satellite television.

There were weekends in Moscow in hotels with good food and hot water, and there were western clothes in the shops, and tables on the pavements outside the cafés. There were handsome salaries and the satisfaction that the deal was bringing in handsome revenues to the firm. But for the people from Price Waterhouse, Togliatti would always be a hardship post.

The Moskvich plant remained closed. GAZ, the Gorky Automobile Works, made the Chaika limousine for the Politburo and the Volga sedan for lesser *apparatchiks*. GAZ was the next casualty on the River Volga rust belt. The company's problems only began when the marketing director shot himself with his hunting rifle.

The GAZ management was in revolt against the kind of privatization process that was taking place at Togliatti. They correctly believed this would jeopardize their 350,000 jobs, their ten thousand cows, their Black Sea sanatorium, their 120 kindergartens, their one-thousand-bed hospital, their fish farm, and their vast stocks of sausages. GAZ was less a company than a Soviet version of FIAT.

GAZ was also broke, and under investigation for fraud and tax evasion. But the management still refused to accept the need for reform: "I'm sitting on a powder keg. It could blow up at any moment," said Boris Nemtsov, the reform-minded mayor of Nizhny Novgorod, formerly Gorky. He was the implacable opponent of the GAZ management: "This is the most difficult problem I want to solve. They are a mafia, an honest-to-goodness Russian mafia."

The mayor of Moscow usually rode in a Zil limousine. He announced that Zil was switching to a four-day week and might shut down altogether.

Zil faced bankruptcy as a result of the payments crisis that threatened thousands of Russian companies. On Autofactory Street, Moscow, assembly lines ground to a halt, chimneys stopped belching smoke, and workers were sent home with severance pay. At the great marble Stalinist main entrance, a fringe Marxist group, the Communist Workers Party of Russia, put up posters explaining the difference between capitalism and socialism. The Interior Ministry put up posters offering Zil workers jobs at 50 percent higher wages in police work. Workers' Moscow, another militant antireform group, put up posters denouncing "bankers, speculators, and the criminal bourgeoisie" and called upon workers to seize back their assets.

In autumn 1994, Prime Minister Chernomyrdin announced that the government had allocated $55 million to develop a new range of Zil limousines. He also said that the government would buy at least twenty-four Zil limousines a year from the Likhachyov plant — the "ecological inferno" on the bend of the Volga in southern Moscow.

A Russian-American Industrial Corporation was established in Geneva, backed by Caterpillar, Pacar, and General Motors. The new corporation planned to invest in a more profitable activity than Zil limousines — namely, a new range of Zil *kolkhoz* trucks. In early 1995, however, all the Zil plants closed down because the company had no more money to buy parts. Zil's general director, Valery Saikin, said the company needed one trillion rubles ($260 million) if it was to reopen.

In August 1994, AvtoVAZ at Togliatti fell short of its production target of 63,000 cars a month. In the same year, costs rose by nearly 100 percent.

In September 1994, AvtoVAZ won a $100-million credit from the British Standard Chartered Bank. The contract would run for seven years and be repaid from AvtoVAZ exports. But, by the summer of 1995, the company was still facing bankruptcy. Hopes rested on Daewoo of South Korea coming to build a new Russian "people's car" at Togliatti.

There was a particular piquancy to this last development. The previous summer, the last Russian soldiers had left Berlin and flown home from a posting that no longer existed to an empire that no longer survived. The cargo holds of their Antonovs were rumored to be filled with BMWs and Mercedes-Benzes.

Prime Minister Chernomyrdin was under increasing attack for the hardship his economic reforms were causing across Russia. The exiled Nobel laureate Alexander Solzhenitsyn had returned to Russia and toured his homeland, excoriating the moral and spiritual effects of opening up the country to the West. The nationalist demagogue Vladimir Zhirinovsky and the commissars of the old Communist Party both made gains in the political void. The economic void was fertile breeding ground for the Russian mafia.

Early in 1996, Togliatti boss Vladimir Kadannikov was appointed by President Yeltsin to head Russia's economic policy, a move which critics of Yeltsin interpreted as a slowdown on the road to reform: "Yeltsin made a point of telling western investors how committed he was to reform," said one banker, "then he appoints this dinosaur to run the economy. What does he expect us to think?" "Look what is happening to VAZ," said a Russian economist, "and you will understand what will happen to Russia."

However uncertain the future, one thing was certain. The Antonovs were coming home from Berlin. However successful the people from Price Waterhouse were at Togliatti, the people at AvtoVAZ were all too aware that the last thing these veterans of Russia's foreign wars wanted to come home to was a Zhiguli.

Alma Ata, Kazakhstan, 1994

In Moscow, Mitsui of Japan was negotiating to export $200 million worth of equipment to the Lenin Komsomol Automotive Plant.

In Bashkortostan, the Ufa plant was still in trouble. In Ukraine, Renault was supplying engines to LAZ, the Lvov bus maker. In

Belorus, Kamaz was starting to make the AvtoVAZ-designed Oka "city car" in Grodno.

In Tatarstan, Daewoo of South Korea was investing $1 billion in a joint venture with the Yelabuga automobile factory. In Uzbekhistan, the first Mercedes-Benz trucks were being built at the Uzbek-German joint venture in Druzhba.

The capitalist road was opening up the autonomous republics, cities, *krais*, and *oblasts* of the new Russian Federation and the exotic lands of what had been Soviet Central Asia. East from Samara, the road led to the Urals, Siberia, and Kazakhstan. Kazakhstan ran from Russia's eastern border to the western flank of China.

Here, fifteen hundred miles southeast of Togliatti and two thousand miles southeast of Moscow, was Alma Ata, the capital of this vast country of more than one hundred ethnic groups. Here, too, on Ablai-Khan Avenue, Price Waterhouse was open for business.

30

Lawless Roads

The Illegal Traffic in Western Cars to Eastern Europe and the Far East

IN THE NEWLY CAPITALIST COUNTRIES of Eastern Europe and the "tiger" economies of the Far East, Mercedes-Benz and BMW cars were being afforded a dubious distinction.

In the former East Germany, they were regarded by newly affluent *Ossis* as essential automobiles. New owners were not too fussy about how they came by their purchase.

In 1993 the trade in stolen Mercedes-Benzes and BMWs within former East Germany reached epidemic proportions. Legitimate owners found it impossible to obtain insurance to drive into former Communist territory. The former Trabant plant at Zwickau serviced Volkswagens. The "other" Germans wanted more — they wanted Mercedes-Benzes and BMWs and they wanted them now.

A secondhand trade arose, which went a short way to alleviating the problem. But although the rising cost of auto insurance in the former West Germany did little for the deepening German recession, that same recession did little to depress the stolen car market. The criminal rings expanded their operations from Germany to Poland, Hungary, and the former Czechoslovakia.

These criminal enterprises were encouraged by the crises that bedeviled automakers whose traditional markets had collapsed with the Iron Curtain. Apart from the crisis at AvtoVAZ at Togliatti, Skoda at Mlada Boleslav, and Tatra at Koprivnica in former Czechoslovakia suffered falling sales, rising costs and uncertain relations with Western partners.

Skoda in Czech means "pity." It had all but closed down once already, when the "Velvet Revolution" of Václav Havel restored democracy to the Czech Republic — and, in doing so, restored freedom to the thousands of political prisoners who made up much of the workforce of the plant.

Sixteen thousand of the fifty thousand inhabitants of Mlada Boleslav still worked there. The importance attached to western alliances by Czech political leaders was such that signs of wavering led to warning lights at high levels. The Czech prime minister, Václav Klaus, was personally reassured by Ferdinand Piech of Volkswagenwerk that the cancellation of a $560-million refinancing program was not the beginning of the end for Skoda as a subsidiary of Volkswagenwerk, which had bought the company. Minister for Trade and Industry Vladimír Dlouhý called on his cabinet colleagues to support domestic production and ride in Tatra limousines.

The smuggling problem had begun for Mercedes-Benz in the 1980s. The Nigerian government had tried to reduce the influx of smuggled cars for its newly oil-rich *Wabenzi* by beginning production of the Nigerian-assembled Volkswagen. By the 1990s, however, the *Wabenzi*, like the market, was a global phenomenon.

The Russia mafia, or *organizatsiya*, and their legal and semilegal counterparts among the *biznismeni* and *nuovorishi*, also wanted Mercedes-Benzes and BMWs and Cadillacs. They too were as unconcerned about the provenance of their purchases as they were about driving licenses and vehicle registration.

A violent reaction awaited not only the overzealous traffic policeman. In Moscow, four-wheel-drive vehicles armed with defensive roo bars went on sale, as well as armored Rolls-Royces and conventional Jaguars and Bentleys.

Oleg Dolganov, a twenty-five-year-old metals and emerald dealer, became the first Russian since Lenin to own a Rolls-Royce legitimately. Dolganov paid 250 million rubles ($212,000). He chartered an Aeroflot aircraft to fly the car to his hometown of Ekaterinburg, six hundred miles east of Moscow in Siberia.

The British ambassador in Moscow forsook his Rolls-Royce for a Range Rover on security grounds.

A lack of security — or armor plating — could be fatal in Russia. The head of Logovaz, the leading luxury car dealer, had already been threatened by the Russian mafia if he did not hand over a share of his profits. He refused to cooperate and narrowly escaped death when a remote-control bomb exploded by his Mercedes-Benz outside his office in a busy Moscow street. His chauffeur was decapitated in the blast.

By the summer of 1994, in north London alone, the Russian mafia had orchestrated the theft of $9 million worth of FIAT Unos, Ladas, and Peugeots in twelve months, all for shipment by sea container to Eastern Europe.

The waiting list in Russia for a Zhiguli was still as much as three years. The average Russian buyer was acquiring a car for life, and a thriving black market also grew up in components and spares. These were cannibalized, not from the plant at Togliatti, but from cars stolen from London and shipped home to Russia. The profit on a smuggled Lada was such that the smuggler could still afford to finance the purchase of his own Mercedes-Benz — or the theft of someone else's.

But the biggest market for the car smugglers, the apotheosis of the *Wabenzi* syndrome, where the new affluence made a Western luxury car a compulsory status symbol and a surefire economic barometer, was southern China.

Hong Kong, 1994

Inspector Jim Mather was frustrated. As a former bomb-disposal expert, he had defused bombs. As a former policeman, he had caught criminals. As a senior member of the Royal Hong Kong Police Anti-Smuggling Task Force, he was supposed to catch smugglers. The trouble was that these smugglers were unlike any others he had encountered before.

To begin with, they were stealing and smuggling cars, and not just any cars, but the latest luxury models. They were stealing those cars to order, right down to the color. They stole them from outside hotels, and from supposedly high-security parking lots here in Hong Kong. They drove them to remote loading docks, and hoisted them into customized speedboats at a deserted wharf near the Chinese border.

Within less than an hour of being stolen from the Hong Kong parking lot, the car would be across the narrow straits and out of the reach of Hong Kong law, in Guangzhou, mainland China.

These smugglers were ingenious as well as super-efficient. They dragged the cars under the waters of the South China Sea in giant waterproof neoprene bags. But the favorite workhorse of these smugglers was the *tai fei*, literally "big flyer." The big, hollowed-out Chinese mainland speedboat, powered by four or more Mercury engines, was capable of carrying a Mercedes 600 across the water at sixty miles per hour.

This was a fast, furious, and sometimes fatal trade, but the profits were phenomenal. China levied a 250-percent import tax on these cars if they were imported in sealed containers in the only available legal fashion to Guangzhou. The men who stole the cars in Hong Kong and drove the *tai fei* boats were paid no more than four hundred dollars a time; the smugglers behind the operation could earn up to fifteen thousand dollars each on a single run.

The Royal Hong Kong Police Anti-Smuggling Task Force patrol boat, a captured *tai fei*, passed beyond the neon lights of the dock and nosed its way out into the South China Sea. It was a windless, moonless night.

Mather's principal weapons were night-vision goggles and a nose for the smell of Chinese two-cycle engine fuel. His crew bristled with arms: bulletproof vests, revolvers at their waists, Heckler & Koch MP5 machine guns and CS gas guns slung over their shoulders. They were taking no chances; a dozen *tai fei* had been captured or sunk; four smugglers had been killed in a high-speed collision with a police boat; two members of the squad had died in similar incidents.

They called Mather "Scrap Man" because he drove a rusting Ford Cortina. His reply was that at least no one was going to steal it and smuggle it to China. He also had a British Leyland Mini-Metro, which was even less likely to be paid the compliment. On his office door were stenciled the black silhouettes of the *tai fei* he and his

206 ∽ CAR WARS

squad had caught. The previous year there had been nearly four thousand suspicious sightings in the shipping lanes. This year the number had dropped to around two thousand.

Mather liked to believe that he and his squad were having a deterrent effect on the Chinese car smugglers. But he had no illusions about the need to maintain vigilance. Besides, there was pressure from local businessmen and politicians whose cars had been stolen, and who had complained to Chris Patten, the governor of Hong Kong.

One thousand twenty-five Mercedes-Benzes worth over $30 million had been stolen in Hong Kong in the preceding year — an average of three a day. BMWs were next in popularity; nineteen had been smuggled in a single night. Close on their heels was the Lexus. The new Mazda appeared at authorized outlets in mainland China, in limited quantities and complete with prohibitive import duties; three days later it was being stolen to order in Hong Kong.

The new mainland Chinese *nuovorishi* — the *dahu* — preferred the Mercedes-Benz and the BMW, the Ferrari and the Lamborghini Diablo, but for some reason did not favor the British Jaguar. This was perhaps why it was enjoying a sudden burst of popularity in Hong Kong. Virtually all the stolen cars, meanwhile, ended up in China. There was no chance of recovery. To the acute discomfort of Inspector Mather, many were driven by policemen.

After two hours, the radio crackled. The captured *tai fei* and its Anti-Smuggling Task Force squad changed course and gathered speed. A Royal Navy ship had spotted something suspicious near Lantau Island. The squad checked their weapons, then turned on first the night-vision goggles, followed by the searchlight. A Chinese sampan swayed offshore; a Chinese man screwed up his eyes in the sudden glare. He was gathering wood washed up on the beach after the recent typhoon.

Two hours later, another call. This time the suspicious craft was a Hong Kong police launch. Another false alarm, another patrol. Another illusory glimpse of a black silhouette in the night. A thousand of the real things in a year. And, occasionally, one more black silhouette — the sign of a "score" — on Inspector Mather's office door.

Shanghai, Southern China, 1994

Six hundred miles northeast of Hong Kong and Guangzhou, up the Huanpu tributary of the Yangtze River, was the destination of many of the cargoes of the nocturnal *tai fei*. This was the rebirth of Shanghai and the industrial and commercial powerhouse of the new China.

Shanghai and its 13 million inhabitants were living through the biggest boom of any city in any country anywhere in the world.

The young Chinese paraded in the latest western fashions on Shanghai's bund along the waterfront. "They're opening anything you'd see on Rodeo Drive or Fifth Avenue," said a westerner who worked here. "They've got Gucci to Pucci — you name it."

In the parks, the old people in their faded Mao jackets struggled to comprehend the transformation that was taking place before their eyes: "Shanghai?" said one old man. "Everyone is making money. I don't know if that's good or bad . . ."

On the Long Wu Road, the main route through Shanghai's industrial district, an entire population seemed to be on the move. Bicycles, motorcycles, cars, trucks, and buses carried them past gleaming new offices and factories that seemed to have sprung up overnight.

This was the hand that jerked the string, that made the puppet move, that stole the Mercedes-Benzes, six hundred miles southwest of here in downtown Hong Kong, and sped across the narrow straits by night in shadowy *tai fei*.

In the nineteenth century, the Americans, Europeans and Japanese built the waterfront commercial enclave that made Shanghai the economic and commercial melting pot of Southern China and the Paris of the Orient. "In no city, west or east, have I ever had such an impression of dense, rank, richly clotted life," observed a western visitor in the 1920s.

Until the Communist revolution of 1949, this seething city moved two thirds of China's trade with the rest of the world. After the revolution, the Communists pointed to Shanghai as the embodiment of all that was corrupt and collusive with the capitalist West.

Westerners had to walk across a covered bridge at Lowu from British Hong Kong to the People's Republic of China. The Chinese government would not permit passenger trains to cross the border. "When you carried your luggage across the bridge, you entered another world," said one of the few westerners to do business with China at that time. "You disappeared into China. For a week or two, you heard nothing whatsoever about the outside world. Anything could have happened to you — and no one would have known. It was eerie — stepping over the brink of civilization."

China closed its doors — and its eyes — to the outside world. The focus of China became the words and deeds of Chairman Mao Tse-tung. In 1957, in his heyday as the great helmsman, Mao announced the "Great Leap Forward." He declared that China was capable of making twenty years' progress in a single day. In three years, Mao declared, China would catch up with America and Britain.

In 1958 the great helmsman sat behind the wheel of the first *Dong Feng* ("East Wind") sedan produced at the Number One Motor Vehicle Plant in Changchun: "At last," said Mao, "I'm sitting in a car made by Chinese."

By the beginning of the 1960s, Chinese housewives ran furnaces in their backyards to make pig iron. China was also making automobiles — but not for the ordinary Chinese. Mao feared freedom and mobility in the Chinese every bit as much as Khrushchev feared it in the Soviet peoples. The Chinese people were barred by law from private car ownership.

The East Wind was joined by the V8 "Red Flag" limousines for Chinese Communist Party bosses, the "Phoenix" sedan, and the ornate "Peace" six-seaters built at a new plant in Tientsin.

Mao's Great Leap Forward ended in economic ruin and political repression. The Cultural Revolution brought a return to the Chinese Year Zero. Shanghai, once the Paris of the Orient, became a gray, shuttered place where it was illegal even to keep a dog.

In the 1970s, America abandoned its policy of isolating China. Deng Xiaoping began to open China up to the West. In 1985 the peace accord between China and the Soviet Union lowered the temperature between the world's two largest countries and led to a change of direction for the People's Liberation Army.

The political climate in China remained capable of sudden and violent reaction of the kind that had sustained forty years of Communism. On June 4, 1989, the government struck back against students and workers who had occupied *Tiananmen Guangchang*, the "Square of the Gate of Heavenly Peace," in the center of Beijing. Troops opened fire and tanks advanced on unarmed civilians. The massacre was seen on television screens around the world.

Five years after the massacre in Tiananmen Square, the leaders of the student revolt were as powerless as the aging autocrats who had ordered their suppression, in the face of the tidal wave of free-market capitalism advancing across China.

Chinese Communism had begun in Shanghai in 1921, with the first recorded meeting of the Chinese Communist Party. One of the twelve delegates in attendance was the young Mao Tse-tung. In 1921 the young revolutionaries had met at a small house near Fuxing Park. In 1949 they had had their revolution. In 1994 the house was a museum. "Few people come here anymore," a Chinese told a western visitor to the museum. "This is dead history. If this was a broker-age house," he added, "they'd be lined up waiting to get in."

The ownership of the future of China had indeed broadened, as Mao had feared, until it no longer lay with the cliques in power in Beijing or on the other side of the barricades in Tiananmen Square. In the new China, the People's Liberation Army owned a multibillion-dollar trading empire of three thousand companies ranging from military equipment to property and nightclubs. In the new China, the future lay with the new capitalists and consumers, the young people parading the latest western fashions on the bund, and the teeming multitudes on the Long Wu road.

Germany. Italy. France. Europe. America. Japan. The Far East. China. The story of the evolution of the automobile industry is the story of company into country, nationalism into internationalism, multinationalism and supranationalism into global market.

In the last days of the twentieth century and in the early twenty-first, this market will be entered by one of the mightiest military and industrial powers the world has ever seen. The perceived threat, posed to America and Europe in the twentieth century, will be posed in the twenty-first century to America, Europe, and Japan by China.

China has all the elements on a unique and colossal scale: an authoritarian government dedicated to converting a collective econ-omy to capitalism; a city — Shanghai — that has been designated by the Chinese government as the trade and banking center, not only of Asia, but of the world, by the year 2010.

China has a domestic market of unparalleled magnitude. A workforce sufficiently cheap and an industrial infrastructure sufficiently developed to attract $50 million a day in foreign investment from around the world. A population of nearly a billion people hungry to become consumers, for whom the first and most potent vehicle of change is the automobile. "It doesn't matter whether a cat is black or white," said Deng Xiaoping, "as long as it catches mice."

Volkswagen Shanghai, anticipated by Major Hirst and established in 1982, was the first Western-Chinese automotive joint venture. After the massacre in Tiananmen Square, the western countries declared a trade boycott. The vacuum was quietly and swiftly filled by the Japanese. Suzuki signed an agreement with China North Industries to produce a small passenger car in Chongqing.

Chrysler, Audi, Daihatsu, and Peugeot-Citroën soon followed. General Motors formed a joint venture with Jinbei in Shenyang, northeast China, to make lightweight pickup trucks. Daimler-Benz planned a bus assembly plant in Shanghai. In the capital of central China's Henan Province, Nissan signed a contract to make one-ton trucks with the Zhengzou Light Truck Company.

Renault combined with the Sanjiang Space Group in Wuhan in Hubei Province to make the Renault Trafic minibus. In Nanjing, FIAT was already making six thousand minibuses a year.

Even Rover of Britain managed to join the end of the line. Rover had already disposed of two other casualties of the suicide of BLMC, the Maestro to Bulgaria and the Montego to India. In a deal reminiscent of Morris and the Hindustan ambassador, Rover sold the tools and production line for the Ital, the last car to carry the Morris badge at the British Leyland Motor Company, to the Chengdu Automotive Company.

The Federal Reserve Bank of Chicago produced a report, "Assessing Global Auto Trends," that examined the prospects for China and pointed to the example of South Korea. In 1980, South Korea had virtually no car industry. In 1993 it had produced 1,600,000 cars and exported 400,000. The bank identified what it believed was a key changing point. Vehicle sales in South Korea "exploded once per capita income reached approximately three and a half thousand dollars a year."

In 1994, annual income levels in southern China rose above two thousand dollars a head, and in the autumn of that year, Alex Trotman of Ford was to be seen in Beijing. Trotman outlined Ford's car and component production plans for China for the coming five years.

Trotman was followed soon afterwards by Jack Smith of General Motors. Smith visited Volkswagen in Shanghai as part of his plan to further General Motors' presence in the Chinese market. The Volkswagen plant spokesman welcomed "the head of the biggest car maker in the world to the biggest car factory in China."

Nobody mentioned "Superlopez."

The Chicago Reserve Bank's report predicted the registration of 40 million cars in China in the coming century, an eightfold increase on the present.

Shanghai, the industrial center of China, is the center of the Chinese automobile industry. This industry is backed by the state and driven by private enterprise. China is placed to join the Japanese in the markets of the Far East, which exceed in size the United States and the European Community put together.

There can be no turning back on the Long Wu road. What Chinese Agnellis and Toyodas are at this moment visiting their equivalents of Detroit's Rouge River? Where is the Chinese Wolfsburg? Who will be the Chinese Ford or Sloan?

Two clues have emerged to the new Chinese road.

In late 1994 the Chinese government called upon eighteen major car manufacturers to attend the Beijing Family Car Congress. The aim was to determine the way ahead for the country that had become the latest and biggest focus for automobile production, with potential sales of 2 million cars a year.

Also in late 1994, the Chinese government called upon one manufacturer in particular to submit designs for "a Chinese people's car."

The closer the year 2000 and the next millennium, the closer comes *ren qui-che* . . . the Chinese *Volkswagen*, or people's car.

In the twenty-first century, labor costs will rise in China as they did in South Korea, Japan, Germany, Britain and America. China, like all those countries, will have to establish bridgeheads overseas if it is to continue to fulfill the expectations of its population at home.

What war or oil shock will trigger its chance? How will it escape the specter of protectionism of governments in recession? Will the experience of Japan in the late twentieth century be the twenty-first-century experience of China?

There is a further, final dimension to the China syndrome. This dimension contains the deep-rooted fear that colors perceptions of Japan, on a far greater scale. It is the specter of the undead empire, of the unfinished business of history, which, just when history seemed to have come to an end, once more rears its apocalyptic head.

In 1957, the year Mao Tse-tung announced the "Great Leap Forward," the Cold War was becoming hotter and the world was closer than ever to nuclear holocaust. In the same year, a witness secretly recorded a conversation in the Kremlin. The conversation was between Mao Tse-tung and the Italian Communist leader Palmiro Togliatti, immortalized in the Russian car plant, Togliattigrad.

Togliatti asked Mao, "But what would become of Italy as a result of such a terrible war?"

Mao looked at him thoughtfully: "But who told you that Italy must survive?" he replied. "Three hundred million Chinese will be left, and that will be enough for the human race to continue."

It doesn't matter whether a cat is black or white . . .

Fifty years after the end of the Second World War, nationalistic terrors and personal fears still lurk near the surface of the new, infinitely sophisticated, posthistorical global marketplace. In such a marketplace, and given the existence of such terrors and fears, can a country such as China really succeed?

Epilogue

The People's Car — Yesterday, Today, and Forever

A S THE WORLD NEARS THE END of the twentieth century, the signs are that in the twenty-first century the focus of economic war and peace between nations will be the activities of the car companies in the global marketplace.

The political developments in Eastern Europe, the "downsizing" — now called "rightsizing" in some quarters — strategies of America and Japan and the rise of the Far East and China all point to activity on an ever greater scale. There will be fewer car workers but more cars, and the number of people will be greater than ever who crave the freedom and mobility of the automobile.

In this sense, never has a man-made product that still provides millions — and indirectly billions — of jobs posed a greater threat to the earth's atmosphere and humanity's well-being. But rumors of an Autogeddon fueled by the infernal combustion engine are as exaggerated as rumors of the death of the automobile.

The evidence suggests that if there is one thing worse than too many automobiles, it is not enough automobiles. The success of the *Mad Max* movies was based on popular empathy with the scenario in which the world — in this case Australia — is driven back to anarchy and barbarism by a shortage of gasoline.

Since the Second World War, the trend has been upward in terms of cars made and sold as a means to economic growth. In the western world, this growth is not necessarily a one-way street to environmental catastrophe. Among the mass of factors that may determine the future, one thing is certain: The shape and substance of the car will be increasingly dictated by legislation.

The Autopia of automobiles and freeways created by General Motors in Los Angeles has turned into a dystopia. The free spirit of L.A. is racked by traffic congestion and choked by smog. The ride that took forty-two minutes by electric train from San Bernardino to Los Angeles takes two and a half hours by automobile today.

The California Air Resources Board (CARB) has already decreed that, by 1998, 2 percent of all automobiles sold there must be "zero-emission vehicles." By 2003 this figure must be 10 percent.

California is the seventh-largest economy in the world. The initiative would have required the major car companies to put at least twenty thousand electric vehicles on Californian roads by 1998, rising to 100,000 within five years. But the insistence of the car companies that such a deadline is impossible has meant that even the mighty CARB has been forced to soften its stance in favor of a plan that would see automobile manufacturers introducing a smaller number of zero-emission vehicles — electric cars — by late 1996.

General Motors has spent an estimated $350 million developing the first mass-produced electric car for the American market, the EV1. The car was unveiled by Jack Smith at the Greater Los Angeles Auto Show in early 1996. Ford and Chrysler have promised to unveil electric cars by 1997. But while the California Air Resources Board currently still clings to the 10-percent requirement by 2003, industry insiders are skeptical about the scale of the commitment of GM and others to zero-emission vehicles, pointing to the relatively high cost, short range, and low numbers of the electric cars that will go on sale at twenty-five dealerships in California and Arizona in the fall of 1996. This is compared with the fact that the best-selling vehicle in America in 1995, a Ford pickup truck, sold to nearly 700,000 people, and the biggest story in the United States car market at the time the GM EV1 was unveiled in Los Angeles was the surge in sales of gas-guzzling four-wheel-drive "sport-utility" vehicles.

In Britain, the Royal Commission on Environmental Pollution called for measures to sharpen the lines between acceptability and unacceptability in the growth of the automobile.

In Germany, BMW is one car company that has tried to redefine the freedom and mobility given to the individual by the automobile by investing in car pools, better road-train links, and subsidized public transport in central Munich. The German government is considering banning all cars without catalytic converters by the year 2000.

Volkswagen's Asian president, Martin Posth, has said of China, "If car ownership reached the levels of the West, there would be an ecological disaster."

The economies of the Pacific, the Far East, and Asia far exceed those of California, Britain, and Germany. Apart from Singapore — an artificial, centrally governed city-state with a commitment to an expensive public transport program aimed at reducing car ownership — these countries show no signs of legislating against environmental catastrophe. Nor do the more volatile economies of Eastern Europe. East or West, however interactive and environmentally friendly the automobile, and however much is invested in public city transport, the driver will never surrender the miracle of freedom and mobility. The car, as tyrant and liberator, will continue to dominate.

North Yorkshire, England, 1994

"It was an operation run by the military government of the Allied Zone. I happened to be a soldier who was seconded to it." Major Hirst, a widower of seventy-eight, lives in a modest house in the North Yorkshire village near where he was born. He steadfastly refuses to succumb to legendary status. "I like to keep a low profile," he says, "except to put the record straight."

After the war, he returned to Britain to work in his family's optical instrument business:

> Some people here suggested I helped damage British industry by helping create a German success story.
>
> My reply is that we got the factory rolling again to help save the British taxpayer money. We began exporting cars for the same reason — to pay for the grain Germany was having to import.
>
> It was up to this country and our car makers to be as efficient as the Germans. I certainly don't believe I've been disloyal. Industry here had its chance and sadly there are cases of missed opportunities.

The head of Volkswagenwerk, Carl Hahn, told an audience at the London Institute of Directors that included Prime Minister John Major: "Without Major Ivan Hirst, my company wouldn't exist."

In Wolfsburg, the Volkswagenwerk company magazine dubbed him "The British Major who Saved Volkswagen."

Hirst drove a Beetle for over a decade. Like the company, he replaced it with a Golf GTi. Volkswagenwerk wanted to give him the new car. Hirst declined the offer. "It wouldn't have been right," he said. "That's not my way."

He did, however, accept the discount offered to Volkswagenwerk workers.

Fifty years earlier, a British army officer and the demoralized workforce of a German car company joined forces on the disputed soil of a shattered country. They accepted a challenge. In doing so, they changed the course of history.

Major Hirst could look back in the knowledge that he had had nothing to lose. On the West Coast of America, in 1994, the stakes were never higher for Volkswagen and J. C. Mays.

Southern California, USA, 1994

J. C. Mays was not a nervous person, but the stress was beginning to get to him. As chief designer at the Volkswagen of America Design Center in southern California, he had been charged with the task of reinterpreting the people's car for the 1990s. The results of his labors had already come under the scrutiny, several thousand miles away in Wolfsburg, of the new head of Volkswagenwerk, the grandson of Dr. Porsche.

In this case, J. C. Mays need not have worried; the pressure was a hundred times worse on Ferdinand Piech. Volkswagenwerk was being described as an industrial dinosaur that would die if it did not introduce leaner methods of production. Wolfsburg was on a four-day week. The "Superlopez" scandal was reverberating throughout America and Germany.

Piech and Lopez had not shown up in Detroit when Volkswagen unveiled the new car at the 1994 American Automobile Show.

The car caused a sensation. In striking similarity to the Beetle, the lemon-yellow car had a perfect three-curve profile and a level waistline. But beneath this miracle of geometry was a front-wheel-drive machine with a choice of three low-pollution, high-economy engines. The company said it "uniquely combined history and the future."

The car caused a similar sensation two months later at the Motor Show in Geneva. Even Hitler would have approved.

They called it "Concept 1." In late 1995, Piech confirmed that the car was to be built at the Volkswagen plant in Puebla, Mexico. The first main target markets for Concept 1 would be the United States, Canada, and South America.

An American in California may have saved Volkswagenwerk with his reinterpretation of a car launched over fifty years earlier. Several thousand miles away, in the Czech Republic, the company led for so long by the other designer who had worked on the original *Volkswagen* was in far deeper trouble.

Koprivnica, Czech Republic, 1994

During the 1970s and 1980s, Tatra had continued to make powerful sedans and trucks for the markets of Eastern Europe and Asia. Tatra also continued to play a role in the secret history of both sides of the Cold War. Forty years had passed since the T87s helped smuggle rocket scientists out of a divided Vienna. The Soviets, too, had exploited the independent, all-around suspension unique to Tatra truck chassis to pursue their own agenda.

In 1990, as the Soviet Union disintegrated, the Iraqi armies of Saddam Hussein invaded Kuwait. Chief among the terror weapons used by the Iraqis was the SCUD missile, which also brought fear to the night skies over Tel Aviv. The SCUDs were fired from a mobile truck launcher that proved elusive even to the Special Forces of the Americans and the British SAS. The vehicle seemed to possess the ability to disappear in even the most featureless and barren terrain.

The reason it was able to do so was the Tatra chassis. The low-slung, eight-wheeled, independent-suspension launcher had a digger mounted at the front, and simply dug itself back and forth into the ground until it was no longer visible.

The progressive disintegration of the Soviet Union did not diminish the interest of western intelligence agencies in Soviet and

Russian military technology. Rare western visitors to the Tatra plant at Koprivnica were often surprised to be contacted, on their return home, by strangers who invited them for a quiet drink in the interests of national security. These encounters were usually fruitless, as the westerner had seen nothing at Koprivnica that might be of interest to the Secret Intelligence Service.

One Briton, however, visited the Tatra plant during this time and impressed the design staff with his knowledge of the company. Browsing through some drawings, he came across what looked to him like a giant tank. The designers confirmed that this was exactly the case. The Soviet super-tank in question was based on a Tatra chassis, and was capable of 112 miles per hour. It could cross a ten-foot ditch without stopping. The strategic plan had been for it to burst across the frontier from East Germany into the West.

The Russians never displayed this astonishing weapon in their annual parades in Red Square. Their reasoning was that it was an offensive weapon, and all their weapons were, officially at least, defensive.

The Tatra designers were rather proud of it.

The British visitor was impressed too. He returned home. Shortly afterwards, his telephone rang and a stranger invited him for a quiet drink "in the interests of national security." Out of curiosity, he accepted. The men from MI6 knew all about his visit to Czechoslovakia, but apparently nothing of the Soviet super-tank. He told them about it and their faces looked ashen, he thought.

"Thank God," said one, "it was only a prototype."

"Yes," said the Briton, "but they told me they had built three hundred of them as well."

The collapse of the Soviet Union and Communism brought an end to Tatra's traditional markets in the Soviet Union and China. Tatra cars were produced in limited quantities, and had not been profitable for years. In 1990, Tatra still sold ten thousand trucks a year. In the first half of 1992, the company sold just eighty. The workforce had already fallen from sixteen thousand to eleven thousand; these, too, were sent home when unpaid component suppliers threatened to cease delivery.

The Czech government hired a team from Detroit to help the Czech management put Tatra back in the black. Gerald Greenwald was a former vice chairman of Chrysler. Greenwald had secured the government loan in 1979 that saved the American company from bankruptcy. The consortium of Greenwald and his colleagues David Shelby and Jack Rutherford was rumored to be paid a combined salary of $120,000 a month. "We have all dealt with Tatra during our careers," said Rutherford. "We can sell these rough, tough suckers anywhere in the world."

The Czech prime minister welcomed the American rescue team. The Czech minister for industry continued to exhort his cabinet colleagues to exchange their Mercedes-Benzes and BMWs for Tatra limousines. By the middle of 1994, Tatra had lost more of its markets in Russia and China to foreign competitors. The company produced just 993 trucks. A month later, Greenwald had left to become president of United Airlines.

Not many people came to the Tatra Museum at Koprivnica at the best of times. These were not the best of times. The museum was closed for two years, some said — maybe indefinitely, said others.

Yet here it still was, in the corner of the room where it had stood for over sixty years — a time machine.

Rear-engined, air-cooled, and unmistakably shaped like a beetle — this was the car in the drawing Hans Ledwinka had handed to Hitler in the Reichsführer's private apartments, more than half a century earlier, and a world away; this was the prototype designed and built by Ledwinka at least two years *before* the prototype built by Dr. Porsche, which Hitler had launched at the huge rally hung with Nazi banners as the Strength-Through-Joy car.

If this was the original *Volkswagen*, did Ledwinka really invent the people's car, only to be robbed of the credit by history and one man in particular? Did Dr. Porsche commit the biggest car theft of all time?

Many thought so.

In the 1990s, the biggest changes will happen in the car companies and not the cars. The car companies have been forced to evolve from national to international, international to multinational, multinational to global players in the global market.

In this global market, the individual company and nation have been superseded by interdependent interests and many-layered blocs of capital. What is sovereignty worth in such a market? Such a world is the ultimate in statelessness for the millions of people who live and work within its evanescent boundaries.

It is a preeminent contemporary irony that the feeling of powerlessness and lack of identity on the part of the individual can only be alleviated for many by getting behind the wheel of a car — produced by the industry that has brought about the market that has induced this feeling of statelessness in the first place.

The end of history in its traditional form, of migration of labor and national and international frontiers, and the beginning of the global market, have brought both peace and the ultimate arena for conflict. Tactical alliances and temporary cease-fires, in the form of mergers and joint ventures, are correspondingly increasing beneath its homogenized surface.

The fruits of these alliances will be manifested in world cars: the Ford Contour/Mondeo, made in the U.S.A. and Belgium; the GM Catera, made in the U.S.A. and Germany; the FIAT 178, to be made in Argentina, Brazil, India, Turkey, Morocco, and South Africa; the SEAT Cordoba, to be made in Spain; the Skoda Felicia, to be made in China, and the IPTN/Rover Maleo, subsequently replaced by a bid from an Australian consortium, to be made in Jakarta, Indonesia; and in the growing "rebadging" of otherwise indistinguishable cars for the purpose of selling them in the same market. In this respect, the map of the world in the form of cars parked down a street will become correspondingly more uniform and featureless to match this terrain.

Looking back from the twenty-first century, it may be possible to identify the key points at which the global players succeeded and failed to make their mark in the global market. By the last decade of the twentieth century, there are no signs that any one player can dominate to the exclusion of the others.

Fifty years after the end of the Second World War, the world is a far safer and far less certain place. In such uncertain times there is virtue in the simple truth. The latest to grasp this simple truth are the Chinese.

The Chinese have called upon one company in particular to submit designs for a Chinese "people's car." The project is code-named C88, and the company is Porsche, founded by the man most commonly associated with the original people's car.

The simple truth to be grasped in uncertain times is that only the durable people's car rules.

This was true of Hitler's Germany, and it is true of the global market of the 1990s. The message is simple, and the moral is clear. Not for nothing did the president of Nissan say to an Englishman that his favorite car — whoever invented it — was the Volkswagen.

Appendix 1

A Selective A–Z of the World's Car Companies

Alfa Romeo, Aston Martin, Astra, Audi, AvtoVAZ, Bentley, BMW, China Motor (Taiwan), Chinese Automobile (Taiwan), Ching Chung Motor (Taiwan), Chrysler, Dacia, Daewoo, DAF, Daihatsu, Ferrari, FIAT, Ford, FSO, GAZ, General Motors, Hindustan Motors, Honda, Hyundai, Indomobil, Isuzu, Jaguar, Jeep, Kia, Kuozui Motors (Taiwan), Lamborghini, Lancia, Mahindra & Mahindra, MAN Nutzfahrzeuge, Maruti, Maserati, Mazda, Mekong Corporation, Mercedes-Benz, Mitsubishi Motors, Nissan, Opel-Vauxhall, Peugeot-Citroën, Porsche, Premier Automobiles, Prince Motor (Taiwan), Proton, Renault, Rolls-Royce, Rover, Saab-Scania, Samsung, San Fu Motors (Taiwan), San Yang Industry (Taiwan), Sbarro, SEAT, Skoda, Ssang Yong, Subaru, Suzuki, Tatra, Toyota, UMW Holdings, United Australia Automotive Industries, Vietnam Motors, Volkswagenwerk, Volvo, Yue Loong Motor (Taiwan), ZAZ, Zengzhou Light Truck Factory, Zil.

Many of the above companies are subsidiaries of, or are controlled by, others: for example, Volkswagenwerk, Audi, SEAT, and Skoda are controlled by Volkswagen; Alfa Romeo, Ferrari, and Lancia are controlled by FIAT; Jaguar and Aston Martin are owned by Ford; Rover is controlled by BMW.

Appendix 2

A Selective A–Z of Overseas Operations and Automobile Alliances

Auto-Alliance (Thailand), Beijing-Jeep Company, Birla-GM, Changan-Suzuki Automobile Company, Daewoo (Pakistan), Daewoo (Philippines), Daihatsu in China, FAW-Volkswagen, Ford of Europe, Ford in China, Ford Lio Ho Motor (Taiwan), Ford of Australia, General Motors Europe, General Motors-FSO (Poland), General Motors Turkiye, Guangzhou-Peugeot, Honda (France), Honda (Italy), Honda (U.K.), Honda (U.S.A.), Honda Atlas Cars, Honda Cars Philippines, Isuzu Motor (Thailand), Italcar Philipinas, Jiangling-Isuzu Motors, Jinbei-GM Automotive Company, MMC Sittipol (Thailand), Mazda (China), Mazda (Philippines), Mitsubishi Motors Australia, Nedcar, Nissan Motor Iberica, Nissan (Australia), Nissan (U.K.), Nissan (U.S.A.), Otosan Otomobile Sanaye (Turkey), Oyak-Renault (Turkey), Pak Suzuki Motor, Peugeot-Dacia (Romania), Philippine Mini Corporation, Pilipinas Nissan, SAW-Citroën, Shanghai-Volkswagen, Siam Automotive Industry, Suzuki Motor España, Tofas (Turkey), Toyota (China), Toyota (Pakistan), Toyota (Turkey), Toyota Motor Thailand, Toyota Motors Philippines Corporation, Toyota (U.K.), Toyota (U.S.A.), Volkswagen (Mexico).

In the twenty-first century, Appendix 2 will grow longer and Appendix 1 will grow shorter.

Notes

Prologue.

D. Yergin, *The Prize*, p. 211.

Chapter 1. Hitler: The Dictator in the Driver's Seat

Interviews with Major Ivan Hirst, Mark Berry, and John Henry, England, 1994 and 1995; *New York Times*, 16 February 1936; P. Wagner, *VW Beetle*, 8–25; D. Marsh, *The Germans: Rich, Bothered and Divided*, 210–12; I. Margolius and J. Henry, *Tatra: The Legacy of Hans Ledwinka*; H. Monnich, *The BMW Story: A Company in its Time*, 292–346; D. Yergin, *The Prize*, 322–23; A. Fisher, "The Beetle Business," *Financial Times*, 20–21 August 1988; J. Woodcock, "Briton's Driving Force Made Beetle a World-Beater," *Daily Mail*, 2 May 1992; K. Eason, "Army Officer who Launched a Legend," *The Times*, 11 July 1992; S. Wood and G. Green, "The Beetle at 50," *Sunday Times*, 22 February 1984; Dr. M. Burleigh, "Beetles in Brown Shirts?" *History Today*, November 1992 and March 1993; H. Mommsen, "Volkswagen and the Nazis — Questions of Guilt," *History Today*, March 1993; G. Borgeson, *Automobile Quarterly*, September 1980; H. R. Trevor-Roper, *The Last Days of Hitler*, 1971.

Chapter 2. Japan: Samurai into Sedans

M. Schaller, *The American Occupation of Japan: The Origins of the Cold War in Asia*, 25–51, 289; M. Walker, *The Cold War*, 78–80; P. Kennedy, *The Rise and Fall of the Great Powers*, 417; T. Jackson, *Turning Japanese: The Fight for Industrial Control of the New Europe*, 78–82; R. Minami, *The Economic Development of China*; E. Dymock, "Cars that Got the Japanese Going," *Sunday Times*, 31 October 1993; P. Dourado, *Independent on Sunday*, 25 April 1993; P. Popham, "Turning Japanese," *Independent Magazine*, 12 September 1993.

Chapter 3. Agnelli, FIAT, and the *Cinquecento*

P. Ginsborg, *A History of Contemporary Italy: Society and Politics 1943–1988*; FIAT: The Big Wheel in Italy's Traffic, *Newsweek*, 20 January 1964; A. Sampson, "The Car Kingdoms," *Observer*, 19 March 1967; "A Society Transformed by Industry," *Time*, 17 January 1969; J. Glancey, "Benvenuto Cinquecento!", *Independent on Sunday*, 21 March 1993.

Chapter 4. Les Chemins de la Liberté et les Deux Chevaux

P. Betts, "Demise of 2CV is a Nostalgic Milestone for French Car Makers," *The Times*, 1 March 1988; J. Champkin, "So Ugly and So Loved!" *Daily Mail*, 14 March 1988; J. Glancey, "Adieu to an Old and Loved French Friend," *Independent*, 16 May 1990.

Chapter 5. A Very British People's Car

Interviews with Jo Burge and Mark Berry, England, 1994; L. Collins and D. Lapierre, *Freedom at Midnight*; M. Carter, "Thirty Years On," *Thoroughbred and Classic Cars*, July 1992; D. Selby, "The Empire Strikes Back," *Your Classic*, September 1992; R. Lustig, "The Car You Love to Hate," *Observer Magazine*, 15 October 1978; C. Dunne, "Magic of the Mighty Minor," *Sun*, 23 April 1981; *Times* (London), 2 August 1982; E. Dymock, "Mini Deserves a New Lease on Life," *Sunday Times*, 12 December 1993; B. Sewell, *Evening Standard*, 29 April 1994; D. Bowen, "Mini Fans Fear the End of the Road," *Independent on Sunday*, 28 August 1994; N. Lyndon, "Over the hill at 35," *Sunday Telegraph*, 28 August 1994; G. Green, *Sunday Times*, 14 October 1984; J. Butterfield, *Daily Express London Motor Show Reports* 1960–64.

Chapter 6. An American in Europe

Sir Terence Beckett in M. Adeney, *The Motor Makers*; C. Levinson, *Vodka Cola*, 212–14; D. Marsh, *The Germans: Rich, Bothered and Divided*, 210–11; L. Iacocca, *Iacocca*; John Barber in *Top Gear*, April 1994; Alex Trotman in *Independent on Sunday*, 24 October 1993.

Chapter 7. *Il Boom*: Italy and Agnelli on the *Autostrada*

J. Glancey, "Benvenuto Cinquecento!", *Independent on Sunday*, 21 March 1993; "A Society Transformed by Industry," *Time*, 17 January 1969; "FIAT: The Big Wheel in Italy's Traffic," *Newsweek*, 20 January 1964; A. Sampson, "The Car Kingdoms," *Observer*, 19 March 1967; C. Levinson, *Vodka Cola*; McGraw-Hill, *Encyclopaedia of Russia and the Soviet Union*, 51, 296; B. Parrott, ed., *Trade, Technology and Soviet-American Relations*, 81–113.

Chapter 8. De Gaulle and "The Goddess"

S. Baker, *Observer Magazine*, 13 December 1992; *Daily Express London Motor Show Reports*, 1960–63; C. Lelouch, *Un Homme et une femme*, 1966; F. Zinneman, *The Day of the Jackal*, 1973; T. Jackson, *Turning Japanese: The Fight for Industrial Control of the New Europe*; A. Horne, *A Savage War of Peace*, 1977.

Chapter 9. Mercedes-Benz and the Economic Miracle

C. Mathews, "Mercedes Magic," *Reader's Digest*, January 1986; D. Marsh, *The Germans: Rich, Bothered and Divided*, 210–11, 345; *Daily Express London Motor Show Reports*, 1960–64.

Chapter 10. BMW and the Pride of Bavaria

H. Monnich, *The BMW Story: A Company in Its Time*; D. Bowen, "Shocked into Excellence," *Independent on Sunday*, 28 June 1992; J. Glancey, "The Essential BMW," *Independent on Sunday*, 8 July 1990.

Chapter 11. Dr. Porsche and Other People's Cars

Interviews with Major Ivan Hirst, Mark Berry, and John Henry, England, 1994 and 1995; I. Margolius and J. Henry, *Tatra: The Legacy of Hans Ledwinka*; H. Mommsen, "Volkswagen and the Nazis — Questions of Guilt," *History Today*, March 1993; Dr. M. Burleigh, "Beetles in Brown Shirts?", *History Today*, November 1992 and March 1993; P. Wager, *VW Beetle*; H. Monnich, *The BMW Story: A Company in Its Time*, 407; S. Ward, *Independent*, 4 June 1988; E. Dymock, *Sunday Times*, 17 June 1990; D. Marsh, *The Germans: Rich, Bothered and Divided*, 210–12, 345; Brock Yates in *Car and Driver* magazine, quoted in R. Banham, *Los Angeles: The Architecture of Four Ecologies*; T. Paterson, "End Credits Roll on Film Star Trabi," *European*, 15 March 1991; T. Lewin, *Independent on Sunday*, 17 February 1991.

Chapter 12. The Men in Motown

D. Landes, *The Unbound Prometheus: Technological Change and Industrial Development in Western Europe from 1750 to the Present*; A. Jay, *Corporation Man*; F. Gladstone, *Business*, July 1986; M. Walker, *The Cold War*; C. Levinson, *Vodka Cola*, 212–14; A. Sampson, *The Seven Sisters: The Great Oil Companies and the World They Made*, 168–9; D. Yergin, *The Prize*; P. Kennedy, *The Rise and Fall of the Great Powers*.

Chapter 13. Auto da Fé: Snapshots from the Suicide of the British Auto Industry

Interviews with Charles Ware and Lady Turnbull, England, 1994 and 1995; J. Wood, *Independent*, 24 December 1992; "Leading Figure in Turbulent Car Industry," *Financial Times*, 24 December 1992; R. Feast, *Automotive International*, October 1994; *Independent*, 2 November 1993; C. Dunne, "Magic of the Mighty Minor," *Sun*, 23 April 1981; R. Lustig, "The Car You Love to

Hate," *Observer Magazine*, 15 October 1978; T. Rocca, "The End of the Morris Minor," *Daily Mail*, 18 April 1970; M. Edwardes, *Back from the Brink*; H. Young, *One of Us*, 361; Tony Benn, Sir Michael Edwardes, John Barber, and Lord Stokes in *Top Gear*, April 1994.

Chapter 14. The Last of the Line Leaves Wolfsburg

Interviews with Major Ivan Hirst, England, 1994; G. Green, "The Beetle at 50," *Sunday Times*, 22 February 1984; C. Burnham, "Beetle-Mania," *Sunday Express Magazine*, 30 November 1986; L. Doucet, "The World's Best-Loved Bug Bites the Dust," *Guardian*, 24 October 1987; A. Fisher, "The Beetle Business," *Financial Times*, 20–21 August 1988; C. Wright, "You and Your Golf," *Daily Star*, 21 July 1989; J. Woodcock, "Briton's Driving Force Made Beetle a World-Beater," *Daily Mail*, 2 May 1992; K. Eason, "Army Officer Who Launched a Legend," *The Times*, 11 July 1992; R. Tyler, *You* magazine, 7 February 1993; P. Wager, *VW Beetle*.

Chapter 15. Collision: The Autocrat and the Commissars

"A Society Transformed by Industry," *Time*, 19 January 1969; G. Hodgson, "Living with the Left in FIAT City," *Sunday Times*, 20 July 1977; F. Rocco, "FIAT Loses Its Grip in the Great European Car Race," *Independent on Sunday*, 23 September 1990; P. Ginsborg, *A History of Contemporary Italy*; J. Haycraft, *Italian Labyrinth*.

Chapter 16. The Coming of Age of the Samurai Sedan

Daily Express London Motor Show Report, 1960; P. Kennedy, *The Rise and Fall of the Great Powers*, 417; M. Walker, *The Cold War*, 239; M. Schaller, *American Occupation of Japan: The Origins of the Cold War in Asia*, 296–98.

Chapter 17. Brand Loyalty and the Bedouin: Mercedes-Benz and General Motors in the Middle East

Author's travels in the Arabian Peninsula; D. Holden and R. Johns, *The House of Saud*, 139–40; L. Mosley, *Power Play: The Tumultuous World of Middle East Oil 1890–1973*; M. Field, *The Merchants: The Big Business Families of Arabia*, 122–32, 150–54.

Chapter 18. Marx, Mao and Motoring: Internal Combustion at Renault and Peugeot

Dodd, K. G., "Experiment at Billancourt," *Guardian*, 27 February 1964; D. Housego, "Why Peugeot's Jobs Mean So Much to So Many," *Financial*

Times, 21 December 1983; P. Betts, "Behind the Battle of Poissy," *Financial Times*, 9 January 1984; P. Betts, "Demise of 2CV Is a Nostalgic Milestone for French Car Makers," *The Times*, 1 March 1988; J. Glancey, "Adieu to an Old and Loved French Friend," *Independent*, 16 May 1990; J. Nundy, "Renault Strikes Back as Militant Car Plant Shuts Down for Good," *Independent*, 1 April 1992; J. Eisenhammer, "Racing Beyond the Famous Names," *Independent on Sunday*, 17 October 1993; J. Nundy, "French State to Hang On to Majority of Renault," *Independent*, 12 September 1994; "Renault Wanted," *Independent*, 5 November 1994.

Chapter 19. Toyota, Mazda, Datsun, and the Drive Upmarket

J. Glancey, "The Essential BMW," *Independent on Sunday*, 8 July 1990; H. Monnich, *The BMW Story: A Company in Its Time*, 408–9; Mazda and Nissan corporate publications.

Chapter 20. Inside Castle Volvo: PG, ET, and the Company that Outgrew a Country

D. Bowen, *Independent*, 26 August 1993; A. Lorenz, *Sunday Times*, 12 September 1993; P. Harrison, *Independent*, 7 September 1993; R. Hotten and D. Bowen, *Independent*, 6 September 1993; M. Brasier, *Daily Telegraph*, 7 September 1993; P. Frater, *Sunday Times*, 5 December 1993; M. Harrison, *Independent*, 3 December 1993; D. Morrison, *Sunday Telegraph*, 11 June 1995.

Chapter 21. Radial Chic: The Coming of Age of Four-Wheel Drive

J. Taylor, *Thoroughbred & Classic Cars*, July 1992; M. Kemp, *Daily Mail*, 23 April 1993; D. Bowen, *Independent on Sunday*, 2 October 1994; A. Wilman, "Who Killed the British Car Industry?", *Top Gear*, April 1994; various trade advertising.

Chapter 22. "How Much of Your Garden Are You Going to Give to the Japanese?": Roger Smith and the New Ghost Towns of the Midwest

T. Dodsworth, "How Japan's Car Makers Have 'Gone Native,'" *Financial Times*, 29 November 1984; F. Gladstone, *Business*, July 1986; M. Hosenball, "General Motors' Private Troubles," *Sunday Times*, 7 December 1986; A. Johnson, "GM Stuck in the Slow Lane," *Business*, April 1989; J. Confino, "Why the Motown Giant is Shaking," *Daily Telegraph*, 20 December

1991; T. Jackson, *Turning Japanese: The Fight for Industrial Control of the New Europe.*

Chapter 23. Fallen by the Roadside: Trabant and Zil in a Disintegrating Europe

J. Kampfner, "A Family that Still Feels Second Class," *Sunday Telegraph*, 6 November 1994; *Go, Trabi, Go*; T. Lewin, *Independent on Sunday*, 17 February 1991; T. Paterson, "End Credits Roll on Film Star Trabi," *European*, 15 March 1991; "Car-Eating Bacteria Feed on the Trabant," *Observer*, 28 April 1991; J. Lloyd, "Zil Heads for the Capitalist Road," *Financial Times*, 4 March 1993; J. Steele, *Eternal Russia*; H. Monnich, *The BMW Story: A Company in Its Time*; *Daily Express London Motor Show Report 1960*; BMW 1993 Company Report; T. Jackson, "Turning Japanese: The Fight for Industrial Control of the New Europe," *Automotive International*, October 1994.

Chapter 24. Contenders: Malaysia and South Korea

Interviews with Lady Turnbull, England, 1994 and 1995; F. Bartu, *The Ugly Japanese: Nippon's Economic Empire in Asia*, 68–78; K. Cooke, *Financial Times*, 3 February 1993 and 31 August 1993; R. Guest, *Sunday Telegraph*, 27 November 1994; *Independent*, 2 November 1993; F. Feast, *Automotive International*, October 1994; H. A. Fredericks and A. Chambers, *Bricklin.*

Chapter 25. "This Is an Economic Pearl Harbor": General Motors and the Downsizing of Detroit

F. Gladstone, *Business*, July 1986; J. Confino, "Why the Motown Giant Is Shaking," *Daily Telegraph*, 20 December 1991; A. Taylor, "GM's $11,000,000,000 Turnaround," *Fortune*, 17 October 1994; T. Jackson, *Turning Japanese: The Fight for Industrial Control of the New Europe*; L. Iacocca, *Iacocca*; M. Kellner, *Collision*; P. Ingrassia and J. White, *Comeback: The Fall and Rise of the American Automobile Industry.*

Chapter 26. Supermodels and "Superlopez": The Catwalk and the Covert Car Wars

Interview with Hans-Georg and Christa Lehmann, Germany, 1995: S. Wood, *Sunday Times*, 12 September 1982; M. Gwyther, *Independent on Sunday*, 11 April 1993; J. Eisenhammer, *Independent*, various reports; D. Gow, "The Big Wheels of Scandal," *Guardian*, 3 September 1993; C. Parkes, *Financial Times*, various reports; P. Bruce, "Local Boy Can Do No Wrong," *Financial*

Times, 21–22 August 1993; I. Jenkins, "The Man Who Drove Too Close to the Edge," *Sunday Times*, 22 August 1993.

Chapter 27. How the Rise of Japan and the Fall of the Wall Brought the Germans to South Carolina

Berndt Pischetsrieder in *BMW Company Report, 1993*; Eberhard von Kuenheim in N. Faith, "Nothing Could be Finer Than a Plant in Carolina," *Independent on Sunday*, 9 May 1993; Edzard Reuter in D. Marsh, *The Germans: Rich, Bothered and Divided*; Peter Bier in H. Walker, "Carolina Plant Crucial to BMW's Global Strategy," *Automotive International*, September 1994; T. Allen-Mills, "Nightmare Engulfs Germany's Good Life," *Sunday Times*, 29 August 1993; M. Jackson, "Mercedes Confronts Japan on Foreign Soil," *Financial Times*, 7 April 1993; T. Jackson, *Turning Japanese: The Fight for Industrial Control of the New Europe*.

Chapter 28. Send for "Motorhead": The Empire Strikes Back

Jac Nasser in J. Randall, *Sunday Times*, 25 April 1993; A. Lorenz, *Sunday Times*, 9 May, 31 October 1993; Alex Trotman in P. Reeves, *Independent on Sunday*, 24 October 1993; A. Lorenz, *Sunday Times*, 31 October 1993; D. Bowen, *Independent on Sunday*, 24 April 1994; *Business Week*, 3 April 1995.

Chapter 29. Capitalist Roads: The Wild East and the New Frontiers

Interviews with Jo Burge, Mark Berry, Keith Arundale, Alice Louis, and Jonathan Glancey, England, 1994; D. Selby, "The Empire Strikes Back," *Your Classic*, September 1992; M. Carter, "Thirty Years On," *Thoroughbred & Classic Cars*, July 1992; Hindustan Motors brochures; S. Wagstyl, "GM in $100 Million India Joint Venture," *Financial Times*, 12 May 1994; C. Urquhart, "Money Opens the Road to Bombay," *Independent on Sunday*, 16 September 1994; A. Roy, *Daily Telegraph*, 15 March 1994; Price Waterhouse, *Doing Business in the Russian Federation*; *Price Waterhouse Services in Russia*; *Price Waterhouse Services in Kazakhstan*; F. Bartu, *The Ugly Japanese: Nippon's Economic Empire in Asia*, 269; J. Eisenhammer, "Mercedes Thinks Time is Right for Swatch Car," *Independent*, 23 February 1994; J. Glancey, *Independent*, 10 March 1994; G. Green, *Independent*, 19 March 1994; L. Boulton, "Lada Car Becomes Victim of Success," *Financial Times*, 25 November 1993; J. Lloyd, "Zil Heads for the Capitalist Road," *Financial Times*, 4 March 1993; J. Lloyd, "Moskvich Car Plant Closes,"

Financial Times, 30 January 1993; B. Parrott, ed., *Trade, Technology and Soviet-American Relations*; S. Sanders, *Living off the West*, 87; J. Hosking, *A History of the Soviet Union*, 366; A. Higgins, "Kremlin's Limo-maker on Road to Oblivion," *Independent*, 14 April 1994; A. Higgins, "Giant Car Firm Steers Chaotic Sell-off Course," *Independent*, 17 March 1994.

Chapter 30. Lawless Roads: The Illegal Traffic in Western Cars to Eastern Europe and the Far East

Interviews with Detective Constable Kieron Freeburn, of the Metropolitan Police Stolen Car Investigation Wing, and Terry Kirby, England, 1994; C. Parkes and K. Done, *Financial Times*, 17 September 1993; M. Campbell, "Russia's Rich Roll Out the Rolls for a Spin in Plush New Suburbia," *Sunday Times*, 22 August 1993; H. Davies, "Russian Mobs Have American Dream in Sight," *Sunday Telegraph*, 20 November 1994; *Independent*, 23 June 1994; C. Seton, *Sunday Telegraph*, 29 September 1993; T. Kirby, "Seven Questioned over £12-Million Luxury Car Thefts," *Independent*, 3 March 1993; J. Bethell, "Mercedes Targeted in £45-Million Car Racket," *Sunday Times*, 18 April 1993; A. Philps, "Bumpy Ride for Russians as Anarchy Rules Roads," *Sunday Telegraph*, 20 March 1994; H. Womack, *Independent on Sunday*, 12 June 1994; Interviews with Inspector Jim Mather, Royal Hong Kong Police Anti-Smuggling Task Force, Hong Kong, 1995; J. Hart, "Wild Car Chase on the China Sea," *Independent on Sunday*, 17 April 1994; T. Poole, *Independent*, 24 May 1993; C. Parkes, "Daimler-Benz Set for China Expansion," *Financial Times*, 8 March 1993; L. Curry, *Financial Times*, 5 June 1993; W. S. Ellis, "Shanghai: Where China's Past and Future Meet," *National Geographic*, March 1994; B. Jamieson, "Shanghai Marches on 21st Century," *Sunday Telegraph*, 23 October 1994; R. Tyerman, "Swords Become Ploughshares as China's Army Muscles In," *Sunday Telegraph*, 25 September 1994; *Sunday Telegraph*, 13 November 1994; Mao Tse-tung and Palmiro Togliatti, quoted in Walker, *The Cold War*, 126; *Car* Magazine, January 1995.

Epilogue. The People's Car — Yesterday, Today and Forever

Interviews with Major Ivan Hirst, Mark Berry, and John Henry in England, 1994 and 1995; *BMW Company Report*, 1993; J. Woodcock, *Daily Mail*, 2 May 1992; *Detroit and Geneva Motor Show Reports*; I. Margolius and J. Henry, *Tatra: The Legacy of Hans Ledwinka*; *Financial Times*, 22 May 1993; *Automotive International*, September 1994; Takashi Ishihara, in *Sunday Times*, 14 October 1984; G. Borgeson, *Automobile Quarterly*, September 1980.

Select Bibliography

Books

Adeney, Martin. *The Motor Makers: The Turbulent History of Britain's Car Industry*. London: Collins, 1988.

Banham, Rayner. *Los Angeles: The Architecture of Four Ecologies*. New York: Harper and Row, 1971.

Bartu, Friedmann. *The Ugly Japanese: Nippon's Economic Empire in Asia*. Singapore and New York: Longman, 1992.

Collins, Larry, and Dominique Lapierre. *Freedom at Midnight*. New York: Simon and Schuster, 1975.

Dwyer, Denis, ed. *China: The Next Decades*. Harlow, U.K.: Longman, 1994.

Elegant, Robert. *Pacific Destiny: Inside Asia Today*. New York: Crown, 1990.

Emmott, Bill. *Japan's Global Reach: The Influences, Strategies and Weaknesses of Japan's Multinational Companies*. London: Century, 1992.

Field, Michael. *One Hundred Million Dollars a Day*. London: Sidgwick and Jackson, 1975.

———. *The Merchants: The Big Business Families of Arabia*. London: J. Murray, 1984.

Fredericks, H. A., and Alan Chambers. *Bricklin*. Fredericton, New Brunswick: Brunswick Press, 1977.

Ginsborg, Paul. *A History of Contemporary Italy: Society and Politics 1943–1988*. London: Penguin, 1990.

Haycraft, John. *Italian Labyrinth*. London: Secker and Warburg, 1985.

Holden, David, and Richard Johns. *The House of Saud: The Rise and Rule of the Most Powerful Dynasty in the Arab World*. New York: Holt, Rinehart, and Winston, 1982.

Horne, Alistair. *A Savage War of Peace: Algeria, 1954–1962*. New York: Penguin, 1987.

Hosking, Geoffrey. *The First Socialist Society: A History of the Soviet Union from Within*. Cambridge: Harvard University Press, 1993.

Iacocca, Lee, with William Novak. *Iacocca: An Autobiography*. New York: Bantam, 1984.

Ingrassia, Paul J., and Joseph B. White. *Comeback: The Fall and Rise of the American Automobile Industry*. New York: Simon and Schuster, 1994.

Jackson, Tim. *The Next Battleground: Japan, America, and the New European Market*. Boston: Houghton Mifflin, 1993.

Jay, Antony. *Corporation Man*. London: Jonathan Cape, 1972.

Kennedy, Paul. *The Rise and Fall of the Great Powers: Economic Change and Military Conflict from 1500 to 2000*. New York: Random House, 1987.

Khrushchev, Nikita. *Khrushchev Remembers*. Translated and Edited by Strobe Talbott. Boston: Little, Brown, 1970.

Landes, David S. *The Unbound Prometheus: Technological Change and Industrial Development in Western Europe from 1750 to the Present*. London: Cambridge University Press, 1969.

Levinson, Charles. *Vodka Cola*. London and New York: Gordon and Cremonesi, 1978.

Margolius, Ivan, and John Henry. *Tatra: The Legacy of Hans Ledwinka*. London: SAF Ltd., 1990.

Marsh, David. *The Germans: Rich, Bothered and Divided*. London: Century, 1989.

Minami, Ryoshin. *The Economic Development of China: A Comparison with the Japanese Experience*. Translated by Wenran Jiang and Tanya Jiang with assistance from David Merriman. New York: St. Martin's Press, 1994.

McGraw-Hill Encyclopedia of Russia and the Soviet Union. New York: McGraw-Hill, 1961.

Monnich, Horst. *The BMW Story: A Company in Its Time*. London: Sidgwick and Jackson, 1991.

Mosley, Leonard. *Power Play: The Tumultuous World of Middle Eastern Oil 1890–1973*. London: Weidenfeld and Nicolson, 1973.

Oppenheim, Philip. *Trade Wars: Japan Versus the West*. London: Weidenfeld and Nicolson, 1992.

Parrott, Bruce, ed. *Trade, Technology, and Soviet-American Relations*. Bloomington: Indiana University Press, 1985.

Sampson, Anthony. *The Seven Sisters: The Great Oil Companies and the World They Shaped*. New York: Viking, 1975.

Sanders, Sol. *Living Off the West: Gorbachev's Secret Agenda and Why It Will Fail*. Lanham, MD: Madison, 1990.

Schaller, Michael. *The American Occupation of Japan: The Origins of the Cold War in Asia*. New York: Oxford University Press, 1985.

Steele, Jonathan. *Eternal Russia: Yeltsin, Gorbachev, and the Mirage of Democracy*. London: Faber, 1994.

Trevor-Roper, H. R. *The Last Days of Hitler*. New York: Macmillan, 1947.

Wager, Paul. *VW Beetle*. London: Magna Books, 1994.

Walker, Martin. *The Cold War: A History*. New York: Henry Holt, 1994.

Womack, James P., Daniel T. Jones, and Daniel Roos. *The Machine that Changed the World*. New York: Rawson Associates, 1990.

Yergin, Daniel. *The Prize: The Epic Quest for Oil, Money, and Power.* New York: Simon and Schuster, 1991.

Young, Hugo. *One of Us: A Biography of Mrs. Thatcher.* London: Macmillan, 1989.

Periodicals

Automobile Quarterly
Automotive International
BMW Company Reports
Car
Classic Cars
Daily Telegraph (London)
Economist, The
European
Evening Standard (London)
Far Eastern Economic Review
Financial Times
Fortune
Guardian, The
History Today
Independent
Independent on Sunday
International Affairs
Le Monde
Middle Eastern Economic Review
New York Times, The
Newsweek
Price Waterhouse Euro News
South China Morning Post
Sunday Telegraph (London)
Sunday Times (London)
Thoroughbred & Classic Car
Time
The Times (London)
Top Gear
USA Automobile Quarterly
Your Classic

Films

Breathless
Bullitt
Day of the Jackal
Go, Trabi, Go
Library Love
Mad Max
Mad Max 2
Mad Max: Beyond the Thunderdome
Roger and Me
The Italian Job
Un Homme et une femme

Index

Adam Opel, *see* Opel
Agnelli, Edoardo, 101
Agnelli, Gianni, 28, 29, 30, 44, 48, 49–50, 52, 53, 55, 78, 95–96, 97, 98–99, 100–101, 181, 193
Agnelli, Giovanni, 28, 30
Agnelli, Giovanni (Giovannino), 101
Agnelli, Umberto, 96, 98, 101
Agnelli family, 28, 53, 95–96, 97, 98, 100
Alfa-Romeo, 56, 123, 128
Algeria, 165
Al Ghanim agency, Kuwait, 113, 115
Allies
  during Occupation: Germany, 8–9, 12, 13, 14, 15, 16, 19, 58, 60, 68, 215; Italy, 30
  World War II operations, 11, 29, 60, 117
Almana, Omar, 114
Amtenbrink, Helmut, 11–12, 13, 93
Andrews, David, 88, 133–134

Arab blacklist, 112, 114
Arabian Peninsula, 109, 112–115
ARAMCO (Arabian American Oil Company), 110
Argentina, 130, 220
"Assessing Global Auto Trends" (FRB of Chicago), 210, 211
Audi company, 130, 165, 210
Austin, Sir Herbert, 23–24
Austin cars
  1100 model, 85
  1300 model, 85
  Allegro, 85
  Seven (1920s), 8, 23, 38, 102, 164
  Seven (Mini), 38–39. *See also* Mini
  Somerset, 102
Austin-Healey, 82
Austin Morris (division of BLMC), 83, 84–85, 87. *See also* Austin Motors; Morris Motors

Austin Motors, 23–24, 37
  on Arab blacklist, 112, 114
  under BLMC, 82, 87
  Qatari market, 114
  See also Austin cars; Austin Morris
Australia, 14, 15, 92, 182
Austria, 68, 77
autobahns, Hitler's vision, 4, 7
Autonacional Biscuter, 166
Autonomia Operaia, Italy, 98, 100
Auto Union, 71, 146
AvtoVAZ, 193–194, 195, 197–198, 199–
  200, 201, 203
  audit. *See* Price Waterhouse
  autos: Lada/Zhiguli, 52, 192, 193, 194,
  195, 198, 200, 204; Lada Niva, 133,
  193, 195; Oka, 201
  Togliattigrad (FIAT-built) plant, 52,
  192–194, 195, 198, 199–200
Avtovelo, takeover of Eisenach
  BMW plant, 10–11, 50, 60, 146,
  174

Bantam company, 132
Barber, John, 46–47, 82, 85
Barton, Bruce, ix–x
Bashford, Gordon, 133
Bashkortostan, 194, 200
Beckett, Terence, 46
Bedouins, 110, 112, 113
Behn, Sosthene, 44
Beijing Family Car Congress, 211
Belgium, 182, 220
Belorus, 201
Benn, Tony, 82
Bentleys, 203
Benz, Karl, 3, 57
Benz company, merger with Daimler,
  57. *See also* Daimler-Benz AG
Berlinguer, Enrico, 98
Berlin Wall, 59; fall of, 144, 147, 148,
  172, 179, 180
Berryman, Richard, 15–16
Bertoni, Flaminio, 34
Besse, Georges, 121

Bier, Peter, 177
Birla, C. K., 188
Birla GM, 188
BLMC. *See* British Leyland Motor
  Corporation
BMC. *See* British Motor Corporation
BMW (*Bayerische Motoren Werke*),
  7–8, 17, 18, 19, 43, 57, 59, 124, 164,
  165, 173–174, 214–215
  aircraft engines, 7, 8, 178
  Allach plant, 8, 60
  autos, 7, 8, 57, 124, 163, 173, 192, 200,
  219; 3-Series, 177; 5-Series, 177;
  318i, 174; 321 model, 10; 326
  model, 3; 501 model, 61; 502
  model, 61; 507 model, 61, 124; 1500
  model, 62; 1600 model, 105; "Dixi,"
  8, 38; Isetta Motor-Coupé, 61;
  stolen, 202, 203, 206; Z3, 177
  Eisenach plant, 8–11, 71, 146–147;
  under Avtovelo, 10–11, 50, 60, 146,
  174
  motorcycles, 7, 8, 9, 10, 61
  Munich plant, 60, 174
  overseas operations, 174, 188;
  Spartanburg, South Carolina, 174–
  178, 182; U.K., 88–89
  postwar revival, 60–63
  Regensburg plant, 177–178
  Rover purchase, 88–89
  V-2 rocket development, 8, 9
  and *Volkswagen* project, 17
Bolshevik Revolution, 50, 51, 189
Bono, Gaudenzio, 49
Boulanger, Pierre, 33, 34, 35, 117
Bradley, Gen. Omar, 103
Brazil, 92, 130, 220
Bricklin, Malcolm, 152, 153
Bristol 400 road racer, 60
Britain
  auto/environmental controls,
  214
  auto imports, 92, 105
  Cold War smuggling operation with
  Tatras, 19–20

government interference in auto
industry, 82, 86–88, 134
number of autos in, 37
Qatari resentment of, 114
and Saudi Arabia, 111–112
in World War II and aftermath, 11,
13, 29, 44
British auto industry
British makers. *See* Austin Motors;
British Leyland Motor
Corporation; British Motor
Company; Morris Motors; Rover
Motor Company
exports to U.S., 79
foreign makers, 88–89, 105, 155, 183.
See also Ford of Britain
Hirst's role, 215
nationalization of, 86–88, 134
people's car, 36–39. *See also* Mini
sports cars, 125
suicide of, 79, 81–89, 125
trade unions, 83, 84–85, 87
British Intelligence, 20, 45, 218
British Leyland Motor Corporation
(BLMC), 46, 81, 82–83, 84–85, 86–
87, 89, 105
downsizing and sell-offs, 88
formation of, 82, 84
models introduced: Maestro, 88,
210; Metro, 88, 205; Montego, 88,
210
name changed to Rover, 88
nationalization of, 86–88, 134
proposed sale to GM, 88, 133
ranking, 81, 82, 118
suicide of, 47, 81–89, 133, 210
*See also constituent companies and
divisions*: Austin Morris; British
Motor Corporation; Jaguar;
Leyland Motors; MG; Rover Motor
Company; Triumph
British Motor Corporation (BMC), 36,
38, 82
Leyland merger, 82
Mini, 38–39, 45, 196

See also Austin Motors; Jaguar; MG;
Morris Motors
British Standard Chartered Bank,
199
bubble cars, 36, 38, 61
Bugatti company, 132
Buick, 78, 112
Bulgaria, 210
Burleigh, Dr. Michael, 66
Bush, George, 158–159

Cadillac, 68, 78, 112, 113, 140, 143, 192,
203
Caine, Michael, 38, 39
California, 67–68, 104–105, 214, 216
California Air Reserves Board (CARB),
214
Callaghan, James, 87
Calvet, Jacques, 119, 120
Campbell, Carroll, 175, 177
Canada, 153, 159, 195, 217
Caterpillar, 199
CGT union, 118–119, 120, 121, 122
Chad, 2CVs in, 35
chaebol, 83, 84, 85, 86, 89, 153
Chengdu Automotive Company, 210
Chernomyrdin, Victor, 194, 199, 200
Chevrolet, 62, 78, 79, 112, 113
China, 207–212, 213
auto industry, 208, 210–211
car smuggling into, 204–206
Communist threat to West, 23, 24, 25,
26, 104
delegation to Volkswagen, 93–94
foreign/global automakers in, 77,
155, 210, 220
people's car (C88), 220
vehicle/person ratio, 187
China North Industries, 210
Chrysler Corporation, 48, 79, 119, 158,
186, 210, 219
autos: electric, 214; Jeep Cherokee,
179; New Yorker, 113
Chung Ju Yung, 83–84, 85–86, 153, 155
Churchill, Winston, 7, 44, 110–111, 112

Citroën, André, 33, 34
Citroën company, 33, 36, 43, 81, 121, 123, 128
  autos, 114, 163; Deux Chevaux (2CV), 33–35, 55, 117, 119, 121; DS 19 (*La Déesse*), 54–55, 56
  FIAT merger, 53, 55–56
  Levallois factory, 34, 118–119, 120–121, 122
  See also Peugeot-Citroën
city cars, 196–197, 201
Clinton, Bill, 141, 142, 158, 184
Cold War, 20, 23, 24, 50, 58, 71, 193, 212, 217
Communism
  vs. Russian privatization, 190, 199, 200
  and trade union unrest, 52, 118–119, 120, 122
  U.S. policies to counter spread of, 16, 23, 24, 31, 103–104
Confindustria, 97
Cooper, John, 45
Czechoslovakia/Czech Republic, 19, 70, 155, 202–203, 217–219. *See also* Skoda; Tatra

Daewoo, 84, 154, 155
  global operations, 89, 155, 188, 200, 201
Daihatsu, 210
Daimler, Gottfried, 3, 57
Daimler-Benz AG, 17, 18, 57, 58, 64, 82, 179
  military production, 58, 76–77
  overseas operations, 188, 210
  proposed purchase of BMW, 61
  See also Mercedes-Benz
Daimler company, 57. *See also* Daimler-Benz AG
D'Ascanio (helicopter designer), 31
Datsun (later Nissan, *q.v.*), 23–24, 26, 27, 123, 125
  assembly of Austin Somerset, 102
  autos: 240Z/My Fair Lady, 124; 510/

  Bluebird, 105; 1600 line, 124; after Austin Seven, 8, 23–24, 38, 102, 164
  exports to U.S., 27, 79, 105
Day, Sir Graham, 88
Day of the Jackal, The (film), 56
Dean, James, 69
Deng Xiaoping, 93, 208, 210
Detroit, Michigan, 24–26, 29, 75, 79–80, 138, 159, 181. *See also* U.S. auto industry
Deux Chevaux (2CV) (French people's car), 33–35, 55, 117, 119, 121
Dlouhý, Vladimír, 203
Dolganov, Oleg, 203–204
Donath, Kurt, 60
Douglas DC-3, 111, 112
Douglas motorcycle, 7
downsizing, 157, 161, 213
Doyle Dane Bernbach, Inc. (DDB), 67
Dufaux, 196
Dulles, Allen, 29
Dulles, John Foster, 103–104

Eastern Europe, 213, 215
  stolen cars, 202, 204
East Germany, 19, 70, 71–72, 202
  people's car. *See* Trabant
Eddy, Col. William A., 111
Edwardes, Michael, 87, 88, 134
Eisenach, Germany, automakers. *See* Avtovelo; BMW; Opel
Eisenacher Motoren Werk (EMW), 146–147, 174
Eisenhower, Dwight D., 103
electric cars, 214
Electronic Data Systems (EDS), 139, 141, 156
Enzmann family, 196
European auto industries
  flaws in, 75
  foreign competition, 4, 43, 49, 183; Ford, 45–47; Japanese, 109, 130, 166–167, 182–183; South Korean, 155

nationalized, 117, 118
sports cars, 126
threats to, 81–82
trade union unrest, 118
utility cars, 45

Far East, 151, 183, 211, 213, 215
FD car, 37
Federal Reserve Bank of Chicago
report, 210, 211
Feltrinelli, Giangiacomo, 97
Ferrari, 53, 206
FIAT (*Fabbrica Italiana Automobili Torino*), 28–32, 36, 39, 43, 48–50, 52–53, 59, 81, 95, 96–97, 98–101, 140, 181, 198
and Alfa-Romeo, 56
autos; 45; 124 model, 51, 52, 124, 194; 178 model, 220; *Nuova Cinquecento* (people's car), 30–32, 37, 39, 48, 71, 101; Spanish clones, 166; Tempra, 163; Topolino ("Little Mouse"), 30; Uno, 100, 204
Citroën merger, 53, 55–56
Ford merger negotiations, 100
global operations, 188, 210; Russia, 28, 50–52, 193, 194
Lingotto factory, 30, 39
Mirafiori plant, Turin, 53, 96, 97, 99–100
production rates, 48, 97
trade union problems, 96, 98–100, 122
during World II and aftermath, 28–30
Firestone, 76, 166
Ford, Henry, 4–5, 13, 14, 15, 44, 45, 185
Ford Asia-Pacific, 184
Ford Motor Company, x, 4–5, 43–45 47, 76, 85, 112, 117, 136, 137, 158, 164, 181–186
autos: Contour/Mondeo (world car), 163, 185–186, 197, 212; Cortina, 46–47, 48, 82, 84, 85, 181, 184, 205; electric, 214; Explorer, 179; Falcon, 45; Ka (city car), 197; Model A, 25; Model T ("Tin Lizzie"), 5, 25, 44, 45, 90, 143, 181; Mustang, 45, 124, 141, 184; Pinto, 79; Thunderbird, 61, 124
FIAT merger negotiations, 100
Jaguar subsidiary, 181
overseas operations, 112, 182, 188, 197, 211; Nazi Germany, 44–45, 76. *See also* Ford of Europe
pickup trucks, 214
Rouge River plant, 4, 25–26, 44, 181
stake in Mazda, 125
Toyota's postwar approach to, 25
Ford North America, 186
Ford of Britain, 36, 45, 46, 183, 184–185
Cortina, 46–47, 48, 82, 84, 85, 181, 184, 205
Ford of Europe, 45, 137, 181, 182–184, 186. *See also* Ford of Britain; Ford of Germany
Ford of Germany/Ford Werke, 45, 46, 183–184
Forster, Paul, 175
Forus Services, 198
four-wheel drive, 132–135
France, 14, 26, 33–35, 114
French auto industry, 122
labor disputes, 115, 118–122
makers. *See* Citroën; Peugeot; Renault
people's car, 43, 46, 65. *See also* Deux Chevaux
Qatari market, 114

Gallieni, Gen. Joseph-Simon, 116
Gaulle, Charles de, 54, 55–56, 103, 114, 118
GAZ (Gorky Automobile Works), 198–199
General Motors Corporation (GM), 15, 43, 45, 75–80, 85, 136, 137–141, 156–157, 158, 159–161, 164, 166, 167, 168–169, 199, 214
acquisitions: EDS, 139, 141, 156;

General Motors Corporation (GM)
(*continued*)
Hughes Aircraft, 156; Pacific
Electric rail system, 76, 214
Arab market, 112, 113–114
autos: Catera, 220; Corvette, 61, 124;
EV1 (electric car), 214; Saturn, 156
divisions (GM Five), 78, 79, 112, 114,
138; Buick, 78, 112; Cadillac, 78,
112, 113, 140; Chevrolet, 78, 112,
113; Oldsmobile, 78, 112; Pontiac,
78, 112
downsizing, 139, 157, 161
financial losses, 136, 157, 160
Japanese competition, 136–138, 156–
157, 161
joint ventures: Hindustan Motors,
188–189; Jinbei, 210; Russian
American Industrial Corporation,
199; Suzuki, 147; Toyota, 139, 140
Kuwait agency, 113–115
lending operations, 138
Lopez affair, 167–171
overseas operations: China, 77, 211;
GM Europe, 147–148; India, 188–
189; Japan, 76, 77; Nazi Germany,
44–45, 76–77, 147; Spain, 168. *See
also* Opel
Perot's views of, 139–140
and Rover, 88, 133, 134
and SAAB, 128
German auto industry
Arab market, 112–113
"bubble cars," 36, 38, 61
foreign/global makers, 155, 220. *See
also* Ford of Germany; Opel
German makers. *See* BMW; Daimler-
Benz AG; Porsche;
Volkswagenwerk
Hitler's vision, 3–7
people's car. *See* Volkswagen
recession, 173–174
after World War II, 8–13
See also East Germany

Germany
Allied occupation, 8–9, 12, 13, 14, 15,
16, 19, 58, 60, 68, 215
auto/environmental controls, 215
auto imports: FIATs, 53;
Volkswagens, 92
Nazi era. *See* Nazi Germany
postwar reconstruction and revival,
16–17, 23, 58, 59
recession, 172–173
reunification, 172, 179
stolen car trade, 202
Wirtschaftswunder (economic
miracle), 57, 59, 60, 61, 62
See also East Germany; German auto
industry
German Jeep, The, 14
Ghidella, Vittorio, 98
Giacosa, Dante, 28, 30, 31, 32, 37, 48,
71, 78
Giugaro, Giorgetto, 91
Godard, Jean-Luc, 55
Goering, Hermann, 8, 18
Goertz, Count Albrecht, 123–124, 125–
126
Golda, Kurt, 61–62
Gorbachev, Mikhail, 145, 146, 193
Go, Trabi, Go (film), 144
Greenwald, Gerald, 218–219
Gromyko, Andrei, 145
Gyllenhammar, Pehr (P.G.), 127, 128,
129, 130

Hahn, Carl, 66, 67, 91, 216
Hahnemann, Paul, 62
Havel, Václav, 203
Hayek, Nicolas, 190–191, 196, 197
Hayes, Walter, 137
Heinkel, 36, 38
Herman, David, 167
Hill, Sen. Lister, 21–22
Hindustan Motors, 188
Hirst, Maj. Ivan, 13–15, 16, 17, 60, 66,
90, 93–94, 210, 215–216

Hitler, Adolf, 3–7, 15, 17–18, 25, 29, 44, 45, 47, 57–58, 64–67, 92–93, 112, 125, 179, 181, 197, 219, 221
Hoffman, Max Edwin, 67, 124
Hofmeister, Wilhelm, 62
Hoglund, Bill, 160
Holland, 5–6, 16, 67
Holland, Dorothea, 169
Homme et une femme, Un (film), 55
Honda, 27, 105
  autos: Accord, 136, 157, 185; Acura, 178; Civic, 137
  overseas operations: India, 188; Marysville, Ohio, 136, 138, 157, 177, 182; Swindon, England, 89
  and Rover, 88, 89, 162
  U.S. production, 136–137
Hong Kong, 204–206, 207
Horch limousines, 71
Howard, Graeme K., 77
Hrdlička, Ales, 22
Hubbert, Jürgen, 178
Hughes, Louis, 147–148, 160, 168
Hungary, 202
Hussein, Saddam, 114, 217
Hyatt Roller Bearing Company, 75
Hyundai Motors, 83–84, 85, 153–155
  overseas operations, 153, 188
  Pony, 86

Iacocca, Lee, 45, 158, 159
Ibn Saud, Abdul Aziz, 110–112
IFI (*Instituto Finanzario Industriale*), 53
India, 155, 187–189, 210, 220
Indonesia, 155, 174, 220
IPTN/Rover Maleo, 220
Iran, 155
Iraq, 114
Isetta company, 61
Israel, 112, 114
Issigonis, Alec, Lord, 36–37, 38, 71, 83, 85, 196, 197
Isuzu company, 133

Italian Job, The (film), 38–39
Italy
  auto industry, 28. *See also* FIAT
  auto ownership, 48, 52
  Brigadi Rossi terrorism, 97–98
  Christian Democrat Party, 31, 95
  and FIAT, 28–29, 31–32, 48–50, 51, 52–53, 95, 96, 100
  people's car, 43, 46. See also *Nuova Cinquecento*
  postwar economic miracle, 28, 31, 49, 96
  trade unions, 52, 53, 96, 98–100, 118, 122

Jaguar, 124, 125, 192, 203, 206
  under BLMC, 82, 87
  E-Type, 124
  under Ford, 181
Japan, 21–27
  auto imports, 24, 125, 187
  Korean attitude toward, 154
  U.S. procurement and aid programs, 26–27, 102, 103–104
  after World War II, 21–23, 24
Japanese auto industry
  downsizing, 213
  exports, 104; banned from South Korea, 154–155; to Britain, 105; to European Community, 182–183; in postwar era, 24; to U.S., 27, 79, 104–105
  founding of, on Austin Seven, 8, 23–24
  global status, 21, 104, 109
  GM wartime operations in, 77
  Kuwaiti market, 113
  makers. *See* Honda; Mitsubishi; Nissan; Toyota
  overseas operations: Britain, 89, 105, 183; Europe, 130, 183; U.S., 105, 136–137, 138, 157, 179, 182
  pressure on U.S. and European industries, 75, 104–105, 109, 130,

Japanese auto industry (*continued*)
    156–157, 161, 166–167, 178, 182–
    183
  production levels, 27, 104
  production methods, 26, 84, 123, 178;
    employed at Eisenach Opel plant,
    147, 148
  sports-car production, 123, 124–126
  traditional auto features, 102
  U.S. role in saving, 26–27, 102
Jeep
  Cherokee, 179
  wartime, 6, 9, 82, 132, 134; cars
    based on, 6, 82, 132–133
  Wagoneer, 134
Jellinek, Emil, 57
Jellinek, Mercedes, 57
Jinbei, joint venture with GM, 210
Joseph, Keith, 88
Juffali brothers, 112–113, 114
just-in-time inventories, 26, 84

Kadannikov, Vladimir, 194, 195, 200
Kamaz company, 201
Kamiya, Shotaro, 25, 27
Kantor, Mickey, 141–142
Kazakhstan, 201
KdF-Stadt ("Strength-Through-Joy
    Town"), 4–6, 11, 12–13, 14, 19, 25,
    64, 65–66, 93, 117, 181
  KdF-Wagen ("Strength-Through-Joy
    Car"), 5, 6, 7, 11, 57, 66, 117, 219
  Kubelwagen, 6, 11, 14
  Schwimmwagen, 6, 11, 14
  Type 87 *Kommandeurwagen*, 7
  For postwar history, see
    Volkswagenwerk: Wolfsburg plant
Kellner, Marryann, 159
Kempka, Erich, 7
Kennedy, John F., 31, 49, 53
Khrushchev, Nikita, 50, 51, 145
Kia company, 84
Kia Ssang Yong, 155
Kim Yung Sam, 155
Kinzer, Al, 177

Kissinger, Henry, 152
Klaus, Václav, 203
Kohl, Helmut, 168
Koprivnica, Czechoslovakia, 18. *See
    also* Tatra
Korea, 24, 25, 83–84. *See also* South
    Korea
Korean War, 25, 26–27, 84, 102, 103
Kosygin, Andrei, 50, 51
Kuenheim, Eberhard von, 62–63, 175,
    176, 177
Kume, Yutaka, 158
Kuwait, 112, 113–115, 217
Kuybyshev, Valerian Vladmirovich, 51

labor unions. *See* trade unions
Lada cars, 52, 192, 195, 198, 204
  Niva, 133, 193, 195
Lagos, Nigeria, 92
Lamborghini Diablo, 206
Lancia, Vincenzo, 28–29
Laos, 174
LaSorda, Tom, 147
Latin America, 174, 198
LAZ, 200
lean production, 26, 84, 178
Ledwinka, Erich, 18, 70
Ledwinka, Hans, 17, 18–19, 65, 70–71,
    77, 219
Lefevbre, André, 33
Lehmann, Hans-Georg, 164–165
Leiding, Rudolph, 91
Lelouch, Claude, 55
Lenin Komsomol Automotive Plant,
    200
Levy, Raymond, 121–122, 128, 130
Lexus, 206
Leyland Motors, 82. *See also* British
    Leyland Motor Corporation
Library Love (film), 125
Libya, stake in FIAT, 96
Likhachev, Ivan Alekseevich, 145
Loewy, Raymond, 123–124
Logovaz dealership, 204
Longuet, Gerard, 129

Lopez de Arriortua, José Ignacio, 161, 165–171, 173, 191, 196, 216
Lord, Sir Leonard, 36, 37, 38
Los Angeles, 76, 214
Lotus Elan, 124, 125
Lotz, Kurt, 91
Lowe Howard-Spink, 163
Luce, Clare Boothe, 31
Luftwaffe, 8, 11, 77
Lutz, Bob, 186

MacArthur, Gen. Douglas, 22
McEvoy, Maj. Michael, 14
MacGregor, Ian, 87
McInnes, Alastair, 14
Mad Max (film), 213
Mahathir Mohamad, Dr. Datuk Seri, 152, 155
Major, John, 216
Malaysia, 151–153, 155, 174
Mao Tse-tung, 3, 208, 209, 212
Marne, "miracle of the," 116–117
Marshall Plan, 16, 23, 27, 58, 61, 69
Maruti company, 187
Marysville, Ohio, Honda plant, 136, 138, 157, 177, 182
Mather, Jim, 204, 205–206
Maunory (Gen. Michel-Joseph), 116
Mays, J. C., 216
Mazda
    autos, 126, 206; Miata/MX-5, 125; MX-3, 125
    Flat Rock, Michigan, plant, 137, 138
Mein Kampf (Hitler), 44, 47
Mercedes-Benz, 43, 57–59, 164, 172, 173, 178–179
    autos, 7, 57–59, 61, 62, 128, 163, 178–179, 192, 200, 204, 219; 600 model, 58, 205; "C" class, 130; stolen/smuggled, 59, 92, 202, 203, 204, 206, 207
    downsizing in early 1990s, 173
    Japanese competition, 178–179
    overseas operations; Alabama, 179, 182; Uzbekhistan, 201

Renault alliance, 130–131
Saudi Arabian agent, 112–113, 114
Swatch partnership 196–197
trucks, 113, 114
See also Daimler-Benz AG
Merlis, Scott F., 186
Messerschmitt, 36, 38, 58, 77
Mexico, 92, 217
MG, 82, 88, 124, 125, 126
Michelin family, 53, 55
Michelotti, Giovanni, 62
Middle Eastern markets, 109–115, 198
Mini (Morris Mini-Minor; Austin Seven; British people's car), 38–39, 45, 71, 83, 87, 89, 196, 197
    Mini-Metro, 88, 205
Mitsubishi, 23, 27, 86, 133
    autos: Lancer Fiore, 152; Sigma wagon, 163
    overseas operations, 152, 188
Mitsui, 23, 24, 200
Mitterrand, François, 119, 120
Miyazawa, Kiichi, 158
Mommsen, Hans, 65–66, 69
Monteverdi, Peter, 196
Mooney, James B., 77
Morgenthau Plan, 12, 13, 15, 16, 21, 23, 58, 61
Moro, Aldo, 98
Morocco, 220
Morris cars
    ADO 15, 37–38
    Ital, 210
    Marina, 84
    Mini-Minor, 38, 39. *See also* Mini
    Minor, 38
Morris Motors, 117
    under BMC, 36–38
    under BLMC, 82, 87
    See also Austin Morris; Morris cars
Moskvich, 51, 146, 194, 195, 198
Motown. *See* Detroit, Michigan
Munich Agreement (1938), 18
Mussolini, Benito, 3, 5, 28–29, 30, 49
Mustang P-51 aircraft, 77

Nasser, Jacques (Jac), 182–184, 185, 191
Nazi Germany
  car ownership, 4
  and FIAT resisters, 29
  Hitler's plans for automobile industry, 3–7, 221
  invasion of France, 33, 117
  slave labor, 6, 8, 11, 14, 60, 64, 65, 117
  wartime production for: Ford, 44–45, 76; GM, 76–77; Renault, 117
Nazi Party, 4, 5, 6, 8, 12, 13, 14, 18, 44, 64, 70, 117, 179
Nemtsov, Boris, 199
Netherlands, 5–6, 16, 67
Nigeria, 92, 203
Nissan (formerly Datsun, q.v.), 23, 27, 105, 133, 158, 164, 221
  autos: Cedric Deluxe, 102, 104; Figaro, 125; Infiniti, 178; Micra, 164
  global operations: China, 210; Smyrna, Tennessee, 137, 138, 156, 157, 182
Nixon, Richard, 104
Nordhoff, Heinrich ("King"), 16, 17, 66, 67, 90–91
North Africa, 165, 195
  guest workers from, 118–119, 121
Novelli, Diego, 97–98, 100
NSU cars, 62
Number One Motor Vehicle Plant, Changchun, China, 208
Nuova Cinquecento (Italian people's car). See FIAT

OAS (Organisation Armée Secrète), 54, 56, 114
Ohno, Taiichi, 26
oil shortages and price shocks
  caused by OPEC policies, 97, 105, 112
  during Suez crisis, 36, 61, 109
  in World War II Germany, 6, 14
  caused by Yom Kippur War, 79, 105

Oldsmobile, 78, 112, 160
OPEC oil shocks, 97, 105, 112
Opel/Adam Opel (GM subsidiary), 16, 147–148, 167–168, 170
  autos, 144; Astra, 188; Corsa, 163, 164; Maxx, 171; "O" car, 167
  Brandenburg plant, 76
  Eisenach plant, 147–148
  Qatari market, 114
  Rüsselsheim plant, 77, 147–148, 168
  World War II production, 58, 76–77
Overney, Pierre, 118

Pacar, 199
Pacific Electric rail system, 76
Palestine, 112, 114
Panhard cars, 62
Patten, Chris, 206
Pearce, Harry, 160
Pegaso sports cars, 166
people's cars, xi, 43, 46, 82, 133, 164, 216, 220–221
  British. See Mini
  Chinese, 211
  East German. See Trabant
  French. See Deux Chevaux
  German. See Volkswagen
  Italian. See Nuova Cinquecento
  South Korean, 86
  Soviet. See Zhiguli
Perot, H. Ross, 139–140, 141
Peugeot cars, 204
  405 station wagon, 163
Peugeot-Citroën, 118–121
  Levallois plant, 118–119, 120–121, 122
  overseas operations, 188, 210
  Talbot plant, Poissy, 119–120, 122
Peugeot company, 65, 82
  Qatari agency, 114
  See also Peugeot-Citroën
Philippines, 155, 174
Pic-Pic, 196
Piech, Anton, 64–65, 66, 117

Piech, Ferdinand, 66, 164, 165, 167, 169–171, 173, 203, 216, 217
Pininfarina company, 105, 124
Pischetsreider, Bernd, 176
Poland, 6, 202
  autos: *Mikrus*, 51; *Smyk*, 51; *Syrena*, 51; *Warszawa/Pobieda*, 50–51
  GM wartime operations, 77
Pon, Ben, 5, 6, 15, 16, 67
Pontiac, 78, 112
  Fiero, copy of, 125
Popp, Franz-Joseph, 7, 17
Porsche, Dr. Ferdinand, 4, 6, 14, 17, 18, 19, 64–66, 68, 69, 70, 91, 117, 169, 219, 220
Porsche, Ferdinand ("Ferry"), 6, 66, 68, 91
Porsche, Fernando Alexander ("Butzi"), 69, 216
Porsche company, 43, 91, 147, 165
  autos: 62, 68–69, 70, 144; 356 model, 68, 69; 550 Spyder, 69; 911 model, 64, 69
  Gmund plant, 68
  patent infringement settlement, 70
  "Targa" roll bar, 123
  U.S. sales, 64, 68
  venture with China, 220
  Zuffenhausen plant, 68
Portugal, 2CV production, 121
Posth, Martin, 215
Price Waterhouse, 189–190, 191–192, 195, 197, 198, 201
Prince Skyline Deluxe, 102
production line assembly, 25–26
Proton (*Perusahaan Otomobil Nasional Bhd*), 151–153
  Saga, 152

Qatar, 114
Quandt, Herbert, 61–63

Radclyffe, Col. Charles, 14
Rao, P. V. Narasimha, 188, 189
Ravenel, Jacques, 121

Red Brigades (*Brigadi Rossi*), 97–98
Reigel, Donald, 158
Renault, Louis, 117
Renault company, 36, 116–118, 121–122, 200
  autos: Caravelle, 118; *Coupés*, 116–117; Dauphine, 79, 118; Five, 98; Four, 118; Trafic minibus, 210; Twingo, 122, 130
  Billancourt factory, 116, 117, 118, 121, 122
  Mercedes-Benz alliance, 130–131
  nationalization of, 117
  privatization of, 122
  Qatari market, 114
  rank, 81, 118
  and Sanjiang Space Group, 210
  and Volvo, 122, 128–130
  during World War II, 117
Renault-Volvo, 129, 131
Reuter, Edzard, 179
Ribbentrop, Joachim von, 44
Ringhoffer family, 70
Roger & Me (film), 140
Rolls-Royce, 16, 77, 111–112, 203–204
Romiti, Cesare, 98–99, 101
Rommel (Field Marshal Erwin), 6, 14
Roosevelt, Elliot, 22
Roosevelt, Franklin D., 6–7, 22, 23, 110, 111, 112
Rootes, Lord, 15
Rootes Motors, 36
Rovan, Joseph, 65–66
Rover cars, 133
  600 model, 162
  Defender, 134
  Ital, 210
  Land-Rover, 82, 88, 89, 133–134
  Maestro, 88, 210
  Montego, 88, 210
  Range Rover, 134, 204
Rover Group (former BLMC), 88, 128
  and Honda, 88, 89, 162
  in India, 188
  privatization of, 88

Rover Group (*continued*)
  proposed sale to GM, 88, 133
  sale to BMW, 88–89
Rover Motor Company, 82, 132–133
Royal Hong Kong Police Anti-
    Smuggling Task Force, 204, 205,
    206
Russia/Russian Federation
  autos and automakers. *See* AvtoVAZ;
    Avtovelo; GAZ; Moskvich; Zhiguli;
    Zil
  FIAT operations, 28, 193, 198
  mafia, 199, 200, 203, 204
  Price Waterhouse in, 189–190, 191–
    192, 195, 197, 198
  privatization of industries, 189–190,
    194–195, 197–200
  See also Soviet Union
Russian-American Industrial
    Corporation, 199
Rutherford, Jack, 219
Rutskoi, Aleksandr, 146
Ryder, Sir Don, 87
Ryder Plan, 87
Ryzhkov, Nikolai, 145

SAAB, 128, 162
  Turbo, 128
Saikin, Valery, 199
Salinas de Gortari, Carlos, 92
Salleh, Mohamad Nadzmi Mohamad,
    151–152, 153
Sampson, Anthony, 53
Samsung, 84, 89, 155
Sanjiang Space Group, 210
Sartre, Jean-Paul, 118, 143
Saudi Arabia, 110–114
Schmuecker, Toni, 93
Schroder, Gerhard, 170
Schweitzer, Louis ("ET"), 128, 130
SCUD missiles, 217
SEAT, 166
  Cordoba, 220
Shah Alam factory, Malaysia, 152
Shanghai, 207–208, 209–210, 211

Shelby, David, 219
Siedler, Albert, 8, 9–10, 11, 12, 19, 60,
    146
Siegfried, Klaus-Jorg, 64
Sikkim, 34–35
Singapore, 215
Skoda, 144, 203
  Felicia, 220
Sloan, Alfred P., Jr., 75–76, 77, 78, 160,
    161, 185
SMH, 191
Smith, John F. ("Jack"), 142, 159–160,
    161, 165, 167, 168, 169, 211, 214
Smith, John T., 77
Smith, Robert, 157
Smith, Roger, 137–138, 139–141, 178
smuggled cars, 59, 92, 202–206
South Africa, 91, 220
South America, 91, 130–131, 195, 217
South Carolina BMW plant, 174–178
Southeast Asia, 103, 104
South Korea, 85–86, 154
  auto industry, 210, 211. *See also*
    Daewoo; Hyundai
Soviet Union
  auto production levels, 50, 193
  autos and automakers: *Pobeida*, 50;
    Zaporogiets, 51; *Zim*, 51. *See also*
    AvtoVAZ; Avtovelo; GAZ;
    Moskvich; Zhiguli; Zil
  collapse of, 194, 218
  FIAT in, 50, 51, 52, 193
  postwar occupation of Eastern
    Europe, 12, 13, 14, 19, 58, 71
  Red Army, 6, 11, 60, 71
  takeover of BMW Eisenach plant.
    See Avtovelo
  Tatra military production for, 217–
    218
  U.S. policies to prevent expansion
    of, 23, 24, 103–104
  See also Russia
Spain, 166, 182, 220
Spartanburg, South Carolina, BMW
    plant, 174–178

Speer, Albert, 4, 7, 66, 92–93
sports car market, Japan's entry, 123–126
sport-utility vehicles, 214
Stalin (Joseph), 3, 6–7, 50, 51, 110, 145
Standard Oil of California, 76
Standard Triumph, 82, 83
    absorbed by Leyland, 82
    See also Triumph
Stempel, Robert, 141, 157, 159
Stokes, Donald, 82, 85
Stryker company, 132
Studebaker, 123
Subaru, 152
Suez War, 36, 61, 109
Suzuki, 105
    Cue, 125
    joint ventures, 147, 187, 210
Swatchmobiles, 191, 196–197
Sweden, and Volvo, 127, 129, 130
Switzerland, 190–191, 196–197

tai fei, 205, 206, 207
Talbot plant, Poissy, 119–120, 122
Tarasov (Soviet minister), 51
"Targa" roll bar. *See* Porsche company
Tatarstan, 201
Tatra company, 17–19, 20, 57, 65, 68, 70–71, 77, 203, 217–219
    autos: T11, 17; T87, 18, 19–20, 70, 217; V-8 sedans, 17; V570 prototype, 18, 71, 219
    SCUD launchers, 217
    Soviet super-tanks, 218
team production, 26
Thailand, 174
Thatcher, Margaret, 87
"3P" movement, 137
Togliatti, Palmiro, 52, 212
Togliattigrad (FIAT-built) plant, Russia, 52, 192–194, 195, 198, 199–200
Toyoda, Eiji, 25, 26, 44, 78, 123, 178, 181
Toyota, 24–25, 27, 105, 133, 164, 181
    autos: Camry, 105, 163; Land Cruiser,

133; Lexus, 178; MR-2, 125; Toyopet Crown Deluxe, 102
    exports to U.S., 27, 79, 102, 105
    joint venture with GM, 139, 140
    overseas operations: Derby, England, 89, 182; Kentucky, 182
    production rates, 97
Toyota Production System, 26, 123
Trabant (East German people's car), 71–72, 143–145, 147, 202
trade unions
    Britain, 83, 84–85, 87
    France, 118–120, 121, 122
    Italy, 52, 53, 96, 98–100, 118, 122
    U.S., 76, 137, 156, 176
Triumph, 82, 83, 88, 124, 125
    Herald, 62
    Spitfire, 62
Trotman, Alex, 46, 47, 184–186, 211
Truman, Harry S., 22, 23
Tukey, Dick, 175
Tupolev bombers, 146
Turin, 39, 97–98
    March of the Forty Thousand, 99–100
Turkey, 220
Turnbull, George, 82–83, 84–85, 86, 88, 133, 153
TZ car, 166

Udet, Ernst, 7, 8, 178
Ufa, Bashkortostan, plant, 194, 200
Ukraine, 200
Ulsan, South Korea. *See* Hyundai
unions. *See* trade unions
United Automobile Workers, 137, 156
United States
    Allied occupation of postwar Germany, 8, 9, 13, 14
    anti-Communist trade and foreign policies, 23, 24, 31, 103–104
    auto imports, 49; BMW, 124; British, 79; Japanese, 27, 79, 102, 104–105; Land-Rover and Range Rover, 134; Porsche, 64, 68; Renault, 79;

United States (*continued*)
Volkswagen, 64, 67–68, 79, 91, 102
best-selling vehicle in, 214
damages paid to producers for Axis Powers, 45, 77
Japanese auto industry saved by, 26–27, 102
Korean War costs, 26–27
and postwar Japan, 21–24
and Saudi Arabia, 110–112
significance of auto in, ix–x
and Vietnam War, 26, 104
in World War II, 8, 14, 29
U.S. auto industry
Detroit makers. *See* Chrysler; Ford Motor Company; General Motors
downsizing, 213
exports: to Japan, 24; Japanese make, 179
first foreign inroads, 79
flaws in, 75, 79–80
foreign/global makers: BMW, 174–178; Honda, 136–137, 138, 157, 177, 182; Mazda, 137, 138; Mercedes Benz, 179; Nissan, 137, 138; Toyota, 139; Volkswagenwerk, 67, 91, 137, 176
Japanese competition, 79, 105, 109, 136–138, 140, 141–142, 158; in luxury market, 178
losses (1991), 157
production levels (1950s), 79
Saudi Arabian market, 110–112
Toyoda's study of, 25
trade unions, 76, 137, 156, 176
U.S. Defense Department, 25
U.S. Secret Service, 77
U.S. Senate Armed Forces Committee, 77–78
U.S. Special Procurements program, 26–27
USS *Quincy*, 110, 111
Uzbekhistan, 155, 201

V-rockets, 6, 8, 11, 58
Valletta, Dr. Vittorio, 28, 29, 30, 31, 48, 49, 50, 51, 98
Varta battery, 61
Vespa motor scooter, 31
Vienna, smuggling rocket scientists from, 19–20
Vietnam, 104, 155, 174
Vietnam War, 26, 102, 104
Volkswagen cars (German people's car), 14–17, 18, 31, 36, 37, 38, 62, 65, 66–68, 69, 70, 121, 132, 162, 163, 202, 221
Beetle, 67–68, 90–91, 92–93, 216
Concept 1, 216–217
Dutch imports, 16
Golf/Rabbit, 91–92, 144
Golf GTi, 216
Golf II, 92
Ledwinka's prototype (V570), 18, 71, 219
non-German manufacture, 92, 203
Passat, 91
Polo, 91
Project EA 266, 91
Scirocco, 91
Type One ("Volkswagen"), 15
Type 3, 91
U.S. imports, 64, 67–68, 79, 102
Volkswagen companies. *See* Audi; SEAT; Skoda; Volkswagenwerk
Volkswagen of America Design Center, 216
Volkswagen Shanghai, 94, 196, 210, 211
Volkswagenwerk, 3, 12, 14–17, 43, 45, 53, 60, 61, 65, 66–67, 70, 81, 90–91, 93, 164–165, 167, 168, 169–171, 173, 181, 203, 216–217
Lopez affair, 167–171, 196, 216
overseas operations, 91, 188, 211, 217; U.S., 67, 91, 137, 176
Soltau dispersal site, 12
subsidiaries: SEAT, 166; Skoda, 203
and Swatchmobile, 196
Wolfsburg plant (formerly KdF-

Stadt), 11, 12–17, 19, 45, 65, 66, 93–94, 167, 170, 171, 216. *For Nazi-era history and autos, see* KdF-Stadt
Zwickau servicing center, 144, 202
See also Volkswagen cars
Volvo, 122, 127–130, 163
and Renault, 128–130

Wabenzi, 59, 92, 203
Wagoner, Rick, 160
Warren, Alfred, Jr., 138
Wartburgs, 146
Webster, Harry, 85
Weekend (film), 55
Wehrmacht, 16, 45, 47, 58, 77
Werner, Helmut, 178
Westrick, Gerhardt, 44
Whittle, Frank, 77
Wilks, Maurice, 132–133
Willys Jeep, 132, 133
Wilson, Charles Erwin, 77–78, 80
Wilson, Harold, 87
Wolfsburg. *See* Volkswagenwerk: Wolfsburg plant
Wolfsburg Under the Swastika symposium (1988), 65

women, auto design for, 37–38
world cars, 185–186, 220
World War I, 7, 28, 75, 116–117
World War II, 5–6
Allied operations, 11, 29, 60, 117
effects on: ARAMCO, 110; German auto industry, 8–13; Tatra, 18–19
production for Axis powers: FIAT, 28; Ford, 44–45; GM, 44, 76–77; Renault, 117

Yalta Conference (1945), 7, 110
Yelabuga, Tatarstan, factory, 201
Yeltsin, Boris, 145–146, 194, 195, 200
Yom Kippur War (1973), 79, 105
Yonker, Greg de, 188–189
Yugo, 152

zaibatsu, 23, 24
Zavod Imeni Likhacheva (ZIL), 145
zero-emission vehicles, 214
Zhengzou Light Truck Company, 210
Zhiguli, 52, 192, 193, 194, 195, 200, 204
Zil, 143, 145–146, 194, 195, 199
Zinneman, Fred, 56
Zwickau, East Germany, plant, 71, 144, 202. *See also* Trabant